AFRICAN AMERICAN
WRITING

WERNER SOLLORS

AFRICAN AMERICAN WRITING

A Literary Approach

TEMPLE UNIVERSITY PRESS   *Philadelphia • Rome • Tokyo*

TEMPLE UNIVERSITY PRESS
Philadelphia, Pennsylvania 19122
www.temple.edu/tempress

Copyright © 2016 by Werner Sollors
All rights reserved
Published 2016

Library of Congress Cataloging-in-Publication Data

Names: Sollors, Werner.
Title: African American writing : a literary approach / Werner Sollors.
Description: Philadelphia : Temple University Press, 2016. | Includes
    bibliographical references and index.
Identifiers: LCCN 2015031431 | ISBN 9781439913369 (hardback: alk. paper) |
    ISBN 9781439913376 (paper: alk. paper) | ISBN 9781439913383 (e-book)
Subjects: LCSH: American literature—African American authors—History and
    criticism. | African Americans in literature. | Race relations in literature. |
    BISAC: LITERARY CRITICISM / American / African American.
Classification: LCC PS153.N5 S64 2016 | DDC 810.9/896073—dc23
LC record available at http://lccn.loc.gov/2015031431

Printed in the United States of America

9 8 7 6 5 4 3 2 1

IN MEMORY OF

Charles Harold Nichols *(1919–2007)*

Robert Bone *(1924–2007)*

Nathan Irvin Huggins *(1927–1989)*

Contents

List of Figures

AFRICAN AMERICAN
WRITING

Introduction

WHEN RICHARD WRIGHT tried to capture the essence of his subject in a lecture titled "The Literature of the Negro in the United States," he said that it should be understood against the background of the story of the global movement from traditional, rural, religiously based, and pre-individual cultures to modern, urban, industrial, secular, and stridently individual societies. It is for this reason that, despite all specificities and differences, Wright said, "One ought to use the same concepts in discussing Negro life that one used in discussing white life." In this context, Wright arrived at one of his most famous quips: "The history of the Negro in America is the history of America written in vivid and bloody terms; it is the history of Western Man writ small. It is the history of men who tried to adjust themselves to a world whose laws, customs, and instruments of force were leveled against them. The Negro is America's metaphor."

Today's students may find Wright's gendered language and the very word "Negro" antiquated, if not reactionary. Yet they may be overlooking the Enlightenment legacy of the language of the "rights of man" that easily could be imagined to stand for men and women: even the Declaration of Sentiments of 1848 spoke of "the family of man" in articulating its hope for gender equality. The term "Negro," too, though it was disparaged by radicals of the 1960s and satirized by LeRoi Jones as "knee-grow," was once a word into which the hope for full equality was inscribed. For Wright, the Negro as America's metaphor was also a memory-inducing mirror for white America. Near the end of his lecture, he said: "The differences between black folk and white folk are not blood or color, and the ties that bind us are deeper than those that separate us. The common road of hope which we have all traveled has brought us into a stronger kinship than any words, laws, or legal claims. Look at us and know us and you will know yourselves, for *we* are *you*, looking back at you from the dark mirror of our lives."[1]

"Negro literature" was a term capacious enough to include writers of African descent anywhere in the world. In fact, from Gustavus Vassa to LeRoi Jones himself, the writers discussed in this book most commonly employed the term "Negro" to describe themselves, as well as people of African ancestry more generally. Early scholarship in the field, much of it written by intellectuals who had to work within the constraints of racial segregation, supported the political struggle for equality and integration. In 1926, Carter G. Woodson (Ph.D., Harvard University, 1912) established Negro History Week during the second week of February to commemorate the birthdays of Frederick Douglass (1818) and Abraham Lincoln (1809), a black man and a white man who together symbolized the end of slavery. Woodson had pioneered in history with such classic studies as *The Education of the Negro prior to 1861* (1915) and *The History of the Negro Church* (1924) and with an early focus on the history of what in the United States is called "miscegenation" (interracial sexual, marital, and family relations). Benjamin Brawley (M.A., Harvard, 1908) published literary histories that included *The Negro Genius* (1937); Eva B. Dykes (Ph.D., Radcliffe College, 1921) demonstrated the significance of the antislavery struggle for English Romantic literature in *The Negro in English Romantic Thought; or, A Study of Sympathy for the Oppressed* (1941); the poet-critic Sterling A. Brown (M.A., Harvard, 1923) critiqued stereotypes and highlighted realistic portrayals in American writing in his *Negro Poetry and Negro Drama* (1937) and *The Negro in American Fiction* (1937); Benjamin Mays (Ph.D., University of Chicago, 1935) pioneered in the study of religion and published *The Negro's God as Reflected in His Literature* (1938); the immensely productive historian John Hope Franklin (Ph.D., Harvard, 1947) offered a helpfully synthesizing textbook to complement American history textbooks, *From Slavery to Freedom* (1947); Frank Snowden, who in 1944 received a Ph.D. in Classics from Harvard with a dissertation written in Latin, "De Servis Libertisque Pompeian-is," focused in his *Blacks in Antiquity* (1970) and other works on the role of blacks in the ancient world, a time that there were no black laws or bans on miscegenation; Hugh M. Gloster (Ph.D., New York University, 1944) wrote his dissertation on "American Negro Fiction from Charles W. Chesnutt to Richard Wright"; and Marion W. Starling, in "The Slave Narrative: Its Place in American Literary History" (New York University, 1946), and Charles H. Nichols, in "A Study of the Slave Narrative" (Brown University, 1949), undertook the first full-scale doctoral work on the slave narrative. Such scholarship had the effect of making visible the African American past, writing blacks into American and global history, rectifying omissions and neglect, and setting the record straight against the then dominant American scholarly opinion that slighted the impor-tance and contributions of blacks.

Due to this early scholarship, interest in previously neglected works and authors grew and received more critical attention. Thus, Robert A. Bone wrote *The Negro Novel in America* (1955), a dissertation for Yale University in which he singled out the achievement of Jean Toomer's *Cane*, new editions of which were published later with full biographical introductions by Arna Bontemps and Darwin T. Turner. Bone soon also called attention to the brilliant structure of Charles Chesnutt's short sto-ries. Paul Edwards brought back Gustavus Vassa/Olaudah Equiano in a marvelously introduced facsimile edition in 1969, in which he highlight-ed Equiano's account of trying to talk to a book. And much scholarship followed, accelerating especially in the 1970s, after the creation of Black Studies Departments.

The best African American writers confronted issues of slavery, seg-regation, and race in one way or another, but their literary interests were broader. These writers commented on positions taken by race leaders and educators, and they engaged in debates with their contemporaries, but they did more than reflect or build on black precursor texts. Per-haps Wright was exceptional in that he read Negro literature system-atically and, in *White Man, Listen!* (1957), published the knowledgeable and argumentative lecture about it referenced above. Wright and these authors generally fought Jim Crow and excoriated lynching. Yet each also lived in an aesthetic universe that was centrally shaped by reading a wide array of materials that included, but was not limited to, Negro literature.

Reading and writing, these authors took part in world literature. Equiano/Vassa read Milton, Pope, Thomas Day, American Quakers, and British abolitionists, as well as the autobiographies by his black British contemporaries James Albert Ukawsaw Gronniosaw and Quobna Otto-bah Cugoano. Frank Webb read Victor Hugo, Charles Dickens, Eugène Sue, and Alexandre Dumas, père. Charles W. Chesnutt read Ovid, Dumas, Thomas Hardy, Pushkin, Henry James, Joel Chandler Harris, George Washington Cable, William Dean Howells, and Albion Tourgée. Jean Toomer read Shaw, Ibsen, Goethe, Dostoevsky, Tolstoy, Flaubert, Baudelaire, and the Imagist poets, and he was inspired by modern art and photography. W. E. B. Du Bois read very broadly, but he remained an unwavering Germanophile who quoted Goethe's *Faust* from memory, viewed his own life path in the light of Goethe's Wilhelm Meister, and wrote in the *Pittsburgh Courier* about Richard Wagner's operas that "no human being, white or black, can afford not to know them, if he would know life." Wright read everything he could get his hands on, including Poe, Kierkegaard, Nietzsche, William James, Proust, Joyce, and Hemingway. He loved Gertrude Stein's "Melanctha" so much that he wrote that he wished he had written it.[2]

Zora Neale Hurston thoroughly disliked Du Bois and opposed being forced into racial groupings such as "skinfolks" rather than "kinfolks." Her favorite authors were Rudyard Kipling, Robert Louis Stevenson, and Hans Christian Andersen, and she adored Norse myths. Ralph Ellison read Wright, of course, considering him a racial "relative," but he viewed Melville, Dostoyevsky, Malraux, Joyce, and Faulkner as his literary "ancestors," and he regularly retyped a Hemingway short story as a warm-up exercise that prepared him for his own writing.[3] Adrienne Kennedy commented on Du Bois and Paul Robeson, and she read *Jane Eyre* and world tragedy; adapted Euripides; specifically mentioned Maurice Maeterlinck, Anton Chekhov, and Tennessee Williams; and intertwined her own stories with famous Hollywood movies she had seen. Before LeRoi Jones became Amiri Baraka, he read Herman Melville, Charles Baudelaire, August Strindberg, William Carlos Williams, Charles Olson, Allen Ginsberg, Jack Kerouac, and William Burroughs's *Naked Lunch*.

Each of these writers confronted the white preoccupation with race but did so by resisting notions of a prescriptive aesthetic and by drawing on a broadly international range of available aesthetic resources. If there was one Negro author read by many others, it was Alexandre Dumas, though generally not his race-themed *Georges* but, rather, *The Count of Monte-Cristo* or *The Three Musketeers*.

This Book

The essays collected here, written over a long period of time, take a literary approach to black writing in an attempt to present writers as readers and as intellectuals who were open to the world. Olaudah Equiano has been considered the progenitor of the African American slave narrative. Yet in his lifetime, he was known as Gustavus Vassa and used the name Equiano only once, when he published his autobiography, *The Interesting Narrative of the Life of Olaudah Equiano, or Gustavus Vassa, the African. Written by Himself* (1789). He spent less time in America than sailing the seas, and he settled in England. He referred to himself as a Negro or "the African." Written in the age of Jean-Jacques Rousseau and Benjamin Franklin, Equiano's autobiography was that of one of the most widely traveled men of his time, who quoted much English poetry from memory. The book, at the center of which was his religious conversion, ended with a plea for free trade. In an open letter to a slavery advocate, Vassa, who married Susan Cullen, an Englishwoman, and left a substantial inheritance to his daughter Joanna Vassa, published what may be the first interracial manifesto, giving interracial marriage its biblical sanction.

Any student who first reads Frank J. Webb's *The Garies and Their Friends* (1857) is surprised by the sheer aesthetic pleasure that this suspenseful novel of manners provides, with its fully realized characters and its ironic narrative tone. To state that this novel was the best fiction published by an African American in the slavery period is hardly an exaggeration. Yet even though the novel first appeared in England with an introductory comment by Harriet Beecher Stowe, and was reprinted as a popular cheap edition that sold twelve thousand copies, no current American anthology gives any room to *The Garies and Their Friends*, and Webb rarely is taught in courses on African American literature. Written in the slavery period but set largely among free colored people in Philadelphia, the novel focuses, quite prophetically, on the etiquette, troubles, and violence of a Jim Crow society that would follow the abolition of slavery. Webb remains the big unknown figure in American literature, perhaps because he is believed to have avoided the representation of slavery, yet a most sarcastic scene with northern candidates who are being interviewed for the job of overseer on a Georgia plantation shows that slavery was also among Webb's concerns. In *The Garies and Their Friends*, Webb aspired to participate in the genre of the social novel, in the spectrum from Eugène Sue to Dickens. Webb also was clearly inspired by Dumas and set a novella at the very site of Dumas's *Man with the Iron Mask*. In that 1870 novella, "Two Wolves and a Lamb," Webb pioneered in creating fiction in which no black character appeared, a form of literary expression that was once called "raceless fiction." It was a mode of writing that provided many later authors with the liberty to experiment with themes they wished to isolate from any overarching obsession with race, such as a psychoanalytic understanding of violence (Wright's *Savage Holiday*), rape (Hurston's *Seraph on the Suwanee*), or a fully realized homosexual plot (James Baldwin's *Giovanni's Room*).

Long ignored in American literary studies, Charles Chesnutt's works have enjoyed a much deserved revival. He was a great master of irony and the most accomplished writer to address the legacy of slavery and the arrival of Jim Crow in forms of fiction that drew on, and transformed, plotlines and formal devices he found in a wide range of great authors, as well as in "plantation school" dialect writing that often leaned toward nostalgia for slavery. Chesnutt's own complex narrative structures laid bare the tragic, comic, and tragicomic potential of the lives of slaves, former slaves, and their descendants and the ways that white characters understood, or misunderstood, those lives. In his Uncle Julius stories, Chesnutt employed a biased narrator for the frame narratives to stage meaningful narrative competitions with Julius's inside tales. Chesnutt also offered an intricate form of dialect transcription that compels the reader to slow down and contemplate the force of the inside story of conjure, involving a magical metamorphosis in slavery days, against the often placid and self-contented analysis offered by the frame narrator. Was not slavery itself a form of magical transformation that changed a person into an animal or a thing, the reader is forced to ask, and what can racial distinctions mean when the color line, though forcefully drawn, is also porous—and can, in any event, be easily crossed by magic? Although sometimes considered merely a concession to a market for dialect writing that Chesnutt supposedly was happy to abandon, the short stories in *The Conjure Woman* (1899), as well as the "goopher" tales that did not make it into that collection, were an extraordinary aesthetic accomplishment in the age of literary realism.

Jean Toomer was a towering figure of American literary modernism. In *Cane* (1923), his very sentences sparkle with synaesthesia and the palpable joy of experimenting with features of poetry, prose, and drama in a mélange of images that trains the reader's eyes and ears on the rural South, the new urban centers of Washington and Chicago, and the intellectual's quandary in dealing with the clash of tradition and modernity. This drama is further complicated by the contemplation of the legacy of slavery and the newly intensified, often violent drawing of the color line in America, embodied by a truly gruesome lynching of a pregnant woman. How can an artist create beauty out of such a painful history, Toomer asks? Yet he attempted to do just that. Toomer also was, and perhaps remains to this day, the most radical questioner of the American belief in race. He attacked the notion of racial difference in countless ways, starting with non-clichéd descriptions of his characters ("her skin was like dusk on the eastern horizon") and including many attempts to broaden the category of "American" to contain all racial groups. This has provoked the strange accusation that Toomer changed his racial self-description out of sheer opportunism: a highly visible, and demonstrably false, claim was made that Toomer supposedly was the only member of his family who ever crossed the color line. In fact, Toomer spent crucial years of his puberty with his mother and stepfather who had married as "whites." His grandfather's sister also encouraged her brother to pass for white, as she did. Coming from a multigenerational, racially mixed family, Toomer was only too aware that talk of blood was a scientistic fantasy employed mostly for sinister ends. He also found support for his prochoice view of race in the contemporary Negro press. His radicalism, combined with his remarkable aesthetic experimentation, has attracted many readers, writers, students, and artists to his work.

African American intellectuals' travels and encounters with radical spirits across the Atlantic, including European pacifists and leftist enthusiasts for black American creativity, challenged them to rethink American notions of race. Two examples of this phenomenon were the cases of Countée Cullen's meeting with Claire Goll and Horace Cayton's self-reported comedy of manners-like near-romance with Nancy Cunard. Similarly, Claude McKay's response to Leon Trotsky in 1923 and Du

Bois's visit to Nazi Germany in 1936 demonstrate these cosmopolitan intellectuals' openness to the world, as well as their critical engagement with the political streams of Soviet Communism and German National Socialism. With his abiding love for Germany and for Wagner's operas, Du Bois offered a most perceptive analysis of the effects of Nazi propaganda in his remarkable, though too little known, essay "The Present Plight of the German Jew."

Zora Neale Hurston was a central figure in the 1930s until Richard Wright took the spotlight in the 1940s. Both were southern-born Negro migrants to northern cities, and both wrote short stories that thematized the conflicts of urban modernity and rural life in the form of adultery tales. However, they rather sharply polemicized against each other's work. Hurston's academic training in the Anthropology Department at Columbia University and Wright's friendship with central figures of the Chicago School of Sociology helped shape their different points of view; Hurston's political conservatism and Wright's leftist radicalism further enhanced their opposition.[4] As a result, they are not often read together and compared, though such comparisons increase our understanding of both of these modern writers' attempts to project prototypical African American stories.

With the Supreme Court's decision in *Brown v. Board of Education* in 1954, the days of legal segregation were numbered. It was somewhat surprising, then, that in 1955 Zora Neale Hurston published an attack on *Brown v. Board* in a southern segregationist newspaper, in which she invoked "the days of the never-to-be-sufficiently-deplored Reconstruction," and polemicized against government by decree, while focusing the core of her essay on the fear of "the evils of Communist penetration" and the worry that school desegregation might be a communist plot designed to prepare the country for interracial marriages (then still banned in many states). The rhetoric of Hurston's essay was strong, even strident. An essay by Hannah Arendt of the same period suggested that the issue of interracial marriage was an explosive one in the 1950s, and this juxtaposition permitted me to draw some tentative conclusions about the changing national mood from the 1950s to the 1960s.

Born three years after the end of the Civil War, Du Bois died the day before the March on Washington in 1963. His reflections in his posthumously published *Autobiography* (1968) offered a review of the history from Reconstruction to the impending success of the Civil Rights Movement. Du Bois gave surprisingly candid accounts of his personal life and depicted his academic and civil rights career vividly, although the book also bore the stamp of Stalinist Cold War rhetoric. Speaking in the voice of a man who had turned ninety when he began his autobiography, Du Bois not only reviewed his life as if it were an unfulfilled bildungsroman, but he also commented scathingly on the American attempt "to reduce life to buying and selling" and even on the puzzling spectacle of Elvis Presley going "through the motions of copulation on the public stage" and driving teenage children into a frenzy. As the youth cult was just taking off in America, Du Bois dryly pronounced the most un-American of maxims: "Youth is more courageous than age because it knows less. Age is wiser than youth because it knows more." That the public recognition the aged Du Bois may have hoped for came only in the form of intense surveillance by the Federal Bureau of Investigation is another cruel irony of his life.[5]

Serious African American drama had entered Broadway in the 1930s with Langston Hughes's play *Mulatto* (1935). The fame of that piece was eclipsed by the enormous success of Lorraine Hansberry's *A Raisin in the Sun* (1959), which was turned into a movie starring Diana Sands, Claudia MacNeil, Ruby Dee, and Sidney Poitier. Half a year after the March on Washington, young black playwrights turned to the more experimental off-Broadway scene where one-act (as opposed to Broadway's multi-act) plays and absurd (as opposed to realistic) drama flourished, and out of which a new black theater movement developed. A pioneer of that movement was Adrienne Kennedy. Her *Funnyhouse of a Negro* (1964) was the opening volley in a theatrical revolution that featured characters who appear to be collages of multiple and contradictory selves, stage props "possessing the quality of nightmares and terror," ritualistic repetitions and variations of identical lines, chorus-like chants taken from Greek tragedy, and enigmatic and troubling images and metaphors ("the race's hair fell out"), all of which evoked the harrowing sensation of divided races, divided families, and divided selves and set the tone for the 1960s. Kennedy's Sarah is a figure that is both black and white, male and female, as Queen Victoria, the Duchess of Hapsburg, Patrice Lumumba, and Jesus make up "her selves." Produced by Edward Albee, *Funnyhouse of a Negro* emerged from a modern drama tradition going back to Maurice Maeterlinck and August Strindberg, Eugene O'Neill, Tennessee Williams, and Eugène Ionesco. Kennedy's many plays made her "totally cool" work (as the playwright Suzan-Lori Parks characterized it) widely known. Kennedy's formal influences are apparent in the plays of many of her American followers, from Ntozake Shange's *For Colored Girls Who Have Considered Suicide When the Rainbow Is Enuf* (1975) to Anna Deavere Smith's *Fires in the Mirror* (1992) and Parks's own early experimental plays, as well as in the international drama scene.

LeRoi Jones/Amiri Baraka's explosive one-act play *Dutchman* (1964) was also produced by Albee. Jones presents a divided self, too, in the middle-class Negro Clay and the white bohemian Lula, both of whom speak lines that Jones also used in essays and poems. With its circular ending, *Dutchman* suggests an eternal repetition of the action: the ritual killing of the Clays by the Lulas creates a Flying Dutchman–like situation in the underground setting of the New York subway. The reader finds echoes of Strindberg's *Miss Julie*, O'Neill's *All God's Chillun Got Wings*, and Ionesco's *Lesson*. Yet Clay delivers a long speech before Lula kills him, and that speech embodies powerful anger and becomes a proto-nationalist manifesto, declaimed by an absurd character who will be killed for his words. Clay, an aspiring artist, sees art as a neurotic perversion and advocates racial violence as the only course of action that will restore the black man's sanity. Clay and Lula are narcissistic mirror images of each other, but their composite self, their "corporate Godhead," has cracked lethally. On the stage, Lula literally kills Clay and, as the ending suggests, will kill more and more Clays. Symbolically, however, the play encourages viewers to cast off their Lulaness, to exorcise their murderous whiteness and femininity to arrive at the "pure heart, the pumping black heart" of an undivided identity. *Dutchman* thus presented a serious challenge to the universalist and integrationist spirit of the postwar years and helped to open up an era of, one could say, "Lula-free" questing for a male-focused racial authenticity. Clay's speech also may have marked the beginning of the gradual end of the common use of the word "Negro."

Based on a conference at the American Academy of Arts and Sciences, the issues of *Daedalus* on "The Negro American" (1965) give the reader a sense of how America's racial future was imagined a half-century ago. At least one of the prophecies—voiced by the sociologist Everett C. Hughes—found its fulfillment in an unexpected way at President Barack Obama's inauguration in 2009. Short stories by Amina Gautier ("Been Meaning to Say" and "Pan Is Dead"), a novel by Heidi Durrow (*The Girl Who Fell from the Sky*), plays by Thomas Bradshaw (*Strom Thurmond Is Not a Racist* and *Cleansed*), and poems by Terrance Hayes ("For Brothers and the Dragon" and "The Avocado") suggest trends in recent works by African American authors who began their careers in the twenty-first century and published in "the age of Obama."

What is the sense of the literature—call it Negro, black, Afro-American, or African American (with or without hyphen)—that emerges as one reads the Enlightenment traveler Vassa, the Philadelphian expatriate to Britain and Reconstruction-time returnee Webb, the self-taught cosmopolitan Chesnutt, the experimenter and radical universalist Toomer, various writers' international encounters and conversations in the interwar period, the antithetical spirits of Wright and Hurston, Du Bois's views of his century, and Kennedy's and Jones's dramatic experiments? The essays in this book, essays that alternate between close readings and broader cultural contextualizations, delineate a literary series of striking works. Even after a half-century of Black Studies, the reader can make fresh and often surprising discoveries in these works, as well as in the authors' encounters and dialogues with others. The transnational and transracial openness of African American writers was remarkable, particularly given the constraints under which they produced "Negro literature," and it has helped to usher in a period in which African American literature has found a truly global audience. The essays in this book attempt to honor that literature's achievement, heterogeneity, creativity, and openness to the world of letters.

The Illustrations

Each essay is accompanied by an image. Gustavus Vassa, painted by William Denton and engraved by Daniel Orme, is shown in the frontispiece of his autobiography as a reader of the Bible, which his hand holds open at Acts of the Apostles 4:12 (Chapter 1). The rarely reproduced daguerreotype of Frank Webb shows him seated on the right with his hands folded in his lap; next to him stands his wife, Mary, whose arm rests on an unidentified man (Chapter 2). A photograph of Charles W. Chesnutt in the library at his home in Cleveland portrays him, too, as a writer who is a reader of many books (Chapter 3). A photograph of Claude McKay speaking at the Kremlin in 1923 illustrates the many international connections of the 1920s and 1930s (Chapter 5); stage photographs of *Funnyhouse of a Negro* (by Roger Pic) and of the cast of *Dutchman* (by Alix Jeffry) give the reader a sense of contemporary productions of those plays

(Chapters 10 and 11, respectively), and a news photograph of Obama's first inauguration accompanies Chapter 12, for a reason that is clarified in the essay itself.

As particular highlights, this book includes examples of the most memorable visual representations of twentieth-century intellectuals and artists in the artwork of the German-born artist and pacifist Winold Reiss and that of the promoter of Negro literature Carl Van Vechten. Reiss did much in the 1920s to define the New Negro visually in numerous portraits and illustrative work. Van Vechten created an archive of four-teen thousand portraits between 1932 and 1964, an archive that includes many black writers, artists, and performers he photographed with his Leica. Three images in this book are color reproductions of Reiss's pastel portraits: *Jean Toomer* (Chapter 4), *W. E. B. Du Bois* (Chapter 6), and *Zora Neale Hurston* (Chapter 8), all from 1925. Reiss, trained by Franz von Stuck at the Munich Art Academy and invited by Alain Locke to serve as chief illustrator of the *New Negro*, often contrasted realistically rendered faces and hands with flat, or at times merely outlined, clothing against a largely empty background with a few lines to suggest shadows that inten-sified the outline. Thus, Reiss's portrait of Toomer represents his brooding face with an almost three-dimensional effect, while the lower half of the image is dominated by the large black jacket that seems to lack any depth. In a similar way, Du Bois's face is so precisely realized as to seem sculp-tured, whereas his white jacket is merely outlined: his thoughtful face and the part of his hand that is visible at the bottom seem to move out of the flat white surroundings toward the viewer. In portraying Hurston gazing down to the right, in profile, Reiss used a square format, left some pencil shadings visible in her face, and let the more sketched quality begin just below her neck, extending to her characteristically flat dress or blouse. In all three cases, the monochromatic surroundings enhance the precision of hair, eyebrows, eyelashes, mouths, and ears of the pensive faces of the writers Reiss portrayed.[6]

Whereas portrait painters often fill in background with telling objects, portrait photographers tend to use white, flat, or otherwise nondescript backdrops. Reiss and Van Vechten seemed to invert this custom. While Reiss chose light, nondescript backgrounds for his painted portraits, Van Vechten worked with numerous props and avoided blank walls, instead using fabrics, wallpapers, and rugs as artificial and often bold backdrops in his photographs. Van Vechten's photograph of Richard Wright (1939) shows him in half-profile, seated in a half-length pose with the prop of a black, presumably African, sculpture, which he holds in both hands and seems to be examining most intently (Chapter 7). His torso and the sculpture are sharply outlined against the faint zebra-striped wallpaper in the back on which his shadow falls. In Van Vechten's portrait of W. E. B. Du Bois (1946), part of a large set of Kodachrome color photographs, Du Bois looks straight at the camera against the backdrop of an undulating red cloth, suggesting a red flag, giving the portrait a strangely warm glow and blurring the contrast between human figure and background (Chapter 9). Like Wright, Du Bois is wearing a suit and tie, but the tie's knot is a bit loose; the tiepin seems to protrude; and a ribbon is dangling toward an inside pocket that may perhaps contain Du Bois's glasses, adding a touch of disarray to the well-groomed figure.[7] That two visual artists so strikingly and memorably portrayed a great many twentieth-century African American writers is a welcome gift to teachers and students of literature.

Figure 1.1. Frontispiece of the 9th edition (1794) of *The Interesting Narrative of the Life of Olaudah Equiano, or Gustavus Vassa, the African. Written by Himself.* (Bavarian State Library, Munich [Bayerische Staatsbibliothek München].)

CHAPTER I

Olaudah Equiano, an Enlightenment Cosmopolitan in the Age of Slavery

July 10, 1766: Gustavus Vassa, twenty-one, buys his freedom for £40 from Robert King, a Philadelphia Quaker merchant.

APPROXIMATELY FIFTY-THREE THOUSAND AFRICANS were transported as slaves to the Americas each year of the 1750s, and many of them died in the process. The total number of Africans who were forced into New World slavery from the sixteenth century to the nineteenth century has been estimated at between eleven million and twelve million.[1] How did these Africans experience their enslavement and the forced Atlantic crossing of the Middle Passage—"the rupture and the ordeal," as Nathan Huggins described the second leg of the triangular voyage among Europe, Africa, and the Americas?[2] One early answer was given by the book *The Interesting Narrative of the Life of Olaudah Equiano, or Gustavus Vassa, the African. Written by Himself*, first published in that memorable revolutionary year, 1789. The memoir, written before the word "autobiography" had been coined, describes the author's life before, during, and after his enslavement. Equiano's haunting account of his experience aboard a slave ship in the 1750s is unforgettable:

SOURCE: Werner Sollors, "Introduction," in *The Interesting Narrative of the Life of Olaudah Equiano, or Gustavus Vassa, the African. Written by Himself: Norton Critical Edition*, ed. Werner Sollors (New York: W. W. Norton, 2001), ix–xxxi. Copyright © 2001 by W. W. Norton and Company, Inc. Used by permission of W. W. Norton and Company, Inc.

The stench of the hold while we were on the coast was so intol-
erably loathsome, that it was dangerous to remain there for any
time, and some of us had been permitted to stay on the deck for
the fresh air; but now that the whole ship's cargo were confined
together, it became absolutely pestilential. The closeness of the
place, and the heat of the climate, added to the number in the
ship, which was so crowded that each had scarcely room to turn
himself, almost suffocated us. This produced copious perspira-
tions, so that the air soon became unfit for respiration, from a
variety of loathsome smells, and brought on a sickness among the
slaves, of which many died, thus falling victims to the improvi-
dent avarice, as I may call it, of their purchasers. This wretched
situation was again aggravated by the galling of the chains, now
become insupportable; and the filth of the necessary tubs, into
which the children often fell, and were almost suffocated. The
shrieks of the women, and the groans of the dying, rendered the
whole a scene of horror almost inconceivable. (1:78–79)[3]

The author offers his life as a "history of neither a saint, a hero, nor a
tyrant" (1:2). He casts himself as a representative African who, although
his suffering was extraordinary by European standards, was still more
fortunate than many of his fellow Africans.

The stages of Equiano's life also represent a model of history. The
development starts with an ideal state in West Africa, which is interrupted by kidnapping, enslavement, and the brutal Middle Passage, and
culminates in freedom of economic enterprise, scientific exploration, and
devout Christianity. This representative life story would help end the
African slave trade and convince readers that it was not only contrary to
Enlightenment principles and incompatible with Christian religion but
also ultimately an impediment to English economic growth. But the
book goes far beyond these two themes as it tells the story of a generally
interesting life.

According to the *Narrative*, Olaudah Equiano (O-lah-*oo*-day Ek-wee-
ah-no) was born in West Africa in 1745. He explains that his first name
means "vicissitude or fortune also, one favoured, and having a loud voice
and well spoken" (1:31). Paul Edwards and Catherine Obianju Acholonu
have tried to identify in present-day Nigeria the precise birthplace Equiano mentions: the vale of Essaka, province of Eboe, kingdom of Benin,

Guinea. When Olaudah was about eleven, he and his sister were kid-napped; after a brief, chance meeting subsequent to their initial parting, the siblings were separated from each other forever. Equiano was taken on board a slave ship to Barbados and sent to a plantation in Virginia. He was soon purchased by the British naval officer Michael Henry Pascal, who took him to England and who, inspired by a popular English play about the sixteenth-century hero of Swedish independence, renamed him Gustavus Vassa. Previously, Equiano had also been called Michael and Jacob, and he at first resisted the new name Vassa but ultimately came to use it more frequently than his Ibo name. With the exception of the *Narrative* itself, a single letter from 1789, and one use of the signature "Aethiopianus," Equiano appears to have signed publications, letters, and legal documents with the name Gustavus Vassa.[4]

Vassa served with Pascal in the Seven Years' War (the American part of it is known as the French and Indian War) and was present at the siege of Louisbourg in Nova Scotia, was then resold into slavery, and worked on ships for a Philadelphia Quaker merchant, Robert King, trading between the West Indies and the mainland American colonies, ultimately earning enough money to buy his own freedom. He lived through shipwrecks, sailed the Mediterranean, and participated in an expedition to the Arctic. He converted to Anglicanism and was admitted to communion in West-minster Church (although he also expressed Methodist leanings). He took part in an English settlement among the Miskito Indians in Central America, sailed to North America again, and was appointed commis-sary for a Sierra Leone settlement by the Committee for the Relief of the Black Poor in 1787, although he lost the appointment for political reasons. He published letters in London newspapers and often expressed his support of the movement to abolish the slave trade. In 1787, he sent a brief to Lord Hawkesbury that was virtually identical to the penultimate paragraphs of the *Narrative*, in which he argued that the slave trade was an impediment to British manufacturing interests. In 1788, he presented an antislavery petition to Queen Charlotte, the Royal Consort of King George III, which is incorporated into chapter 12 of the *Narrative*.

After the publication of his book—which went through nine English editions; was reprinted in America; and was translated into Dutch, Ger-man, and Russian—he continued to live in England and remained con-nected with opponents of the slave trade. In 1791, for example, he spoke in Ireland, where nearly two thousand copies of his book were sold. In

1792, as he proudly added to later editions of the *Narrative*, he married Susan Cullen of Ely, Cambridgeshire, with whom he had two daughters, Ann Maria Vassa (who died in infancy) and Joanna Vassa. Susan Cullen Vassa was buried on February 21, 1796, and Gustavus Vassa died on March 31, 1797. Upon her father's death, Joanna Vassa inherited a fair amount of money.

The Slave Trade Opposed and Africa Remembered

The author of the *Narrative* lived in the intellectual ambience of English anti-slave trade activists. As Charles Nichols pointed out, it was Equiano who called the British abolitionist Granville Sharp's attention to the so-called *Zong* massacre, the case of a captain who in November 1781 had ordered 132 ailing African slaves drowned alive during the Middle Passage and who then collected the insurance premium on them. (In 1789, Sharp was among the subscribers whose support made the publication of the *Narrative* possible.) Gustavus Vassa knew British public figures of African origin with whom he formed the "Sons of Africa," and he co-signed public appeals with Ottobah Cugoano (a subscriber to the *Narrative*), Yahne Aelane, Jasper Goree, and others. Equiano knew, quoted, and defended celebrated abolitionists such as Thomas Clarkson and James Ramsay against pro-slave trade attacks. (Clarkson and Ramsay also were subscribers to the *Narrative*.) In 1789, Equiano wrote a letter to the Committee for the Abolition of the Slave Trade in which he commented on the famous illustration of the cross-section of the slave ship *Brookes* that had accompanied Clarkson's essays and that was frequently reproduced. The committee attempted to move the British Parliament to curb and ultimately abolish the lucrative slave trade, a campaign that began in 1788 and did not come to a successful end until 1807. Equiano's book also strengthened John Wesley, the founder of Methodism, in his opposition to slavery.

Equiano's contemporaries were, with varying degrees of enthusiasm, drawn to the *Narrative*. Here was a first-person singular account by a man who had been captured and taken away on a slave ship and who was an eyewitness to both the enormous and the subtle cruelties that accompanied the slave trade. This was not just a book written against the slave trade; it was a book written by an African who had firsthand memories of his childhood in West Africa.

In his vivid account of customs and staples, Equiano provided all readers interested in West African origins with rich details such as the following:

> We compute the year from the day on which the sun crosses the line, and on its setting that evening there is a general shout throughout the land; at least I can speak from my own knowledge throughout our vicinity. The people at the same time make a great noise with rattles, not unlike the basket rattles used by children here, though much larger, and hold up their hands to heaven for a blessing. (1:29).
>
> The natives are extremely cautious about poison. When they buy any eatable the seller kisses it all round before the buyer, to shew him it is not poisoned; and the same is done when any meat or drink is presented, particularly to a stranger. We have serpents of different kinds, some of which are esteemed ominous when they appear in our houses, and these we never molest. I remember two of those ominous snakes, each of which was as thick as the calf of a man's leg, and in colour resembling a dolphin in the water, crept at different times into my mother's night-house, where I always lay with her, and coiled themselves into folds, and each time they crowed like a cock. (1:36)

The fact that Equiano could not only remember so much but also recorded his observations makes the *Narrative*, as Charles Nichols stressed, one of the "rarest historical documents, for millions of the men, women, and children who crossed the Atlantic during two or three centuries of the slave trade have left no word of their experiences."[5] Edwards and Acholonu have traced and identified features such as scarification, cam wood, and salt made of wood ash, all mentioned in the *Narrative*. Equiano's memories symbolically bridge the rupture of the Middle Passage.

The parts of the *Narrative* that seem to have affected its audience most were the descriptions of African life and of the Middle Passage in the first three chapters, the account of the atrocities of slave life in the West Indies in chapter 5, and the episode in which the author buys his freedom in chapter 7. Contemporary reviewers, later American abolitionists such as Lydia Maria Child, and modern-day critics all tended to focus on these passages.

Readers who shared Equiano's faith or were interested in religious autobiography were also moved by the account of his conversion in chapter 10. But those who, like Mary Wollstonecraft, were Enlightenment freethinkers wished that Equiano had stopped before getting religion and had ended the book at the moment he purchased his freedom on July 11, 1766. For Equiano, however, these themes were intimately connected.

Literacy and Religion

Since the slave trade was a great *moral* evil (though very profitable for those who were engaged or invested in it), Vassa firmly believed in Christian education for Africans, as well as in the need to turn those who were Christians in name only into true believers. Part of this process included his acquisition and use of literacy. Equiano draws on the comic potential of the old topos of the book that is encountered by someone who does not know how to read:

> I had often seen my master and Dick employed in reading; and I had a great curiosity to talk to the books, as I thought they did; and so to learn how all things had a beginning: for that purpose I have often taken up a book, and have talked to it, and then put my ears to it, when alone, in hopes it would answer me; and I have been very much concerned when I found it remained silent. (1:106–107)

Equiano's "account of how he tried to talk to the book" was pioneeringly analyzed by Paul Edwards as "one of the most striking passages" in the *Narrative* and placed in the context of Vassa's contemporary sources, James Albert Ukawsaw Gronniosaw (1770) and Quobna Ottobah Cugoano (1787). "To most Africans at that time," Edwards wrote in 1969, "the idea of communicating in words other than orally would be unimaginable, and the movement of the lips of an indifferent silent reader would certainly be interpreted in these circumstances as 'talking to the book.'"[6] This passage, later famously reexamined by Henry Louis Gates Jr. as the "trope of the talking book," was common in encounters of orally communicating with lettered cultures in colonial and postcolonial texts—for example, "El Inca" Garcilaso de la Vega's *Royal Commentaries of the Incas and General History of Peru* (1609).[7]

The initiation into the magic of the lettered world interests Equiano most especially in connection with his meditations on the Bible. In fact, he tells us when the book finally speaks to him that the one remaining "silent" at first was God. Equiano's conversion occurred at that very moment. He is reading Acts 4:12, the page to which the Bible in his hand is open in the frontispiece—"And there is salvation in no one else, for there is no other name under heaven given among men by which we must be saved"—when he finds that "the scriptures became an unsealed book. . . . The word of God was sweet to my taste, yea sweeter than honey and the honeycomb" (2:146–147). This experience makes the Bible his "only companion and comfort" (2:150):

> I prized it much, with many thanks to God that I could read it for myself. . . . Whenever I looked in the bible I saw things new, and many texts were immediately applied to me with great comfort, for I knew that to me was the word of salvation sent. (2:150)

In faith, the book has really spoken to Equiano, and resting on this revelation he can dare to write his own book. It is after his conversion, too, that Equiano—who interlaced his *Narrative* with snippets from poets, including Milton and Thomas Day, and who wrote an appreciative letter to the poet Samuel Jackson Pratt—presents a long poem of his own, a religious meditation that culminates in the phrase "Salvation is by Christ alone!" freely adapted from Acts 4. For any religious reader, this section must constitute the center of Equiano's book. Incidentally, Equiano also contemplated Islam and Judaism as possible religions and rejected a Spanish offer to study for the Catholic priesthood on the grounds that Catholics do not read the Bible enough. And as a reader-believer he was shocked to see Portuguese Catholics banning Protestant Bible translations.

The *Narrative* devotes much space to registering surprising deliverances and providential reversals as well as to describing the wonders of seafaring and of the whole natural world. And it is telling that of the two illustrations that accompany the first edition, one showed Equiano holding the Bible, the other the wreck of the slave ship *Nancy* in a storm at Bahama Banks in 1767, subtitled with a text taken from Job 33:14–30. Vassa's tale is undoubtedly a spiritual autobiography, and the turning point of his life is his conversion and religious rebirth on October 6, 1775.

Equiano's Transatlantic World

Although spiritual autobiography can be quite otherworldly, Equiano takes a deep, naturalistic, and scientific, interest in the secular world, for it was not only God's book that spoke to him but others, as well. He was obviously someone who enjoyed books more generally. The *Narrative* is also a memoir by a seaman who, during his travels around the globe, observes flying fish (amazingly, right from the slave ship that takes him to Barbados), whales, and flamingoes; the customs of Central American Indians; the volcano Mount Vesuvius; the wonders of the Arctic; and the mysteries of human skin color. If Vassa marshals the power of literacy and writing against the slave trade, he also writes in heterogeneous literary traditions. He is well versed in the Old and New Testaments and is clearly inspired by St. Paul in the Acts of the Apostles and by St. Augustine's *Confessions*. But he also writes in the novelistic manner of Daniel Defoe;[8] he freely quotes the classics, from Homer to Shakespeare and Milton, as well as contemporary English poets; and he draws on travel and scientific literature, as well as religious, political, and scientific tracts, following the scholarly procedure of indicating several sources in footnotes.

Equiano's literary language made his book much more than a generic attack on African slavery or a conversion narrative, for at a peak period of the culture of the printed book, here was one written by an African writer and reader whose image, holding the Good Book, must have appealed to an audience that he impressed by his self-conscious employment of literary devices and allusions. Equiano's particular command of literacy helped to strengthen his case against the slave trade by establishing him not only as a representative African but also as a well-rounded cosmopolitan and well-read Christian—or in short, a "bourgeois subject" whose views deserved serious attention and whose very abilities were a refutation of racist justifications of the African slave trade.[9] In this sense, his many asides on topics such as bullfighting or George Whitefield's style of preaching, his amazing interest in a Shropshire coal pit or in the Portuguese Carnival, are not distractions from his central political and religious subjects—the need to end the slave trade and to find universal salvation in Christ. His random observations, such as his reaction to seeing snow for the first time, and his spontaneous, and at times quite humorous, comments, instead help to get the central, serious points across.

Equiano is remarkably comparative in his contribution to inter-pretations of the Atlantic World in which he lived. For example, Afri-can dances remind him of oppressed Greeks whom he later observed in Turkish Smyrna, the Ibo robes are reminiscent of Scottish highland plaid (which he saw in the Seven Years' War), and even the snake's color in landlocked Essaka is described to the reader in terms of a dolphin. Equiano was impressively broad in his global framework of perception.

Rousseau, Montesquieu, Woolman, and Benezet

Among the many strains of philosophical, political, and religious thought that permeated Equiano's intellectual world, three reached him through a source he cites in the *Narrative*.

First, Equiano's representation of Africa was in part a response to the theme of the "noble savage" and a close fit to the Rousseau–inspired Euro-pean predilection for a natural simplicity that was not yet contaminated by the depredations of urban luxury and education.[10] Jean-Jacques Rousseau made the argument in *A Discourse upon the Origin and Foundation of Inequal-ity among Mankind* (1753; English translation, 1755) that "savage Man" or "Man in a State of Nature" had strength, courage, and good health; how-ever, "As he becomes sociable . . . he becomes weak, fearful, mean-spirited, and his soft and effeminate Way of Living at once completes the Enervation of his Strength and of his Courage."[11] With property comes selfishness, destroying man's original goodness and unlimited ability to empathize. This belief—that would have held an obvious appeal to Equiano—pervad-ed European intellectual life in the last decades of the eighteenth century and particularly inspired authors of travel writing who were fond of finding Rousseau's natural men in Africa and the Americas. Although Rousseau had said little on the subject of slavery, the Rousseauvian view of Africa was an argument against the pro-slave trade faction that tended to disparage Africa as backward.

Second, Montesquieu offered a rationalist critique of slavery as incompatible with any form of government except despotism. Charles Louis de Secondat Montesquieu made the important argument in *The Spirit of the Laws* (1748; English translation, 1750) that slavery must not exist under a monarchy, in which it is decisively important not to subject human nature to oppression and indignity; in a democracy, where all humans are equal; or even in an aristocracy, in which laws attempt to equalize men as much as that form of government permits. Montesquieu made his case not only as a matter of principle—an important one, for it permitted intellectuals to view slavery as incompatible with democracy and monarchy and to describe a slaveholding society as a tyranny—but also in a strong, ironic passage directed at supporters of slavery on racial grounds. "It is impossible to imagine that those people," Montesquieu appears to be parodying the pro-slavery position on Africans, "could be human beings, for if we considered them humans we would have to start doubting whether we ourselves are Christian men."[12] Other readers believed this passage was serious and an "instance of the prejudice under which even a liberal mind can labor." Although Montesquieu's position on slavery and on the climate theory of human character was full of contradictions—in the eyes of Montesquieu's antislavery readers, African slavery was contradictory to political principles, served only the undeserved luxury of Europeans, and stemmed from a hypocritical violation of that same human empathy in which Christians professed to believe. This, too, would have been a congenial platform for Vassa to adopt.

Third, the Pennsylvania Society of Friends felt that the contradiction between Christian faith and African slavery was simply unsustainable.[13] The Philadelphia Quaker John Woolman began to articulate this tension in his diary in 1742, and in 1754 he published the tract *Some Considerations on the Keeping of Negroes; Recommended to the Professors of Christianity, of Every Denomination*. Filled with a "real sadness" when contemplating the fate of "these poor negroes," Woolman cited the shared human origin in Adam and Eve as evidence that "all nations are of one blood" (Acts 17:26). He emphasized the golden rule as the core of Christian doctrine: "Whatsoever ye would that Men should do unto you, do even so to them" (Matthew 7:12). He quoted Christ's maxim, "Forasmuch as ye did it to the least of these my brethren, ye did it unto me" (Matthew 25:40). He invited Christian readers to imagine themselves in the Africans' place, to "make their case ours." He proceeded with a novel consideration that proved persuasive to many readers in the second half of the eighteenth century. Woolman examined the effects of slaveholding on *whites* and focused perceptively on the danger of a rise of racial prejudice. In contemplating the effects of slavery on a Christian commonwealth, Woolman feared for the loss of "that humility and meekness in which alone lasting happiness can be enjoyed."[14] Beginning in 1761, Quakers were increasingly exhorted to release their slaves and to cease all participation in the slave trade. It is no coincidence that Equiano's master, who permitted him, however reluctantly, to buy his freedom in 1766, was a Philadelphia Quaker. Even though Equiano did not wish to become a Quaker himself (he seemed to prefer Bible reading to silent meetings), he held Quakers in highest esteem.

These different strands of mid-eighteenth century thought coalesced perfectly in the once extremely popular (though now less well known) work by the Pennsylvania Quaker abolitionist quotation gatherer Anthony Benezet, *Some Historical Account of Guinea* (published in 1771 and reprinted many times). Benezet, who also founded a Philadelphia Free School for colored children that Equiano visited in 1785 (see chapter 12 of the *Narrative*), absorbed from his sources many positive and admiring descriptions of Africa; he devoted a section to a praise of Montesquieu's critique of slavery, and, following the Quaker tradition of worrying about the effects of slavery on Christianity, he opposed slavery vehemently from a Christian universalist position. The long title of his book included the programmatic phrase *An Inquiry into the Rise and Progress of the Slave-Trade, Its Nature and Lamentable Effects*, and his opening epigraph on the title page is taken from Acts 17: "God that made the World—hath made of one Blood all Nations of Men." He also included long descriptions of the extraordinary cruelties toward African slaves on the West Indian islands and extracts from Granville Sharp's attack on slavery.

Benezet was a strong presence in the writings of English opponents to the slave trade who were rallying to their cause in the 1780s. This is certainly true for Thomas Clarkson's important work *An Essay on the Slavery and Commerce of the Human Species, Particularly the African* (1786), in which the author "traced the situation of man from unbounded liberty to subordination" to attack African slavery as "contrary to *reason, justice, nature, the principles of law and government, the whole doctrine, in short, of natural religion, and the revealed voice of God.*"[15] Clarkson invoked Woolman and named Benezet's *Account* as one of his central sources. "In this precious book I found almost all I wanted," he stated.[16] Appeals to original goodness, a natural right to liberty, human oneness ("one blood"), the golden rule, and the incompatibility of slavery with Christianity pervaded antislavery writing, and Benezet also influenced Tom Paine and John Wesley. It was impossible for Equiano not to encounter and appreciate Benezet's glowing account of Africa. With his footnotes to Benezet,

Equiano signals his participation in this tradition of anti–slave trade and antislavery writing.[17]

Equiano's Voice

Equiano's voice is both that of "the African" (as the title page of his book promises) and that of a European.[18] He is the African who cherishes his past and the culture within which he was raised and who, when he sees Europeans for the first time, can describe his fear of being "eaten by those white men with horrible looks, red faces, and loose hair" (1:72). And he is the English intellectual who can speak with the voice of Ajax in Pope's translation of the *Iliad* or describe the hell of slavery in Montserrat in the words of *Paradise Lost*. In fact, his English erudition appears well before he describes his first encounter with Englishmen. It is manifest right from the rhetorical opening—where he expresses feigned worry that a writer of memoirs might be considered vain—to the sources through which he represents Africa. It reaches extreme moments, as when he describes his fear of perishing in the African woods while escaping his capture by a neighboring nation. "Thus was I like the hunted deer," he writes:

> —Ev'ry leaf and ev'ry whisp'ring breath,
> Convey'd a foe, and ev'ry foe a death. (1:56)

To have a repertoire of even minor literary quotations available—this one adapted from John Denham's *Coopers Hill* (1642)—and to employ them even in situations charged with emotions (for example, great anxiety) reveals not merely literacy but a close approximation of a contemporary literary ideal. Equiano's literary sophistication and rhetorical skills do not constitute a contradictory interference with his "Africanness." Instead, they help to define the terms in which he came to present and view African life.

Yet Equiano could not assume a readily available collective identification ("Afro-Briton"? "Anglo-African"?). This causes a certain instability of the first-person singular observer and of the pronouns he uses to describe collective belonging. Both "they" and "we" may refer to Equiano's Africans, as well as to Europeans. The following sentences from chapter 1 are representative:

> As to religion, the natives believe that there is one Creator of all
> things, and that he lives in the sun, and is girted round with a
> belt that he may never eat or drink; but, according to some, he
> smokes a pipe, which is our own favourite luxury. They believe
> he governs events. (1:27)

There is a subtle distinction between "our own" luxury and what "they" believe.[19] The Ibo sun god referred to may be Chukwu, as Edwards suggested. However, the presence of a pipe-smoking god also makes for a certain humor here, as it points to a post-Columbian origin of this "original" custom (in a part of the world in which Indian corn had also become a staple). The appeal to Rousseauvian ideas of simplicity is explicitly articulated: "Our manner of living is entirely plain; for as yet the natives are unacquainted with those refinements in cookery which debauch the taste" (1:13).

If for Equiano "Africa" meant, on the one hand, the presence of natural man, simple, unrefined, and still capable of empathy unmediated by selfishness, his land of birth was, on the other hand, also associated with biblical origins. Equiano explicitly casts the Ibos as typologically related to the biblical Israelites. "We practised circumcision like the Jews, and made offerings and feasts on that occasion in the same manner as they did. Like them also, our children were named from some event, some circumstance, or fancied foreboding at the time of their birth" (1:30–31). Equiano repeatedly mentions examples of African-Jewish parallels and even offers a general observation concerning, as he puts it, "the strong analogy . . . in the manners and customs of my countrymen and those of the Jews, before they reached the Land of Promise" (1:38).[20] Equiano here followed contemporary efforts to connect all human history to the biblical story. This reinforced the perception that Africans were living in an earlier, more original, positively conceived "primitive" state: "Like the Israelites in their primitive state, our government was conducted by our chiefs or judges, our wise men and elders; and the head of a family with us enjoyed a similar authority over his household with that which is ascribed to Abraham and the other patriarchs" (1:39). This simile casts Africans as the symbolic ancestors of the British, what the Hebrew patriarchs were for Christianity. This analogy also created an expectation of a possible return, on a higher, Christian level, to this state of nature he describes, and to a realm of full, unselfish empathy, of which Christian Africans might be the harbingers.

Equiano ends both chapter 1 and chapter 2 with strong exhortations of European readers that are augmented by the familiar biblical quotations ("one blood" from Acts 17:26 and the "golden rule" of Matthew 7:12):

> Let the polished and haughty European recollect that his ances-
> tors were once, like the Africans, uncivilized, and even barbarous.
> Did Nature make *them* inferior to their sons? And should *they too*
> have been made slaves? Every rational mind answers, No. . . .
> If, when they [the Europeans] look round the world, they feel
> exultation, let it be tempered with benevolence to others, and
> gratitude to God, "who hath made of one blood all nations of
> men for to dwell on all the face of the earth." (1:43–44)

And

> O, ye nominal Christians! might not an African ask you, learned
> you this from your God, who says unto you, Do unto all men as
> you would men should do unto you?" (1:87)

Free Trade

Whether or not African aborigines lived in an original state of nature (as the English aborigines once did), that state was brought to an abrupt and brutal end by the slave trade. One thinks that this experience might generate a nostalgic wish in Equiano for a return to origins or the development of a position from which *all* British trade would be attacked as destructive of original goodness. Yet far from yearning for a return to an original state of repose,[21] Equiano actually cherishes the hustle-bustle of the world of modern free trade in which *only* the slave trade is an obstacle to an otherwise thoroughly appreciated and endorsed free exchange of goods and the opening of untapped markets. As Houston A. Baker Jr. stressed, the very fact that Equiano *purchased* himself was a sign of his recognition "that only the acquisition of property will enable him to alter his designated status *as property*."[22] It was thus Equiano's ability to trade that freed him from his slave status. "As the inhuman traffic of slavery is to be taken into the consideration of the British legislature," he states in his *Narrative*, and adapting passages from a letter he had written to the president of the English Board of Trade, Lord Hawkesbury, he continues:

> I doubt not, if a system of commerce was established in Africa, the demand for manufactures would most rapidly augment, as the native inhabitants will insensibly adopt the British fashions, manners, customs, &c. In proportion to the civilization, so will be the consumption of British manufactures. (2:249–250)

He believes that the "manufacturing interest and the general interest are synonymous" (2:252) and it is in the area of consumption growth that African history will repeat English history:

> It cost the Aborigines of Britain little or nothing in clothing, &c. The difference between their forefathers and the present generation, in point of consumption, is literally infinite. The supposition is most obvious. It will be equally immense in Africa—The same cause, viz. civilization, will ever have the same effect. (2:250)

Civilization and property spelled the end of Rousseau's state of nature, but Equiano deemed such progress beneficial.[23] Hence the slave trade appears to be not only morally wrong but also bad for all commerce— except the trade in shackles and chains, as Equiano sarcastically adds.

Cultural Relativism

Equiano's autobiographical self had multiple perspectives: the eyewitness of Ibo life and of the slave ship; the extoller of primitive man; the writer, reader, and Protestant convert; the political abolitionist and economic free-trade advocate. These various aspects of Equiano's autobiographical self do not easily merge into a single point of view. Speaking with different voices, he is also remarkably curious about many of the details of the worlds he encounters in his largely episodic book. He is, as Geraldine Murphy writes, an "accidental tourist" who finds something to marvel at wherever he goes—from the predictable to the unexpected.

In his observations, Equiano provides some evidence of cultural relativism, most pronounced in his explicit and implicit comparisons between black and white, African and English. He writes that "in regard to complexion, ideas of beauty are wholly relative" (1:21), an idea to which some English intellectuals also gave currency, going back at least to Thomas Browne's study *Pseudodoxia* (1646). Browne had stressed that Africans take so much content in blackness "that they esteem deformity by other colours, describing the Devil, and terrible objects, white," and concluded that "beauty is determined by opinion, and seems to have no essence that holds one notion with all."[24] Equiano supports a similar observation by his own life: "I remember while in Africa to have seen three negro children, who were tawny, and another quite white, who were universally regarded by myself, and the natives in general, as far as related to their complexions, as deformed" (1:21–22).

His relativism is less clear-cut when he observes other cultures. He is often inclined to see the world through British eyes. His anti-Catholicism is pronounced; his double-edged reference to the "morality and common sense of a Samaide or a Hottentot" (1:219) does not betray an African point of view; and in such decisive cultural markers as monogamy, Vassa can come out on different sides of the issue. He describes the Ibo men understandingly as not preserving "the same constancy to their wives, which they expect from them; for they indulge in a plurality, though seldom in more than two" (1:8). Yet when he is offered two wives by a Turkish officer in Smyrna, he comments with irony, but now also from a firmly Western point of view, "I refused the temptation" (2:94). (He added in a later edition that he thought "one was as much as some could manage, and more than others would venture on.")

Language, Free Black Life, and Interracialism

Equiano, who views himself as an open-minded observer, renders many other interesting aspects of eighteenth-century Atlantic life that a modern reader may enjoy. His observations on language, free black life, and on interracialism are examples. He is, from childhood, quite accustomed to language difference, and he continually comments on languages. Scholars have endeavored to offer additional explanations of Equiano's Ibo terms such as "Embrenche" and "Ah-affoe-way-cah." Yet his memory of his mother tongue also serves to support the theory of natural goodness: "I remember we never polluted the name of the object of our adoration; on the contrary, it was always mentioned with the greatest reverence;

and we were totally unacquainted with swearing, and all those terms of abuse and reproach which find their way so readily and copiously into the languages of more civilized people" (1:31). Still, switching from one natural language to another was not difficult. "From the time I left my own nation I always found somebody that understood me till I came to the sea coast. The languages of different nations did not totally differ, nor were they so copious as those of the Europeans, particularly the English. They were therefore easily learned; and, while I was journeying thus through Africa, I acquired two or three different tongues" (1:59).

This (idealized) family resemblance of various African languages ("we understood each other perfectly" [1:64–65]) changes radically when he has his first encounter with Europeans, who are absolutely different in "manners, customs, and language" (1:66). More than that, "The language they spoke (which was very different from any I had ever heard)" (1:71) strengthens his belief that they must be bad spirits, not human beings at all. Yet as his fear of Europeans disappears, he can also master English: "I could now speak English tolerably well, and I perfectly understood everything that was said. I now not only felt myself quite easy with these new countrymen, but relished their society and manners" (1:132).

One could probably add that Vassa particularly relished the language of the sea and that modern readers could assemble a whole phrase book from his *Narrative*, including, for example, vessels such as wherry, punt, drogger, hoy, sloop, frigate, snow, privateer, schooner, man of war, or fire ship; abbreviations from the compass such as S.W. and E.N.E.; and nautical terms such as quadrant, ensign, sounding, battery, press-gang, half-musket shot, quarter-deck, jib, gunwale, lee-beam, mizzenmast, and maintop gallant mast-head. He even liked to spin sailors' yarns, like the story of his seahorses "which neighed exactly like any other horses" (2:106).

How cosmopolitan this multilingual African becomes in the course of the book is driven home by another Rousseauvian encounter that he has when he takes part in an English expedition to Central America. In the same manner in which he described his own West Africans, he viewed the Miskito Indians as original men: "Upon the whole, I never met any nation that were so simple in their manners as these people, or had so little ornament in their houses. Neither had they, as I ever could learn, one word expressive of an oath" (2:182). Yet in Indian eyes Equiano seems to be an Englishman, even if somewhat better than the others. He reports the double-edged comment by a Miskito who is struck by the many curse words that were used by the English Christians: "How comes it that all the white men on board who can read and write, and observe the sun, and know all things, yet swear, lie, and get drunk, only excepting yourself?" (2:176).

Natural people speak natural languages that are proto-Protestant and pure. "The worst word I ever heard amongst them when they were quarreling, was one that they had got from the English, which was 'you rascal'" (2:182). Adopting English can thus be a mixed blessing. But from there Equiano proceeds to make pronouncements about the negative effect of culture contacts on pure languages, and his reading of aspects of Creole language is not admiring: "The Musquito people within our vicinity . . . made entertainments of the grand kind, called in their tongue *tourrie* or *dryckbot*. The English of this expression is, a feast of drinking about, of which it seems a corruption of language" (2:187–188). This may not be good etymology, but it does raise questions about Equiano's view of multilingual encounters. Does culture contact bring about better understanding or does it merely corrupt? Are natural people purer and more truly Christian than they become after mingling with nominally Christian Englishmen?

Vassa's answer to this question is different when he considers race rather than language. Again, his answer, informed by free black life, does not easily fit into a predictable mold. Equiano was aware that the issue of race had a dynamic of its own that could unfold outside and after slavery, too. He was perceptive in describing the difficulties and legal oppression of free blacks such as the Georgia carpenter who was imprisoned when he asked for his pay, or the free Mulatto sailor Joseph Clipson from the Bermudas who was wrongfully reenslaved. Equiano's legal efforts to regain the liberty of his friend, the cook John Annis, were thwarted, for Annis was kidnapped on the river Thames and taken to St. Kitts where he was, "according to custom, staked to the ground with four pins through a cord, two on his wrists, and two on his ancles, was cut and flogged most unmercifully, and afterwards loaded cruelly with irons about his neck" (2:122–123).

Equiano states forcefully that the liberty of free blacks is "nominal, for they are universally insulted and plundered without the possibility of redress" (1:249–250). John Wesley (whose antislavery position was aroused earlier when he read Benezet's *Account of Guinea*) reacted with particular empathy when he learned in Equiano's *Narrative* of the curtailment of the rights of free blacks who were not permitted to bear witness against whites in court. Like John Woolman, Equiano understood the dangerous nature of racial prejudice, but unlike Woolman, Equiano himself was repeatedly exposed to racial injustices in the colonies after his manumission. When a Mr. Hughes ties and hoists him up, intending to sell him as a slave in Cartagena, Equiano comments: "Thus I hung, without any crime committed, and without judge or jury; merely because I was a free man, and could not by the law get any redress from a white person in those parts of the world" (2:196). It is significant that in chapter 5 Equiano explicitly expresses his sympathy for Moses, who found redress only by slaying an Egyptian (as in Exodus 2:11–12). In this discerning allusion to Moses, Equiano supports militant, violent retaliation to racial injustice as one of the expectable and understandable responses. It is as if Equiano had said, "By any means necessary." The year was, after all, 1789, and bourgeois and colonial subjects were rallying to the cause of Revolution.

Vassa also examined the meaning of reciprocity implied by the golden rule to advocate a course of action that would seem to make him a prophet of the modern interracial movement. His theoretical starting point is the premise from the abolitionists' favorite passage in Acts 17 that all human beings are "of one blood" and that racial differences are of secondary significance and are due to different climates. He invokes John Mitchell's "Essay on the Causes of the Different Colours of People in Different Climates" (1744), which had argued that both blacks and whites "were descended from people of an intermediate tawny colour; whose posterity became more and more tawny, i.e., black, in the southern regions, and less so, or white, in the northern climes."[25] From Clarkson, Equiano adopts Mitchell's example of the Spaniards in America who had become "as dark coloured as our native Indians of Virginia" (1:41). Given the original "tawny colour" of Adam, Eve, and Noah, there was really no "black" or "white" in the world—there was only more or less "tawny." Hence, Equiano saw interracial marriage, on which he commented in the *Narrative* and in one of his public letters, as a desirable expression of human nature.[26]

Of course, Vassa was aware of the opposition to interracial unions that was particularly strong in the colonies and that was articulated by pro-slavery authors. He describes, for example, the "curious imposition on human nature" in an episode in St. Kitts, when "a white man wanted to marry in the church a free black woman":

The clergyman told him it was against the law of the place to marry a white and a black in the church. The man then asked to be married on the water, to which the parson consented, and the two lovers went in one boat, and the parson in another, and thus the ceremony was performed. (1:241)

As this episode suggests, Equiano did not favor the "curious imposition" of intermarriage restrictions. He not only lived an interracial life, he also advocated a general program of intermarriage. In an open letter to the *Public Advertiser* (January 28, 1788), he wrote that the "mutual commerce of the sexes of both Blacks and Whites" would help the situation of black women who are sexually exploited because of the legal restraints on intermarriage. He asked the London reader, "Why not establish intermarriages at home, and in our Colonies? and encourage open, free, and generous love upon Nature's own wide and extensive plan, subservient only to moral rectitude, without distinction of the colour of a skin?" In Equiano's eyes, interracial "mutual commerce" was part of the free flow of commercial activity that he generally favored.

Here he again adopts his favored typological role model of Moses, this time as the loving husband of an Ethiopian woman, the Midianite Zipporah (Exodus 2; Numbers 12), rather than as the militant slayer of an Egyptian.

That ancient, most wise, and inspired politician, Moses, encouraged strangers to unite with the Israelites, upon this maxim, that every addition to their number was an addition to their strength, and as an inducement, admitted them to most of the immunities of his own people. He established marriage with strangers by his own example—The Lord confirmed them—and punished Aaron and Miriam for vexing their brother for marrying the Ethiopian—Away then with your narrow impolitic notion of preventing by law what will be a national honour, national strength, and productive of national virtue—Intermarriages![27]

Gustavus Vassa's work may not have been the ideal prototype of the American slave narrative, for as Charles T. Davis put it so memorably, the *Narrative* was "neither an Afro-American work nor a slave narrative."[28] But Olaudah Equiano did participate in the eighteenth-century project of self-representation in autobiographic writing, of which Rousseau's *Confessions* and Benjamin Franklin's memoirs also were a part.[29] Proud of Africa, tireless in his opposition to the slave trade, and serious about spiritual matters, he led an active life and wrote an autobiography of true political significance. In Equiano's openness in encountering the whole world of the eighteenth century and in representing it in the different voices he developed in his *Narrative*, he has left posterity a remarkable legacy that is as intriguing for today's readers as it was for his contemporaries.

Reception

While there were many editions of the *Narrative* between 1789 and 1819, and the next English edition appeared only in 1964, Vassa was not forgotten in the intervening years. His memory was kept alive by American abolitionists. The last two editions published in the nineteenth century appeared in the United States, in 1829 and 1837, respectively; Lydia Maria Child drew on Equiano's sympathetic depiction of African manners in her short story "Jumbo and Zairee" (1831) and included a one-page sketch of Equiano, "better known by the name of Gustavus Vassa," in *An Appeal in Favor of that Class of Americans Called Africans* (1833); and Wilson Armistead's *A Tribute for the Negro* (1848) gave a forty-page summary of the *Narrative* and cited Vassa's appeal to Queen Charlotte. Although I surprisingly have not been able to find any reference to Equiano in Frederick Douglass's writing, efforts at stocktaking of the African American tradition have continued to remember Equiano. For example, Gertrude Mossell's "Sketch of Afro-American Literature" (1894) mentions him; Arthur Schomburg's bibliography in Alain Locke's *The New Negro* (1925) lists the American edition of 1791 "with portrait by Tiebout"; Vernon Loggins offers a positive appraisal in *The Negro Author* (1931); in *The Negro Genius* (1937), Benjamin Brawley sketches Gustavus Vassa's life and quotes a page from chapter 2 of the *Narrative*; Benjamin E. Mays, *The Negro's God as Reflected in His Literature* (1938), gives a one-page account of the *Narrative*; and Sterling Brown, Arthur P. Davis, and Ulysses Lee's *Negro Caravan* (1941) lists the book in the chronology. Dorothy Porter, who had assisted in the production of Brown's path-breaking anthology, pioneered in sorting out more than a dozen different editions in "Early American Negro Writings: A Bibliographical

Study" (1945). In 1942, no fewer than three books devoted some space to Vassa. Eva Beatrice Dykes's *The Negro in English Romantic Thought* and Wylie Sypher's *Guinea's Captive Kings: British Anti-slavery Literature of the XVIIIth Century* discuss Equiano, while Joel Rogers's *Sex and Race* includes Equiano's image with a few accompanying words. The dissertations by Marion W. Starling (1946) and Charles H. Nichols (1949) opened up the field of African American autobiography in the slavery period. Despite this continued recognition, Vassa remained a minor figure in historical and literary scholarship until his text was republished in the 1960s, reexamined in the 1980s, and widely anthologized in the 1990s.

The turning point in the reception of Equiano is easily marked by the definitive facsimile of the first edition that was prepared and magisterially introduced by Paul Edwards in 1969. Starting with the Edwards edition, it has also been more common to discuss the author under his African name Equiano than under the name the author himself used far more frequently, Gustavus Vassa. American readers and students began to pay more attention to Equiano after Arna Bontemps included the full *Narrative* in his collection *Great Slave Narratives* (1969).

Since the autobiography itself remains the most important source of Equiano's life story, much of the critical literature has offered summaries of the author's account, interlaced with excerpts from the *Narrative*. However, this state of affairs has inspired readers from Edwards to Acholonu to locate related historical documents, and the question of the book's reliability has been raised more than once. Equiano's authenticity has been disputed repeatedly from 1792 (when rumors circulated that Equiano had been born in St. Croix rather than in West Africa) to the present. For example, Edwards noticed a problem in the text concerning Equiano's age. More recently, Vincent Carretta, working with British Admiralty records, has found Equiano truthful in many of the details of his life he represented. However, Carretta also reopened the question of the place and date of Equiano's nativity. Carretta did so, not in the edition he prepared, but in separate essays, in which he pondered

> the tantalizing possibility that Equiano's African identity may have been a rhetorical invention. . . . In 1792 he vigorously disputed an assertion in a London newspaper that charged he was not born in Africa but rather in the Danish West Indies. In the documentary evidence of his baptism and naval records while serving

with Pascal, Equiano had no control over the name recorded or the baptismal location of his nativity "in Carolina." But on the voyage to the North Pole, he was a free man and presumably the only source of the information in the muster book of the *Racehorse* identifying him as "Gustavus Weston" (non-English names were often misspelled), an able seaman, aged 28, who had been born in South Carolina.[30]

This raised the question of "why, if he had indeed been born Olaudah Equiano in Africa, he chose to suppress these facts." Carretta surmised that "Pascal must have bought Equiano from Campbell, and renamed him Gustavus Vassa in early September 1754"—that is to say, "two years earlier than the date Vassa offers in the *Narrative*."[31] Carretta added that these disparities were particularly odd in the case of an autobiographer who was so verifiably accurate about the later stages of his career. If Carretta's hypothesis of Equiano's Carolina birth were ever to be fully substantiated, Equiano might just turn out to be one of the very first black American expatriates in Europe. This would, of course, also require a new interpretation of the *Narrative*.

Figure 2.1. Mary E. and (*on the right*) Frank Webb with an unidentified man.
Daguerreotype, ca. 1850s. (Harriet Beecher Stowe Center, Hartford, Connecticut.)

CHAPTER 2

The Philadelphian Novelist Frank Webb Anticipates the Future

October 5, 1855: On account of their color, Frank and Mary Webb are denied passage on the bark Sam Slick *from Philadelphia to Rio de Janeiro.*

WHO WAS FRANK WEBB? Relatively little is known about the Philadelphian of color who published *The Garies and Their Friends* with George Routledge and Company in London in 1857, one of only four African American novels written before the Civil War and easily the best of the four. Thanks to the painstaking efforts by Allan D. Austin, Rosemary Crockett, Roy E. Finkenbine, Eric Gardner, and Philip Lapsansky, we now know that Frank Johnson Webb was born in Philadelphia on March 21, 1828, the son of a Virginia-born father and a Pennsylvanian mother; that he may have worked in a clothing store and in the printing trade; and that he participated in the activities of a colored debating society called the Banneker Institute, where he delivered a lecture on "The Martial Capacity of Blacks." In 1845 he married Mary E., whose full maiden name remains unknown. Webb later wrote that his wife had been born in New Bedford, Massachusetts, the daughter of a runaway African slave woman from Virginia and "a Spanish gentleman of wealth" whose efforts to purchase the freedom of Mary's mother had

SOURCE: Werner Sollors, "Introduction," in *Frank J. Webb: Fiction, Essays and Poetry* (New Milford, CT: Toby Press, 2005), 1–24. Copyright © 2005 by Werner Sollors.

been unsuccessful but who continued, until Mary was six or seven, to support her and her mother lavishly. Both Frank and Mary were well-educated, were seventeen years old when they married, and were classified as Mulattoes in the 1850 Census.[1]

In 1855, after Webb's business failed, Mary, who had studied oratory and had become an excellent reader of poetry and drama, began to give public reading tours in cities along the East Coast, from Philadelphia to Boston and Salem, attracting the attention of listeners such as Charlotte Forten, William Lloyd Garrison, Henry Wadsworth Longfellow, William Cooper Nell, Harriet Beecher Stowe, and John Greenleaf Whittier. Stowe wrote "The Christian Slave," an adaptation of *Uncle Tom's Cabin*, expressly for Mary's readings. Mary's further repertoire included scenes from Shakespeare's *Romeo and Juliet*, excerpts from Monk Lewis, and most especially Henry Wadsworth Longfellow's "Hiawatha," which, as Webb reported, Mary "read whilst arrayed in the picturesque costume of the North American Indians, which adds greatly to the effect." Mary Webb became publicly known as "the colored Siddons," a tag comparing her to the famed British Shakespearean actress Sarah Siddons.

In the fall of 1855, the Webbs were planning to go to Brazil, but their plans were thwarted when the captain of the bark *Sam Slick* refused to give them passage from Philadelphia to Rio de Janeiro because of Frank Webb's skin color. In June 1856, the Webbs traveled to England on the Enoch Pratt shipping line, carrying with them letters of introduction by Stowe and Longfellow. In Britain, Mary continued her readings to great success, and one of her performances at the Duchess of Sutherland's was featured in an article in the *Illustrated London News*, while Frank wrote the novel for which Stowe and Henry Lord Brougham provided prefaces. Dedicated to Lady Noel Byron, *The Garies and Their Friends* was well received in England and sold two thousand copies of the regular edition, as well as twelve thousand copies in Routledge's "cheap series." It was reviewed in the *Sunday Times*, the *Athenaeum*, and the *National Review*. In the United States, however, no extended contemporary comments on the novel have been found. Neither Frederick Douglass nor *The Liberator* seems to have responded to Webb's interesting novel in any way, though a brief report on the "disgraceful conduct" of the captain of the bark *Sam Slick* had appeared in *Frederick Douglass' Paper* in 1855. ("I allow no man whose complexion is darker than my own to take passage with me," the captain was reported as saying.)

Mary's pulmonary ailment necessitated the couple's relocation, and in 1858, after spending some winter months in southern France, the Webbs moved to Kingston, Jamaica, where the Duke of Argyle had offered Webb a position in the post office. On their way from England to Jamaica, the Webbs stopped in Philadelphia, where Mary gave another reading. She continued her public performances in Kingston and Spanishtown, but her health soon took a turn for the worse, and she died of consumption on June 17, 1859.

Frank remained at the post office in Kingston and, in December 1864, married the Jamaican Mary Rosabell Rodgers; they were to have four Jamaican-born children between 1865 and 1869 and two more American-born children later, for Webb went back to the United States in 1869, took courses at Howard University Law School, and worked as a part-time clerk for the Freedmen's Bureau. In a letter he claimed that he saw Frederick Douglass every day, chatting over old times.[2] He also returned to his writing career and in 1870 published two novellas, two poems, and some political commentary in the African American weekly the *New Era* under the editorship of J. Sella Martin. Webb also mentioned in a hopeful letter of 1870 to the writer Mary Wager Fisher that he had sent his second novel, a five hundred page manuscript entitled "Paul Sumner," to Samuel Stillman Conant at *Harper's Weekly* and that he deemed it superior to his first novel. Yet it remained unpublished; the manuscript has not been found; and there seems to be no paper trail of it in the Harper archives. Webb stopped contributing to the *New Era* just before Douglass took over the editorship and renamed the paper the *New National Era*.

Around 1870, Webb relocated to Galveston, Texas, where once again he worked for the post office and became more active in Republican Party politics. In 1881, he became principal and teacher at the Barnes Institute School, a public school for colored children. He was also a licensed lay reader at St. Augustine's Protestant Episcopal Church; his second wife lectured and wrote papers in support of racial uplift. He died in Galveston on May 7, 1894. The obituary in the *Galveston Daily News* mourned him as an "esteemed resident of this city," and he was buried at Lake View Cemetery.

The Garies and Their Friends

Webb's only extant novel, *The Garies and Their Friends*, is not yet well known to general readers. Strangely, sections of it are not typically included in the big anthologies that tend to determine college reading lists, and Robert Reid-Pharr is right when he writes that this work "continues to be not so much forgotten as ignored."[3] Yet Webb's novel commands attention for a whole variety of reasons, for it is many things at once: a suspenseful Philadelphia novel that seethes with city life; a book of social critique and political protest that confronts the reader with a sharply drawn exposé of Philadelphia's system of color discrimination in the pre–Civil War period; a domestic tale of interrelated families, some of whose members cross the all-important color line; a rare, and possibly the first, representation of a successful free black businessman as one of the central characters; the first African American novel about the theme of racial "passing"; and possibly also the first American novel about a legally married interracial couple.

We meet the Garies, an interracial couple from Savannah. Clarence Garie is an unusual figure in pre–Civil War literature: a slaveowner who actually wants to marry his freed slave mistress, Emily Winston, so that their children, also named Clarence and Emily, will be safe and free and so that the third child Emily is expecting can be born free. Emily's cousin George Winston connects them with the Ellises, a free black family in Philadelphia who have roots in Georgia and help the Garies settle in the city. The Ellises form the sentimental family center of everyday life, with the carpenter Charles Ellis as paterfamilias and practical man, and his wife, Ellen, the maternal figure watching over the children: the courageous Esther; her younger sister, Caddy; and Charlie. This thoroughly bourgeois novel takes delight in the culture of the Garies' and Ellises' domestic meals: a southern dinner and a Philadelphia wedding feast are described in lavish detail. Then there is Mr. Walters, a successful real estate investor who embodies black pride and a new urban philosophy of self-defense. Although he is immensely wealthy, his actions are governed by social consciousness and a sense of responsibility for poorer blacks. As Carla L. Peterson writes, Walters is among the characters who "attend to the collectivity, returning surplus value to the community rather than serving their own special interests."[4] It is a sign of his activist spirit that his house boasts a portrait of the Haitian revolutionary Toussaint L'Ouverture. Walters is a black role model, unmistakably "the most exemplary male character in the novel," as Blyden Jackson put it, and possibly based in part on the black Philadelphia sailmaker and activist James Forten.[5] There was a distant family connection between Webb and the Forten family: Charlotte

Forten Grimké had a maternal aunt, Annie Woods Webb, who was married to Frank Webb's brother.

As the novel unfolds, one feels a narrative presence that would probably make this book interesting to contemporary writers (though I can think only of Charles Johnson's brief allusion to it in his novel *Oxherding Tale* and of Jamaica Kincaid's excitement at teaching it). There is remarkable subtlety in such small touches as a child's experience of northward migration: when the young, Savannah-born Clarence Garie beholds his first snow in the northern city, it seems to him "as if the town was built of salt." The narrator has a particular, Dickensian fondness for child characters, among whom young Kinch stands out: with his humorously misspelled letter ("I had a sord on; and the next Mornin we had a grate Brekfast"), one could easily imagine him in a novel by Mark Twain (though *Tom Sawyer* and *Huckleberry Finn* would be published two or three decades later). Even when Kinch grows up, he is almost mythically hungry ("two bites of cake . . . slipped down his throat as if it was a railroad tunnel and they were a train of cars behind time"). Webb represents children playing marbles and giving quick-witted replies to adults. Kinch and Caddy also seem to follow the example of Quasimodo from Victor Hugo's *The Hunchback of Notre Dame* when they concoct a mixture of cayenne pepper and hot water and pour it over attacking rioters, helping to drive them away from the sanctuary that is Walters's house. Printed in London and following British spelling conventions ("coloured"), the narrative is sprinkled with such French words as *coup de pièce, ennui, dénouement, mêlée, blancmange,* and *biscuit glacé,* creating a cosmopolitan flair and making an ironic counterpoint to the deluded patriotism that prevents Garie from taking his beloved Em and their children to safety in Europe. ("No, no," he says, "that would never do—give me a free country.") Webb also takes a moment in Charlie Ellis's difficult job search to amuse the reader with a Mr. Western of the firm Twining, Western, and Twining at Waterstreet, who puffs wreaths of cigar smoke while speaking and who actually wants to give the young black boy a chance ("Let us cweate a pwecedent, then. The boy wites wemarkably well"). The omniscient narrator foreshadows, occasionally flashes back, leaves a central character "for a few years engaged in his new pursuits," and meditates self-consciously about the nature of Father Time. Webb refuses to render a lovers' dialogue and offers the following account instead: "They walked to the window, where they stood, saying, no doubt, to each other those little tender things which are so profoundly interesting to lovers, and so exceedingly stupid to everyone else." Another couple's wedding preparations make the narrator deliver a prose-poem-like page about mantua-makers and milliners, drapers and jewelers, punctuated by exclamations and addresses to the lovers. Hair-raising coincidences drive the plot, and some spectacular high points are emphasized by dramatically capitalized exclamations.

If *The Garies and Their Friends* is a good nineteenth-century black bourgeois novel, it is also a novel about the extraordinary difficulties black progress runs against, especially in the cities of the free North (though it would be a mistake to infer from this northern urban focus that Webb was not strenuously opposed to slavery). As Rosemary Crockett has argued, this book marks the beginning of the historical shift in black writing from the theme of slavery to that of color discrimination. Slavery and the South are left behind when the Garies leave Savannah for Philadelphia, and there emerges a predominantly urban novel that questions the dream of the free North—and does so some years before slavery was abolished, thereby anticipating themes of later nineteenth- and twentieth-century novels by and about African Americans in post-slavery urban situations. The city of Philadelphia comes to life in these pages, often hauntingly so. Webb's firm narrative hand takes the reader through the streets of nineteenth-century colored South Philadelphia, from the Ellis residence at 18 Little Green-street to Mr. Walters's house at 257 Easton Street, corner of Shotwell. Webb also mentions 10th Street improvements, Christian-street between 11th and 12th Streets, Baker-street, Bedford-street, and the colored area around Sixth, Seventh, and Eighth Street. There is the shady poor-white Whitticar Tavern, and there are the fancier outlying areas at Winter Street near Logan Square, where the Garies settle, identifiable sites in Philadelphia. A new urban sensibility is present, a sense that many stories coexist in a large nineteenth-century city. For example, as young Charlie Ellis sends out a letter to a possible employer, he ponders the many kinds of letters that must be streaming down the "ever-distended and insatiable brass throat" of a mailbox. Characters cannot read one another easily in the city: a black dialect speaker who expresses his sadness at no longer being a slave ("hain't got no kind marster to look after me here, and I has to work drefful hard sometimes") turns out to be putting on an act for a man he wrongly believes to be a white southerner, and the most minstrel-like appearance of any character in the novel is that of a white who has been beaten up and tarred.

For its black and biracial residents and for interracially married whites, city life means the brutal confrontation with mob violence and urban riots, one of which the novel portrays at its center. No reader of this novel is likely to forget the traumatic mob attacks on the central characters, the shouts of "Down with the Abolitionist—Down with the Amalgamation-ist!" and the brutally violent and murderous acts, followed by a "cry of triumphant malignity" from the crowd, or the city dwellers' "wending their way to the lower part of the city" one day later "to gratify their curi-osity by gazing upon the havoc made by the rioters during the . . . night." Robert S. Levine praised the novel for its bracing realism and placed the chapters on the riot "among the most disturbing (and spectacular) accounts of violence in antebellum literature."[6] In the first twenty years of Webb's life, the years he spent in Philadelphia, there were, Theodore Hershberg has written, "half a dozen major antiblack riots and many more minor mob actions" in the City of Brotherly Love. While Philadelphia's white population grew by 63 percent in the decade from 1840 to 1850, there was a net loss in the Negro population, a decline in the number of black property holders, and a rise in residential segregation. In one of four black households there lived a former slave, and black class stratification was sharp: the top 10 percent owned 70 percent of the total wealth (the top 1 percent held 30 percent), while the bottom half had only 5 per-cent. Hershberg stresses that these data and the general poverty of the black population point to "the destructiveness of the urban experience for blacks in nineteenth-century Philadelphia" and that some of the problems blacks faced were not due merely to the history of slavery but "may more accurately be traced to the processes of urbanization, industrialization, and immigration, occurring in a setting of racial inequality."[7] Such was the social background of the novel, in which the tenuousness of black life is omnipresent and class stratification is apparent. Interestingly, however, Webb represents instances of cross-class intraracial solidarity in the black community, most especially in the relationship of the Ellises with the rich but race-conscious Mr. Walters. They all have to confront the white hostility that all forms of boundary crossing may evoke—the quest for upward mobility, even just the search for employment, but most especial-ly the crossing of racial lines in interracial marriage or in a mixed-race person's passing for white.

The theme of racial passing appears in not one but two subplots: George Winston represents the comic variant, and young Clarence Garie represents the tragic. George is taken for white by a high-standing New York who has "a holy horror of everything approaching to amalgamation" and prides himself "on being able to detect evidences of the least drop of African blood in any one." This scene is social satire, not upon the character who passes but upon the social pretense on which condemnation of racial passing must rely. Ellis warns George that if he settles down he must be "either one thing or other—white or coloured" and that "passing for white" represents a great risk, for if he is found out he will be "shunned" as if he were "a pestilence." The tormented Clarence echoes Ellis's advice in his own experience: "I can't be white and coloured at the same time; the two don't mingle, and I must consequently be one or the other." It is when he falls in love with Anne Bates ("little Birdie") that his agony begins, for he cannot make himself tell her the truth about his background, yet he loathes himself for his weakness and feels that he is betraying the memory of his mother. It is important to remember that Walters opposed the scheme that led to Clarence's passing in the first place.

Driving the central drama is the scheming, racist, hypocritical, intemperate, and ruthless upstart George Stevens, a Satanic figure who acts out of envy and in retaliation for being a descendant from a slighted branch of the Garie family. He comes out of the tradition of melodramatic villainy and of the urban Gothic plots of collusion between seemingly upstanding pillars of society and the seedy world of thuggery, crime, and murder, plots that became quite popular in the wake of Eugène Sue's *Mystères de Paris*. Two published mysteries of Philadelphia, George Lippard's *The Quaker City* and the anonymous and fragmentary German-language novel *Die Geheimnisse von Philadelphia* invite comparison with Webb's book. In *The Garies and Their Friends*, it is the villain Stevens who in fact engineers the violent racist mob riot, while his wife, Jule, cannot tolerate the idea of integrated schools, calls the Garie children "white niggers," and advocates a colonization scheme for free blacks. Can a couple fleeing from the prohibition of interracial marriage in slaveholding Georgia find a minister who will marry them in free Philadelphia? Will they be able to build a better world for their children? Is there a recipe for black middle-class survival to be drawn from Walters's sense of racial pride and readiness to embrace a program of self-defense? These are among the important questions that this novel asks the reader to contemplate.

Philip Lapsansky has suggested that the Ellis family was "possibly modeled on Webb's family" and that perhaps Webb's autobiographical material was inserted into the figure of Charlie Ellis.[8] If one follows that lead, one can also attempt to find certain resemblances between young Em and Webb's wife, Mary. And perhaps Webb played around with "Em Garie" and "Mary E." in choosing her surname and titling the whole novel for the Garies, for "The Ellises and Their Friends" also would have worked. Did Webb's father have an experience similar to Charles Ellis's in one of the Philadelphia riots? Without more biographical data, such questions have to remain unanswered, of course.[9]

The book gives the reader an encyclopedia of manifestations of racial hatred and segregation from cradle to grave, affecting all the areas that would remain at the focus of the struggle for black civil rights for more than a century after the novel was published: the denial of equal employment opportunities, of equal access to education, to public libraries, and to public transportation—all of which the novel depicts, making it the fullest American antisegregationist protest novel of the nineteenth century. Webb also clearly sees the core of racist sentiment in the violent hostility to interracial intimacy: noticing black and white children kissing each other can generate revulsion and disgust in a white parent, and an interracial couple cannot even be buried together in Philadelphia. "Love a colored woman! I cannot conceive it possible," a white character proclaims with a "look of disgust," adding, "there is something strange and unnatural about it." In the face of so much racism, it is no wonder that Caddy speaks of "white devils" and says, "I wish there were no white folks," for "they are all, I believe, a complete set of villains and everything else that is bad"—but her wiser sister Esther replies, "Don't be so sweeping in your remarks." There are, after all, also some decent and extraordinarily generous white characters in the novel, the most unforgettable among them perhaps Mrs. Bird, who treats Charlie Ellis lovingly like a surrogate son. White characters are on the right track when they can learn to say, as does Mrs. Burrell, who empathizes with Charlie Ellis and imagines what her life would be like if she were colored. "I think . . . we treat coloured people with great injustice." Webb's white readers were probably meant to follow suit.

Essays, Poems, Novellas

Webb's uncollected writings help to give the modern reader a fuller sense of his range and of his activities in the years before and after the publication of *The Garies and Their Friends*. In 1870, he published two poems in the *New Era*, "None Spoke a Single Word to Me," about the feeling of being a social outsider, and the romantic "Waiting," dedicated to his second wife, Mary Rodgers Webb. In an article on a planned exhibition, Webb asks whether "we, the colored men" shall not "make an effort to further demonstrate, in some substantial manner, our ability to contribute to the material prosperity of this great Republic, of which we form no inconsiderable part?" And in another article, on a bill for school integration in Washington, DC, Webb raises the question "whether, in this District at least, the white and colored children cannot breathe the air of the same school room, romp in the same play ground, compete in the same classes, and be flogged by the same teacher, without the safety of the country being imperilled thereby." He gives the prophetic answer: "The day will come when people will smile at the fact that this question could have been discussed with so much acrimony of spirit." A third article, "An Old Foe with a New Face," is an attack on the Democrats who were contemplating changing their name to "Conservatives."[10]

The *New Era* also serialized two novellas by Webb. "Two Wolves and a Lamb" is a Gothic tale of spiritualism and domination set among expatriates in Paris and southern France that makes problematic the easy distinction between good and evil, between sanity and madness, and between a sense of justice and sadism. Gus, whose love of food connects this tale with *The Garies and Their Friends*, introduces Philip Braham, the narrator, to Laura Burrows (the "lamb"); to Marie Goffe and her sister, Laura's mischievous cousins (the "wolves"); and to Laura's fiancé, Mr. Walton. The drama that unfolds culminates in an almost surrealistic scene of absolute horror and death. "Marvin Hayle," told by the female narrator, Ella, is a story of a deep and reciprocated love that unites the wealthy Ella and the proud and struggling artist, in spirit if not in reality, for social rules prohibit them from showing their love to the world or to each other. The novella is set in London and the same area of southern France around Cannes and the Île Sainte-Marguerite where Webb's "Two Wolves and a Lamb" takes place, but now we find an international and polyglot group of characters that includes Arabs. The two novellas that are as different in spirit as a male-narrated tale of horror and female-narrated love story can be, but they are also united by the presence of such background figures as the Chevalier D'Oyen and Dr. Saddler, by culinary details, by numerous French words and phrases, and by a wealth of literary allusions, among them to Alexandre Dumas's *Man with the Iron Mask*, to Edward Bulwer-Lytton's *The Lady of Lyons; or, Love and Pride*, to poems by Alexander Smith and Longfellow, and to Shakespeare. The representation of evil characters that concerned Webb in *The Garies and Their Friends* has been deepened and complicated in "Two Wolves and a Lamb," and whereas the theme of interracial marriage was important for Webb's earlier novel, it is a class-crossing love threatening to lead to a misalliance that "Marvin Hayle" examines. While readers will find certain stylistic and thematic parallels between these novellas and *The Garies and Their Friends*, they will also notice the absence of racially marked characters in the literary works of 1870. Rather than interpret this thematic choice as an "escape" from racism, one should see in it a demonstration that a black writer "can claim these subjects," as Eric Gardner has rightly suggested. It is also possible that these pioneering examples of what would be called "raceless fiction" in the 1950s permitted Webb to write about personal matters in a way that would not be obvious because of the apparent disguise. What Marvin Hayle says in that novella about another writer might also apply to Webb: "Under the shield of other names" (and, one could add, a Euro-American cast of characters), he "has told the story of his own life." If that is the case, then these novellas can be considered precursors of Zora Neale Hurston's *Seraph on the Suwanee* and of James Baldwin's *Giovanni's Room*. And who knows what surprises the manuscript of Webb's second novel might hold if "Paul Sumner" were to resurface one day.

In 1969, Arthur P. Davis introduced the first reprint of *The Garies and Their Friends* with an essay that marked the beginning of critical attention to Frank Webb. Praising it as an "exciting and significant novel," Davis concludes, "As an early work that foreshadows later important developments in Negro American fiction, it should be much better known."[11] In the intervening years, some biographical details and other writings by Webb have become known to scholars, though not to general readers, and more secondary literature has appeared in print. However, even today one can only second Davis's wish. I do hope that the intriguing and fascinating writer Frank J. Webb becomes a better-known representative of nineteenth-century American urban literature.[12]

Figure 3.1. Charles W. Chesnutt in his library, 9719 Lamont Avenue, Cleveland. (Photograph of Charles W. Chesnutt, gift of Helen Chesnutt, 1970. Cleveland Public Library Digital Gallery.)

CHAPTER 3

The Goopher in Charles W. Chesnutt's Conjure Tales

Superstition, Ethnicity, and Modern Metamorphoses

I went by the field of the slothful, and by the vineyard of a man void of understanding; And, lo, it was all grown over with thorns, and nettles had covered the face thereof, and the stone wall thereof was broken down. Then I saw, and considered it well: I looked upon it, and received instruction.

—Proverbs 24:30–32

If a Negro loses his rabbit's foot charm, he will turn white.
—*Popular Beliefs and Superstitions: A Compendium
of American Folklore* (no. 4636, 1958)

August 1, 1887: "The Goophered Grapevine," the first of Charles W. Chesnutt's Uncle Julius tales, appears in the Atlantic Monthly.

I N 1899, the free-born and light-skinned Afro-American author Charles W. Chesnutt (1858–1932) published a volume of seven short stories entitled *The Conjure Woman*.[1] His title refers to the character Aunt Peggy, who appears in several (although not all) tales, working her roots and spells and "goophers." "Goopher" (also "goofer" or "guffer") is a word of African origin. Chesnutt was erroneously thought to have introduced it into print in English. Etymologically akin to the Mende word "ngafa" (spirit, ghost), the Ewe "gafe" (shrine of a god), and the Fon "kafo" (iron

SOURCE: Werner Sollors, "The Goopher in Charles Chesnutt's Conjure Tales: Superstition, Ethnicity, and Modern Metamorphoses," *Letterature d'America* 6, no. 27 (Spring 1985): 107–129.

fetish), "goopher" denotes a curse or spell, as well as the conjure man who performs it. Derivatives of the word appear in the English language in the shape of "goofer dust" (graveyard dirt), "to be goofed" (after smoking grass), "goofing" (making a mistake), "goofy," and "goofball."[2] Goophers frequently bring about magical transformations. Chesnutt's goopher stories are set in the old slavery days near "Patesville," based on Fayetteville, North Carolina, where both of Chesnutt's parents had been born.[3] In all, Chesnutt published fourteen interrelated conjure tales from 1887 to 1900, seven of which remained uncollected in his lifetime but were included in Sylvia Lyons Render's *The Short Fiction of Charles W. Chesnutt.*[4]

In an attempt to call attention to Chesnutt's short fiction—which was all but forgotten in 1962, although selections appear in most anthologies for survey courses in American literature today—Robert Smith characterized the stories this way:

> Interwoven in Chesnutt's stories are the humor, weal, woe, and pathos of the slave and his plantation life, colored by blind igno-rance and belief in voodooism. The author tells tales of simple people who had nothing practical on which to depend. To them the slightest phenomenon was inexplicable and was deemed to be the work of the conjurer. . . . A reader is invariably charmed [!] by the simple humor which permeates these naive stories.[5]

Smith apologizes for the ignorance of voodooism and for Chesnutt's naïveté. Yet the antithesis between "reason" and "blind ignorance" is cul-turally charged, and as many later observers have noted, there is nothing simple about Chesnutt's short stories. In an early review, the perceptive William Dean Howells compared Chesnutt to Turgenev and Maupassant.[6]

The stories are told by a white narrator and ardent believer in "rea-son," John, who was born in Ohio (as was Chesnutt) and who has come to North Carolina after the Civil War (as did Chesnutt). His wife, Annie, is frail and benefits from the southern climate—her health prompted John, the narrator of the frame stories, to move south—while John him-self thinks of schemes to make a profit and to expand his enterprises and landholdings. In the course of each tale, the white couple encounters the former slave Uncle Julius, who usually tells the inside story, always a goopher tale of the old slavery times (usually set forty or fifty years earlier than the "rationalist" frame narrative).

The story "Sis' Becky's Pickaninny" is representative of Chesnutt's oeuvre. Although Richard Baldwin complained about the aesthetic inferiority of this tale, other readers—such as Robert Bone and Robert Hemenway—consider "Sis' Becky's Pickaninny" a significant and outstanding work and have argued their case compellingly.[7] At the beginning (the "outside story") of "Sis' Becky's Pickaninny," Annie's health has taken a turn for the worse. Not even the best country doctor can cure her melancholy, and John's efforts to read novels to her, or his ordering the field hands to serenade her with plantation songs, fail to divert her depression. Julius, however, appears with "some small object" (*TCW*, 134) that turns out to be a rabbit's foot. This happened at a time, the narrator adds, that rabbits' feet "had not yet outgrown the charm [!] of novelty." The Yankee empiricist John disapproves, and the following dialogue ensues:

> "What do you do with it?"
>
> "I kyars it wid me fer luck, suh."
>
> "Julius," I observed, half to him and half to my wife, "your people will never rise in the world until they throw off these childish superstitions and learn to live by the light of reason and common sense. How absurd to imagine that the fore-foot of a poor dead rabbit, with which he timorously felt his way along through a life surrounded by snares and pitfalls, beset by enemies on every hand, can promote happiness or success, or ward off failure or misfortune!"
>
> "It is ridiculous," assented my wife, with faint interest.
>
> "Dat's w'at I tells dese niggers roun' heah," said Julius. "De fo'-foot ain' got no power. It has ter be de hin'-foot, suh,—de lef' hin'-foot er a grabeya'd rabbit, killt by a cross-eyed nigger on a da'k night in de full er de moon." (*TCW*, 134–135)

The resourceful dialect speaker Julius has shifted gears. While the entrepreneuring John can only comment, in his somewhat dry standard English, that such rabbits' feet must be "very rare and valuable," Julius has entered the world of what is called "superstition." What John regards merely as an "object," as the occasion for an object lesson to his wife and to Uncle Julius, is a living power for Julius and of curative value to Annie.

Although Chesnutt "made up" his goopher tales (except "The Goophered Grapevine," to which a folktale was "the norm"), Julius's rabbit's foot comes straight from American folklore as recorded by Newbell Niles Puckett in 1926 and in Ohio instances as late as in 1959. "Among most Negroes," Puckett writes,

> it is the left hind foot of a graveyard rabbit killed in the dark of the moon, though the left hind foot of an ordinary rabbit is by no means despised. Others add that such a graveyard rabbit must be killed by a cross-eyed person.

Puckett further reports that one rabbit's foot charm he purchased in New Orleans had with it a printed slip containing a graphic illustration of the rabbit in the act of being shot and the following inscription: "This little luckie is the left hind foot of a graveyard rabbit killed in the full of the moon by a red-headed, cross-eyed nigger at 12 o'clock at night, riding a white mule."[8] The compilers of *Popular Beliefs and Superstitions: A Compendium of American Folklore* give many instances from Ohio.[9] For example:

> If a child is born on Friday the 13th, he brings bad luck to the family. To cure this, it is necessary to have a cross-eyed farmer kill a rabbit at midnight and cut off its foot. The child must carry the foot with him all his life. (No. 1128, 1958)
> Use a rabbit's foot to keep away the hoodoo. (No. 26086, 1958)
> If a rabbit was killed under a full moon by a cross-eyed person, and you cut off the left foot, it will ensure you a lucky life. (No. 25361, 1959 [a Negro janitor])
> To have good luck, you must carry a left hind foot of a rabbit killed in the dark of the moon in a cemetery with a silver bullet. (No. 25360, 1955)

Chesnutt, incidentally, was the amused owner of such a rabbit's foot. In view of such evidence, it is no wonder that the folk-wise Julius is surprised when the doubting John asks for *proof* of the rabbit's foot's power, which raises the general problem of the (un)testability of superstitions.[10] "Law, suh! You doan hafter prove 'bout de rabbit foot! Eve'ybody knows dat; leas'ways eve'ybody roun' heah knows it" (*TCW*, 136). The proof is in the community that Julius represents and in the stories that circulate in it. Hence, Julius proceeds with the inside tale of Sis' Becky and her pickaninny, which he offers precisely as proof of the rabbit's foot's power.

In the old days, the story goes, Becky was a slave of Colonel Pendleton (a plantation owner who figures in several tales). Her husband was
sold away by his master, so that all Becky had left was her "pickaninny,"
little Mose. Colonel Pendleton had a weakness for horses, and one day he
bought a racing horse, offering to pay with a slave in lieu of the requested
$1,000. The owner of the horse picked Becky but had no use for Mose.
He comforted Pendleton with the remark, "I'll keep dat 'oman so busy
she'll fergit de baby; fer niggers is made ter wuk, en dey ain' got no
time fer no sich foolis'ness ez babies" (*TCW*, 142). Pendleton, Chesnutt
lets Julius report ironically, "was a kin'-hea'ted man, en nebber lack' ter
make no trouble fer nobody,—en so he tol' Becky he was gwine sen' her
down ter Robeson County fer a day er so, ter he'p out his son-in-law in
his wuk; en bein' ez dis yuther man wuz gwine dat way, he had ax' 'im
ter take her 'long in his buggy" (*TCW*, 142). Becky has to learn the cruel
truth as a shock, without any preparation. Paralleling Annie's melancholy
in the outside story, Mose gets ill and depressed.

It is now that the goopher comes in and, significantly, as Hemenway
has suggested, not for sinister purposes but for the good. Paid by Aunt
Nancy, the boy's nurse, the conjure woman Aunt Peggy transforms Mose
first into a humming bird, and later into a mocking bird. He flies to his
mother and sings to her with all his might—and no paid hands' sere-
nades, either! Becky, who is also depressed by the separation, is able to
"'magine" (*TCW*, 147, 149) that each bird is her Mose, and the power
of music and of the imagination succeed for a while.[11] But to cure the
melancholy permanently, Becky has to be conjured back. Aunt Peggy
gets a hornet to sting the racehorse (for which Becky was traded), sends a
sparrow with some roots for Sis' Becky, and stops further bird excursions
of little Mose. Pendleton now wants to return the horse. After some hesitation, the trader who sees how ill Becky has meanwhile become agrees.
(Like John, the trader is, in Julius's words, "one er dese yer w'ite folks
w'at purten' dey doan b'liebe in cunj'in" [*TCW*, 155]). The inside tale
comes to a happy ending, with freedom and exodus for mother and son
thrown in, which is not at all the rule in Chesnutt's stories.

The last three pages close the frame of John's outside tale. He reports
his wife's interest (in marked difference from her response to his own
efforts), sympathy, and satisfaction with the story. When he tells Julius that
it was "a very ingenious fairy tale" (*TCW*, 159), Annie objects severely
that "the story bears the stamp of truth, if ever a story did."

"Yes," I replied, "especially the humming-bird episode, and the mocking-bird digression to say nothing of the doings of the hornet and the sparrow."

"Oh, well, I don't care," she rejoined with delightful animation; "those are mere ornamental details and not at all essential. The story is true to nature, and might have happened half a hundred times, and no doubt did happen, in those horrid days before the war." (*TCW*, 159)

John finally plays what he thinks is his trump card: the story simply fails to prove "that a rabbit's foot brings good luck." Julius, however, can firmly count on Annie's support now, as she gives the correct answer: "Sis' Becky had no rabbit's foot" (*TCW*, 160).[12] Although John remains unconvinced, Annie's condition starts to improve this very day, and when she is fully recovered several weeks later, John finds an "object" in one of her pockets, ending the story with the sentence: "It was Julius's rabbit's foot" (*TCW*, 161).

In most of Chesnutt's conjure tales, John narrates the modern outside story and Julius tells the inside tale, which has a magical transformation at its center. Robert Bone has illustrated the pattern (see Figure 3.2).[13] As in "Sis' Becky's Pickaninny," Annie is always more receptive to the inside tale than John who remains genteelly aloof and superior.

In Chesnutt's first conjure tale, "The Goophered Grapevine," originally published in the *Atlantic Monthly* in 1887 and later expanded to provide a broader frame for *The Conjure Woman*, Julius tells the harrowing story of the slave Henry who becomes like a grapevine, nearly dying each fall and flourishing again in the spring, thus prompting his shrewd owner to sell him profitably each spring and to buy him back for very little in the fall. In this story, John first encounters Julius and describes him in a racially patronizing way: "There was a shrewdness is his eyes, too, which was not altogether African, and which, as we afterwards learned from experience, was indicative of a corresponding shrewdness in his character" (*TCW*, 10). In "Po' Sandy," the inside tale of which concerns a man who has been turned into a tree so he can stay near his wife, Tenie, yet is cut into lumber when she is away, John muses: "Some of these stories are quaintly humorous; others wildly extravagant, revealing the Oriental cast of the negro's imagination; while others, poured freely into the sympathetic ear of a Northern-bred woman, disclose many a tragic incident of the darker side of slavery" (*TCW*, 40–41).

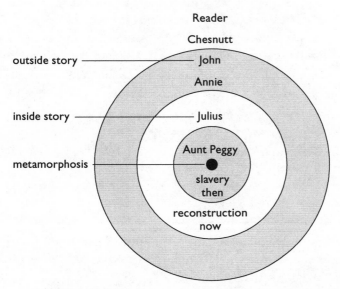

Figure 3.2. Outside and inside narratives in Chesnutt's conjure tales.

The narrator's patronizing tone is also unmistakable in "Dave's Neck-liss," the powerful story of a slave who symbolically turns into the ham that his master had fastened to his neck as a punishment and who hangs himself in the plantation smokehouse. Here John muses about Julius:

> Whether the sacred name of liberty ever set his soul aglow with a generous fire; whether he had more than the most elementary ideas of love, friendship, patriotism, religion—things which are half, and the better half, of life to us; whether he ever realized except in a vague, uncertain way, his own degradation, I do not know. I fear not; and if not, then centuries of repression had borne their legitimate fruit. But in the simple human feeling, and still more in the undertone of sadness, which pervaded his stories, I thought I could see a spark which, fanned by favoring breezes and fed by the memories of the past, might become in his children's children a glowing flame of sensibility, alive to every thrill of human happiness or human woe. (*TSF*, 133)

This tone has offended some readers who, like James R. Giles, blame not only John but also Chesnutt for racial condescension and insincerity.[14] John's attitude furthermore is part of a larger pattern of shallow, complacent self-indulgence that surfaces in his reflections not only on Uncle Julius but also on his wife and himself. "I possessed a passable baritone voice," he states in "The Conjurer's Revenge" (*TCW*, 103); he notes that the possibilities of a frog pond (haunted, according to Julius) "as a source of food supply suggested themselves to my somewhat practical mind" ("Tobe's Tribulations," *TSF*, 97). In "Lonesome Ben," John explains: "My wife came of a family of reformers, who could never contemplate an evil without seeking an immediate remedy" (*TSF*, 114). He observes that she "liked to hear the end of a story" ("Lonesome Ben," *TSF*, 110), that she was "of a very sympathetic turn of mind" ("Po' Sandy," *TCW*, 40), and that Annie "wanted a kitchen in the back yard" "for some occult [!] reason" (*TCW*, 37).

To be sure, John's language is pedantic, and he often seems offensive, although Giles's complete identification of John and Chesnutt as condescending storytellers is hasty. Opposing views have been voiced by readers such as Theodore Hovet, who saw the stories as "microcosms of imperialism" in which John's at times racist and sexist narration is merely the untrustworthy ideology of an expanding enterprise that Chesnutt wishes to criticize.[15]

At other times, however, John *can* be perceptive and full of genuine understanding of, and admiration for, Julius and—correspondingly—critical of slavery. In "The Marked Tree," John states:

> I suspected Julius at times of a large degree of poetic license—he took the crude legends and vague superstitions of the neighborhood and embodied them in stories as complete, in their way, as the Sagas of Iceland or the primitive tales of ancient Greece. I have saved a few of them. Had Julius lived in a happier age for men of his complexion the world might have had a black Aesop or Grimm or [E.T.A. Hoffmann]—as it still may have, for who knows whether our civilization has yet more than cut its milk teeth, or humanity has even really begun to walk erect? (*TSF*, 144)

In a passage in "Tobe's Tribulations," one can observe a shift in John's tone:

> [Julius] had seen life from what was to us a new point of view— from the bottom, as it were; and there clung to his mind, like barnacles to the submerged portion of a ship, all sorts of extrava-

gant beliefs. The simplest phenomena of life were to him fraught with hidden meaning.

These beliefs may have come from diverse origins, John muses:

> But from his own imagination, I take it—for I never heard quite the same stories from anyone else—he gave to the raw material of folklore and superstition a fancifulness of touch that truly made of it, to borrow a homely phrase, a silk purse out of a sow's ear. (*TSF*, 98–99)

Such a comment makes John a far more intelligent interpreter of Afro-American folklore than Puckett—who traced black superstitions back to European origins (similar to the way some linguists accounted for Afro-American peculiarities by invoking English regional dialects). More important, in such passages John sounds precisely like Chesnutt, who published the important essay "Superstitions and Folklore of the South" in 1901, parts of which could have been written by John:

> Relics of ancestral barbarism are found among all peoples, but advanced civilization has at least shaken off the more obvious absurdities of superstition.

Or, quite in John's tone of amusement, Chesnutt reports:

> I procured, from an equally trustworthy source, a genuine grave-yard rabbit's foot. I would seem to be reasonably well protected against casual misfortune.[16]

Are we to equate John and Chesnutt? Are we to trust the narrator? Or are we supposed to look through him? Robert Stepto has emphasized the explosive issues involved in interpretations of John as the Afro-American writer's white mouthpiece.[17] Yet the fact remains that at times John echoes Chesnutt's sentiments, while at other times Chesnutt employs John's voice ironically.

Whatever John's frame narratives represent, Julius's inside tales can be read as their counterplots. Several readers have looked at Julius's tales as demythologizing John's and have emphasized Julius's economic motives in telling his tales. This is less apparent in "Sis' Becky's Pickaninny," in which Julius only lends Annie his rabbit's foot, perhaps for a fee. In "Dave's Neckliss," however, he gets a ham; in "A Deep Sleeper," probably a watermelon; and in "Po' Sandy," the infamous lumber. In "The Goophered Grapevine," he attempts, but fails, to keep control over his grapes. Robert Smith concluded in 1962, "Uncle Julius's *raison d'*être is to protect himself and his income."[18] William Andrews seconded the motion in 1974 with an approving interpretation of Julius's ulterior motives (something that distinguishes Julius from the uncles of genteel southern fiction of the plantation school and most especially from Joel Chandler Harris's popular Uncle Remus):

> Julius's often remarked technique of adapting a story to prevent his employer's intentions from clashing with his own interests does constitute one individualizing trait in him. . . . More often than not the motive behind Julius's story telling is not nostalgia for the old times . . . or a delight in entertainment . . . , but rather the economic self-interest of old Julius himself who, as the businessman gradually learns in *The Conjure Woman*, has no intention of allowing the white man's economic encroachment on his holdings to go unchallenged.[19]

Is the trickster Julius merely a selfish manipulator, a juggler who acts on ulterior motives? However seriously such readings of conjure tales are offered as counter-texts to John's narrative, they, too, still follow John's lead. As Jules Chametzky argues, Julius's serving of his own interest is, after all, a motive John "benignly understands."[20] John believes in nothing more than economic self-interest; he notes Julius's shrewdness (which, as we saw, he ascribes to the non-African part of his ancestry) and concludes "The Goophered Grapevine" with the comment

> I found, when I bought the vineyard, that Uncle Julius had occupied a cabin on the place for many years, and derived a respectable revenue from the product of the neglected grapevines. This, *doubtless*, accounted for his advice to me not to buy the vineyard, though whether it inspired the goopher story I am unable to state. (*TCW,* 34–35; emphasis added)

Even more forcefully, John views "The Gray Wolf's Ha'nt" as a tale told by Julius to keep his honey supply:

> The gray wolf's haunt had *doubtless* proved useful in keeping off too inquisitive people, who might have interfered with his monopoly. (*TCW*, 194; emphasis added)

That Julius is not a child of nature and that slavery as well as freedom meant living in the economic world is clear. However, the very fact that John regards Julius as an economic schemer, and the probability that the word "doubtless" was used ironically in those passages, should prompt us to look for more than shrewd profit motives in Uncle Julius. For this reason, it is good to focus on "Sis' Becky's Pickaninny," where that motive is not directly present.

Melvin Dixon reads the rabbit's foot as a phallic symbol that accounts for the wife's "satisfaction" in the manner of a seduction tale—which loosely fits into the theme of self-interest, I suppose.[21] Of course, it goes without saying that the rabbit is a fertility symbol and has specific sexual and procreative connotations in much folklore. Claudia de Lys, for example, explains:

> The mystic potency of the foot has always been used symbolically in relation to sex, and the hindfoot of an animal as prolific as the hare or rabbit added to the potency of the amulet.[22]

It is also meaningful that Annie and John are childless, whereas it is as a mother that Becky suffers in the inside tale. Thus, one can easily guess what a Freudian could make of the fact that John pulls Julius's foot out of his wife's pocket. Yet it is the whole explanation of Julius's character that is problematic here.

David Britt argued strongly against an exclusive focus on John's ulterior motive (and we might include the ulterior sexual motive):

> It is a mistake to view a few jugs of wine or a crock of honey [and, we might add, Annie's "pocket"] as the prime objectives of Julius' maneuverings. . . . Julius' tales are not aimed at manipulating John in the way the surface narrative implies.[23]

The struggle is not between ideology and profit, but between differing and conflicting ideologies, expressed in different forms of narration.

In this broader sense the stories can be viewed as tales of seduction (though not necessarily sexual seduction), of verbal persuasion, of attempted manipulation in more than monetary aspects. Robert Bone sees this as the connection, not only between inside and outside tale, but also among Julius, John, and Chesnutt. The role of the black writer, "conveyed through the metaphor of conjuration," is to "bewitch the white folks" with the help of fiction, to open their eyes to truth and imagination. In "Sis' Becky's Pickaninny," for example, Mose's singing is parallel to John's and Julius's tales and to Chesnutt's story. The story is thus, as Bone puts it, a "tribute to sorrow songs." The rabbit, too, as demonstrated by John's first question about the rabbit's foot, parallels the slave—as the Brer Rabbit tradition documents:

> If Brer Fox, like Colonel Pendleton and the white narrator, is a symbol of power without imagination, Brer Rabbit, like Sis' Becky and Uncle Julius, is a symbol of the imagination without power, which sometimes manages to turn the tables, but always enables its possessor to endure.[24]

According to Bone's reading, Becky's rabbit foot is imagination, and Julius's is the "charming" power of storytelling.

To sway the reader (Chesnutt's dream was to undermine the garrison of white resentment), Chesnutt darkens John's world of imaginative "reason" and lightens the occult of Julius's conjuring. In Chesnutt's stories, as Robert Hemenway points out, conjure

> never finally represents evil, because conjure is placed in a context in which the omnipresent evil is slavery itself. The terror in Chesnutt's tales comes not from the transformations of nature, fears of night, the irrationality of supernatural force, but from what men do to each other in the name of race.[25]

The evil of slavery itself appears as a voodoo that transforms men into commodities—whose value fluctuates seasonally and according to the market—or into people who are "socially dead." Chesnutt's stories are full of illustrations of not only the owners' cruelty, avarice, and thoughtlessness but also the slaves' denial of stability ("Po' Sandy," *TCW*, 45) and learning ("A Dumb Witness," *TSF*, 160). Some scenes give vivid testimony to the slaves' experience of radical alienation and reification; in "Lonesome Ben," for example, Julius describes Ben's estrangement from himself:

> Well, po' Ben didn' know what ter do. He had been lonesome ernuff befo', but now he didn' eben hab his own se'f ter 'so'ciate wid, fer he felt mo' lak a stranger 'n he did lak Ben. (*TSF*, 113)

In "Dave's Neckliss," the ham on Dave's neck is like a "cha'm" (*TSF*, 137) that gives him a reified identity:

> W'en de ham had be'n tuk off'n Dave, folks kinder stopped talkin' 'bout 'im so much. But de ham had be'n on his neck so long dat Dave had sorter got use' ter it. He look des lack he'd los' sump'n fer a day er so atter de ham wuz tuk off, en didn' 'pear ter know w'at ter do wid hisse'f. (*TSF*, 138)

The dehumanizing processes of slavery outdo the most horrifying charms, spells, and metamorphoses. The slaves' goopher in Julius's tales is often directed against this state of affairs, and it is no threatening power but a tool for liberation—or, at least, for fending off the worst of slavery. Whenever it is thus politicized, the occult tends to be less demonic and satanic than under other conditions.[26]

John shares his belief in "reason" with the horse trader who finally surrenders Becky, thinking that "a lame hoss wuz better 'n a dead nigger" (*TCW*, 156), and with the owners of the ancien régime of slavery, yet he fails to feel implicated. John's and the former slaveowners' perceptions reduce life to commodities; conversely, what they disparage as mere goophers, as fetishes, superstitions, amulets, or talismans, can transform the reified objects back to life.[27] John's rationality, Hemenway says, "becomes a function of his racism for he is incapable of granting conjure the dignity of belief."[28] John's blindness extends to his own world and to objects he believes he controls. In a frequently invoked scene in "The Gray Wolf's Ha'nt," John reads the following passage to his bored wife:

> "The difficulty of dealing with transformations so many-sided as those which all existences have undergone, or are undergoing, is

such as to make a complete and deductive interpretation almost hopeless. So to grasp the total process of redistribution of matter and motion as to see simultaneously its several necessary results in their actual interdependence is scarcely possible. There is, however, a mode of rendering the process as a whole tolerably comprehensible. Though the genesis of the rearrangement of every evolving aggregate is in itself one, it presents to our intelligence"—

"John," interrupted my wife, "I wish you would stop reading that nonsense and see who that is coming up the lane."

I closed my book with a sigh. I had never been able to interest my wife in the study of philosophy, even when presented in the simplest and most lucid form." (*TCW*, 163–164)

What John reads is, of course, a theory of metamorphoses, the existence of which he so vehemently denies in Julius's tales. Hemenway comments perceptively, "John reads, but does not understand, Julius 'knows' but does not require abstractions for 'proof.'"[29] Julius's "goopher" is what John can only imagine in the abstract, in Herbert Spencer's dry language, never as part of himself. John fails to connect "who is coming up the lane" with what he reads and believes he owns as if it were his racial patrimony.

Chesnutt's stories thus may appeal to the fear that the Western spirit (of the classical and biblical tradition) has been lost to the dead letter of form. The Pharisaic John reads abstractions about metamorphoses—to build a static sense of stable selfhood and to feel superior to Julius, as well as to his wife, who empathizes with Julius's stories of victims of metamorphoses. Julius, not John, is the new Ovid. "The Goophered Grapevine" is reminiscent of Bacchus (*Metamorphoses* 6:125), and "Po' Sandy," of Daphne (1:452–567).[30] Julius's tales are art á la Horace: John himself calls Julius "entertaining" and "useful" (*TCW*, 65).[31] Ironically, then, the slaves are identified with the classical tradition, which John merely invokes as a possession, as shallow form. More important, the same opposition also applies to the biblical allusions in Chesnutt's stories. The slaves are the salt of the earth and abide in God's vine (John 15:1–5), whereas John wants to leave no grapes for the poor and for the stranger, as God had instructed Moses (Numbers 19:10). Chesnutt's "John" does not understand little "Mose." As Monika Plessner has argued, the territory between superstition and rationality is filled by Chesnutt with reminders of Christ's suffering as a hope for redemption and reconciliation. Thus, Chesnutt transformed Fayetteville into "Patesville"—literally Golgotha (Matthew 27:33); the "scuppernong" grapes seem to echo Capernaum, where Jesus preached parables and performed miracles (Matthew 17:24, 8:5, 13:18, 24); and "The Goophered Grapevine" alludes to the parable of the house-holder's vineyard (Matthew 21:33–44).[32] Although John wonders what Christianity may mean for former slaves, they live the spirit of the Bible that the complacent John arrogantly claims as his racial property. John is a Pharisee, a scribe, but Julius has a truly Christian moral vision to which John fails to respond. No wonder that Chesnutt emphasizes the "good" goopher, conjuring against the evils of slavery, ownership, complacency, and lack of empathy. Chesnutt shows with his ironic method that a pro-prietary relationship to truth is a lie.

Interestingly—as Gustav Jahoda points out—modern attitudes to-ward superstition are always characterized by the hope that superstitions are dying out and will give way to rational progress.[33] In this sense, "superstition" is opposed to "modernity" in the same way "ethnicity" is commonly considered a thing of the past. More than that, the first occur-rence of the word "ethnicity" recorded in the *Oxford English Dictionary* is of 1772 and in the sense of "pagan superstition": "From the curling spume of the celebrated Egean waves fabulous ethnicity feigned Venus their idolatress conceived." "Ethnicity" and "superstition" are based on divisions, boundaries between an in-group (sacralized in the process) and an out-group. Although he thinks that he represents universal common sense, John constructs, and fails to see his own construction of, social boundaries. He cannot recognize much of himself in Julius. Although John thinks of the goopher as a vestige of darker ages, in Julius's tales it functions as a modern assault on John's artificial separation between his white male selfhood and all forms of otherness. The conjure wom-an's (and Chesnutt's) goopher dissolves prematurely hardened boundaries around self, gender, and race; it can change any form into any other form, it can turn masters into slaves and children into birds; and it can surely melt hardened hearts.[34] Even an "object," a thing, such as a rab-bit's foot can rescue humans from being mere commodities and fixities. In Chesnutt's world, the goopher spells process against reification and human wholeness against ethnic and sexual division, and it reconciles human beings with their mortality.[35] It is no coincidence that Chesnutt placed the goopher at the very center of his short stories, which, I sup-pose, have rightly been called "charming."

Figure 4.1. Winold Reiss, *Jean Toomer.* Pastel on illustration board, ca. 1925. (National Portrait Gallery, Smithsonian Institution/Art Resource, New York. Courtesy of Renate Reiss.)

CHAPTER 4

Jean Toomer's *Cane*

Modernism and Race in Interwar America

> Oracular.
> Redolent of fermenting syrup,
> Purple of the dusk,
> Deep-rooted cane.[1]

August 21, 1905: Jean Toomer's mother marries Archibald Coombs, both identified as "white" on the marriage certificate.

FROM THE BEGINNING to the ending of *Cane*, the reader is drawn into a magical and mysterious world of pine needles and clay, of autumn leaves and dusk, of spiritual striving and human failing, of love and violence, but also of the movement from country roads to city streets and from natural to industrial sounds. Enigmatic and memorable formulations mark the shift from country ("Time and space have no meaning in a canefield" [19]) to city ("The flute is a cat that ripples its fur against the deep-purring saxophone" [149]). *Cane* is a remarkable expression of the modernist movement in literature that swept the United States and Europe in the first half of the twentieth century. Published in 1923 (before Ernest Hemingway's and William Faulkner's first important books were to appear), *Cane* was a powerful contribution to the stream of modernism that had begun with Gertrude Stein's *Three Lives* and James Joyce's *Dubliners* and continued with Sherwood Anderson's *Winesburg,*

SOURCE: Werner Sollors, "Jean Toomer's *Cane*: Modernism and Race in Interwar America," in *Dream-Fluted Cane: Essays on Jean Toomer and the Harlem Renaissance*, ed. Geneviève Fabre and Michel Feith (New Brunswick, NJ: Rutgers University Press, 2001), 18–37. Copyright © 2001 by Werner Sollors.

Ohio, Waldo Frank's manifesto *Our America*, Hart Crane's poem *The Bridge*, and Eugene O'Neill's plays—a movement that was amplified by Alfred Stieglitz's photographs, Georgia O'Keeffe's paintings, the montage technique of the silent film, and the modern sounds of the blues and of jazz. The cultural historian Henry F. May called the watershed between Theodore Roosevelt and O. Henry, on the one side, and Greenwich Village and T. S. Eliot, on the other, a "cultural revolution."[2] The "revolution" in literature was spread by a younger generation of writers who loved the adjective "new," who chose many modern themes and settings, and who often looked to the other arts for inspiration. *Cane* is on our side of this transformation toward aesthetic modernism, psychological scrutiny, bohemian self-searching, increasing ethnic expression, and engagement with new ideologies.[3]

The author with the enigmatically androgynous name Jean Toomer (1894–1967) took up, but never completed, studies in history, anthropology, agriculture, and physical training; he was early attracted to atheism and socialism, later to the mystical and introspective Gurdjieff movement, to the Quakers, and to an Indian guru; and he spent important years in such artists' colonies as Greenwich Village; Taos, New Mexico; and Carmel, California. He participated in an early experiment in group psychology in Portage, Wisconsin, that neighbors suspected was a free love movement. He published poems, plays, and prose pieces on the pages of all the right small, experimental, and often radical literary magazines, such as *Broom*, *Liberator*, and *Modern Review*. Toomer submitted a play to O'Neill's Provincetown Playhouse, befriended Sherwood Anderson and Hart Crane, and was intimate with Georgia O'Keeffe; his second wife, Marjorie Content, had previously been married to the editor of *Broom*, who was caricatured as Robert Cohn in Hemingway's *The Sun Also Rises*.

Toomer was a searcher among the modernist intellectuals of his time. His writing, most excellently embodied by *Cane*, represents an attempt to answer his close friend Waldo Frank's demand that American writers "study the cultures of the German, the Latin, the Celt, the Slav, the Anglo-Saxon and the African on the American continent: plot their reactions one upon the other, and their disappearance as integral worlds."[4] Frank and Toomer spent some time together in Spartanburg, South Carolina. On the basis of this trip, Frank published his novel of perverted interracial lust and violence, *Holiday*.[5] Toomer had previously worked as an acting principal in a black school in Sparta, Georgia, for two months—his first extended stay in the rural South—during which time the idea for *Cane* germinated. (In *Cane*, he called the town "Sempter.") He read the town newspaper, the *Sparta Ishmaelite*, and lived in an old cabin. This is how Toomer remembered his emotional reaction to Sparta later on:

> There was a valley, the valley of "Cane," with smoke-wreaths during the day and mist at night. A family of back-country Negroes had only recently moved into a shack not too far away. They sang. And this was the first time I'd ever heard the folk-songs and spirituals. They were very rich and sad and joyous and beautiful. But I learned that the Negroes of the town objected to them. They called them "shouting." They had victrolas and player-pianos. So, I realized with deep regret, that the spirituals, meeting ridicule, would be certain to die out. With Negroes also the trend was toward the small town and then toward the city—and industry and commerce and machines. The folk-spirit was walking in to die on the modern desert. That spirit was so beautiful. Its death was so tragic. Just this seemed the sum of life to me. And this was the feeling I put into *Cane*. *Cane* was a swansong. It was a song of an end.[6]

Published the year before Horace Kallen coined the term "cultural pluralism," *Cane* is a meditation on what Toomer felt was the disappearing African culture on the American continent.

It is a book whose very form resists classification. Is *Cane* a novel? A mélange of experimental pieces of differing length? A synthesis of various forms of experimentation? A mosaic? Overall, it is a book sui generis, an experimental but highly readable fusion of poetry, prose, and drama (in "Bona and Paul" and "Kabnis"). Toomer employs a carefully orchestrated system of verbal repetition and musical progression in a text that appeals to all senses, by presenting strong visual images, creating rhythmic effects, evoking smells, tastes, tactile sensations—all the while expressing a strong sense of beauty as well as powerful feelings of pain and suffering. Its very form is an attempt at finding a literary equivalent for the dislocations that modernity had wrought, by moving people from soil to pavements, making them ashamed of their traditional folk culture or changing it into commercial entertainment and radically altering the epic pace of sun and seasons, of sowing and reaping, into the accelerated and syncopated rhythm of trains and cars, the staccato of quickly shifting images and thoughts. Despite all the apparent variations in genres, the book has the effect of a long poem that is held together by recurring images. *Cane* reflects on the country without idyllic nostalgia and on the city without teleological hope. Both are historically changing worlds of failed human understanding and of at times horrifyingly brutal encounters, since Toomer locates his work in the aftermath of World War I and in the white-black racial violence of the South and North. The modernist book *Cane* thus vies for the space of the spirit, of the human soul, that seems threatened under the rule of modernity—in both the country and the city. "We have two emblems, namely, the machinegun and the contraceptive," Toomer writes regretfully.[7] Can the lost soul of a fertile peasant past be found again in the elusively modernist form of a book that artistically, even artificially, reconstitutes life-asserting wholeness by resisting easy generalizations and a priori assumptions? *Cane* makes an attempt to do just that, even though Toomer articulated his keen awareness that there is no possibility of going back to a shared past:

> The modern world was uprooted, the modern world was breaking down, *but we couldn't go back*. There was nothing to go back to. Besides, in our hasty leaps into the future we had burned our bridges. The soil, the earth was still there, even under city pavements and congested sky scrapers.
>
> But such peasantry as America had had—and I sang one of its swan songs in *Cain* [sic]—was swiftly disappearing, swiftly being industrialized and urbanized by machines, motor cars, phonographs, movies. . . . "Back to nature," even if desirable, was no longer possible, because industry had taken nature unto itself. Even if he wanted to, a city person could not become a soil person by changing his locale and living on a farm in the woods.
>
> So then, whether we wished to or not, we *had to go on*.[8]

Toomer's answer to this problem could not lie in a return to traditional values—be they monarchy, religion, or mere conservatism—for "those who sought to cure themselves by a return to more primitive conditions were either romantics or escapists." No, going on, going on to create, searching for aesthetic wholeness and a new vision in a fragmented modern world—that was the only viable answer. His critique of modernity impelled Toomer to move forward the project of modernism.

Cane makes its readers self-conscious to let them yearn for a fresher and fuller look at the world. This effort is captured in the book's repeated allusions to St. Paul's Epistle to the Corinthians—"For now we see through a glass darkly; but then face to face; now I know in part; but then shall I know even as I am known"—a passage that Ralph Waldo Emerson and Nathaniel Hawthorne had also cherished and that Henry Roth and Ralph Ellison were to draw on later. Is it possible to have full knowledge and self-knowledge in the modern world? In pursuing this question in the United States, Toomer also searched for a more cosmic understanding of the wholeness of a polyvocal America as it was once sung by Walt Whitman and now proclaimed by Waldo Frank. And like many visionaries before him, Toomer espoused the fragmentary as the necessary part of larger totalities.

The interrelatedness of fragmentation and quest for wholeness structures Cane. The book is divided into three parts that are marked by parentheses-like curves (,), and (). "Between each of the three sections, a curve. These, to vaguely indicate the design," Toomer wrote to Waldo Frank on December 12, 1922.[9] The two segments realign and aim for a circle without fully achieving its closure in the third part.

Part 1 is set in Georgia, the rural South. It is mostly focused on women, starting with Karintha, whose very name may represent a nod into the direction of Gertrude Stein's "Melanctha" or may allude to St. Paul's "Corinthians," and ending with Louisa in "Blood-Burning Moon." "Karintha" originally appeared in the context of the drama Natalie Mann (1922) in which Toomer's mouthpiece Nathan Merilh reads "Karintha" as evidence that historically grown, black sacred art remained a valid and important source of inspiration to the intellectual who found himself surrounded by modern Marxist and nationalist interrogators.[10] Yet Karintha is more of a modern Mary Magdalene than a conventional sacred figure. Men bring her money, and her imagistic constitution is that of a woman whose running is a "whir" and whose "skin is like dusk on the eastern horizon, . . . when the sun goes down" (1)—a leitmotif of the story in the repetition of which Toomer visibly blurs the line between poetry and prose: it is typeset as a prose sentence and as a poem. In the play, Therman Law, a young man who is also the friend of Nathan Merilh, who in turn is presented as the author of "Karintha," reflects:

What should be the most colorful and robust of our racial segments is approaching a sterile and denuded hypocrisy as its goal.
What has become of the almost obligatory heritage of folk-songs?
Jazz on the one hand, and on the other, a respectability which is
never so vigorous as when it denounces and rejects the true art of
the race's past. They are ashamed of the past made permanent by
the spirituals. My God, imagine the look on the face of Dvořák.[11]

The poems and the portraits of rural women that follow intensify the
reader's sense of hearing Toomer's "swan song," of experiencing fragments of a passing rural world, in which religious sentiments and natural
images, especially those of sunsets and autumn, increasingly give way to
such intrusions of modernity as railroad tracks and factories and to scenes
of violence. Becky, introduced with a paradoxical subtitle reminiscent
of Bertolt Brecht's plot-summarizing dramatic strategies as "the white
woman who had two Negro sons" (8), lives on a "ground islandized
between the road and railroad track" (9). Fern is presented as if narrator
and reader were seeing her from a train thundering by:

Besides, picture if you can, this cream-colored solitary girl sitting
at a tenement window looking down on the indifferent throngs
of Harlem. Better that she listen to folk-songs at dusk in Georgia,
you would say, and so would I. Or, suppose she came up North
and married. Even a doctor or a lawyer, say, one who would be
sure to get along—that is, make money. You and I know, who
have had experience in such things, that love is not a thing like
prejudice which can be bettered by changes of town. Could men
in Washington, Chicago, or New York, more than the men of
Georgia, bring her something left vacant by the bestowal of their
bodies? . . . .
    I ask you, friend (it makes no difference if you sit in the Pull-
man or the Jim Crow as the train crosses her road), what thoughts
would come to you . . . had you seen her in a quick flash, keen
and intuitively, as she sat there on her porch when your train
thundered by? Would you have got off at the next station and
come back for her to take her where? Would you have completely
forgotten her as soon as you reached Macon, Atlanta, Augusta,
Pasadena, Madison, Chicago, Boston, or New Orleans? (28–30)

Esther, who has come to sexual maturity, walks into a jeering crowd like a somnambulist, and the story ends like a Franz Kafka tale: "She steps out. There is no air, no street, and the town has completely disappeared" (48). The undercurrent of violence, which emerges with the blood-stained blade of the scythe that has cut a rat in the poem "Reapers," erupts in "Blood-Burning Moon" at the end of the first section as the factory town mob lynches Louisa's black lover Tom Burwell, whose steel blade had slashed across his white rival Bob Stone's throat. The story is ominously preceded by the short poem "Portrait in Georgia," in which each line begins with an invocation of a woman's body (hair, eyes, lips, breath) but ends with imagery of lynching.

In part 2, *Cane* takes us to cities, especially Washington and Chicago in the age of mass-migration and urbanization. The rhythm changes abruptly in this world that is characterized by postwar disillusionment, by a proliferating entertainment industry, and by the syncopation of jazz that Toomer incorporates into his prose to render a life that is "jazzed, strident, modern. Seventh Street," located in black Washington, "is the song of crude new life. Of a new people."[12] The surrealistic Rhobert, who wears his house like a diver's helmet, is an urban counterpart to Becky, as the narration again repeats prose sentences as poems. The image of the man who sinks is connected with the World War I experience that reduced God to "a Red Cross man with a dredge and a respiration-pump" (74) and makes the singing of the traditional spiritual "Deep River" seem out of place:

Lets build a monument and set it in the ooze where he goes down.
A monument of hewn oak, carved in nigger-heads. Lets open our
throats, brother, and sing "Deep River" when he goes down.
    Brother, Rhobert is sinking.
    Lets open our throats, brother,
    Lets sing Deep River when he goes down. (75)

The self-conscious narrator of "Avey" resembles that of "Fern."[13] Again, the wish for a performance of the spiritual "Deep River," this time by the Howard University Glee Club, marks the contrast to rural religion, a contrast that shapes also the vignette of the young woman on the street in "Calling Jesus." "Theater" continues the jazz theme, and Toomer adopts some blues lines here: "Arms of the girls, and their limbs, which . . jazz,

jazz . . by lifting up their tight street skirts they set free, jab the air and clog the floor in rhythm to the music. (Lift your skirts, Baby, and talk t papa!)" (92).[14] In "Box Seat," Dan Moore reflects on a man who saw the first Oldsmobile but was born a slave: "He saw Grant and Lincoln. He saw Walt—old man, did, you see Walt Whitman?" (125). The new urban world is not even one lifetime removed from Civil War and slavery, and this recent history casts its shadow over the failed interracial romance between Bona and Paul in the story that ends the second part and corresponds most directly to "Blood-Burning Moon." Just as Bob Stone wanted Louisa because she was black and "went in as a master should and took her. Direct, honest, bold" (59), so Bona in the new world of a Chicago gymnasium and the nightclub Crimson Gardens is attracted to Paul because she suspects he is black: "That's why I love—" (135). Bona's (and Toomer's) lyrical labels "harvest moon" and "autumn leaf" cannot displace the racial slur "nigger"—which is, for Bona, however, an ambivalent source of attraction. The weight of such historical racial categories ("a priori" recurs here) impinges on the consciousness of the youths: "Bona is one window. One window, Paul" (137). The urban setting changes Toomer's prose, but it does not free the characters from their preconceptions.

In part 3, "Kabnis," the artist himself is *seen* rather than having merely a stronger or weaker presence as observer. Like Toomer, Kabnis is a secular urban intellectual who goes to rural Georgia to teach. Partly inspired by Joyce's *Portrait of the Artist as a Young Man*, "Kabnis"—written as a play and submitted to O'Neill's Provincetown Players associate Kenneth Macgowan—shows the development of a tortured mind through encounters with nursery rhymes, religion, and the various role models such as a teacher, preacher, cartwright, radical, and visionary. There are many things Kabnis has to face about society, history, and himself, but the core of what he must come to terms with is a legacy of violence. When drunk and self-critical, Kabnis attempts to articulate his aesthetic against the avalanche of words that makes the country go down: "I want t feed th soul—I know what that is; th preachers dont—but I've got t feed it" (224). When he adds, "I wish t God some lynchin white man ud stick his knife through it an pin it to a tree" (224–225), he likens his soul to the child of Mame Lamkins, whose story the preacher Layman had told him earlier:

They killed her in th street, an some white man seein th risin in
her stomach as she lay there soppy in her blood like any cow, took
an ripped her belly open, an th kid fell out. It was living; but a
nigger baby aint supposed t live. So he jabbed his knife in it an
stuck it t a tree. An then they all went away. (178–179)[15]

Even in the face of such horrors, the ending of "Kabnis" resembles a
rebirth, as the book ends with a glorious sunrise: "Gold-glowing child,
it steps into the sky and sends a birth-song slanting down gray dust streets
and sleepy windows of the southern town" (239).

The three parts of *Cane* confront the divisions of South and North,
women and men, as well as black and white, whereas the structure of the
book tends to bridge such divisions and strive toward unity. In a letter
to Waldo Frank dated December 12, 1922, Toomer suggested another
sequence in which one might read the book:

Cane's design is a circle. Aesthetically, from simple forms to complex ones, and back to simple forms. Regionally, from the South
up into the North, and back into the South again. Or, from the
North down into the South, and then a return North. From the
point of view of the spiritual entity behind the work, the curve
really starts with Bona and Paul (awakening), plunges into Kabnis, emerges in Karintha etc. swings upward into Theatre and
Box Seat, and ends (pauses) in Harvest Song. Whew![16]

The book may then be said to follow at least a double curve: one
that goes from beginning to end, and one that starts in the middle and
ends with "Harvest Song." Yet *Cane* could also be read in many other
sequences, since many parts resonate with many other parts because of
the book's poetic structure. Toomer's method also resembles film montage technique, as it juxtaposes sequences that the reader-viewer must
put together, must "suture." Unity is achieved by various repetitions and
leitmotifs that create a sense of thematic cohesion and rhythm and shape
the design of the text.[17]

Toomer aims for a particular kind of lyrical specificity expressed in
strong and often enigmatic images that recur in repeated words, phrases, and shorter or longer sentences throughout the book. Although the

precise meaning of an instance on a given page may be hard to define, the very fact that words are repeated throughout the book gives the reader a sense of acoustic and visual familiarity, a phenomenon reminiscent of Gertrude Stein's *Three Lives*. For example, *Cane* is a book of repeated "thuds," harsh knocking sounds that syncopate the reading from "Becky" to the end of "Kabnis." In "Blood-Burning Moon," the thud is the sound of Bob's body falling and of the mob's action, giving a menacingly violent undercurrent of meaning to such later thuds as those in the gymnasium in "Bona and Paul." Similarly, there are trees throughout the book, but it is the tale of Mame Lamkins in "Kabnis" that gives them their precise sense of eeriness. *Cane* is a book full of sunset and dusk imagery that is virtually omnipresent in the poems and the prose, thus calling particular attention to the emphatic sunrise at the end. Karintha is described as a "November cotton flower"; that is also the title of a poem that appears a few pages later.[18] The repetition of "pines whisper to Jesus" in "Becky" anticipates "Calling Jesus" and the whispering nightwind in "Kabnis." Read this way, the book is woven of recurring sounds and images in such words as sawmill, pine, cotton, dixie pike, street, smoke, wedge, window, moon, cloud, purple, cradle, sin, and, of course, cane. Robert Jones has stressed how Gertrude Stein's love for "ing" forms also affected Toomer; he focused on "Seventh Street" with its reiterated "zooming cadillacs, / Whizzing, whizzing down the street-car tracks," its "thrusting unconscious rhythm"—all coming to a climactic moment in "black reddish blood. Pouring for crude-boned soft-skinned life, who set you flowing?" And "flowing down the smooth asphalt of Seventh Street, in shanties, brick office buildings, theaters, drug stores, restaurants, and cabarets? Eddying on the corners? Swirling like a blood-red smoke up where the buzzards fly in heaven?" (71–72).[19]

In addition, many sections contain further patterns of repeated phrases and sentences within a single story or vignette. At times (as in "Becky" and "Calling Jesus"), the phrasing with the central set of images appears at the beginning and the end, as prose or poetry. In stories such as "Blood-Burning Moon," the internal repetition is remarkable; one can see how this works in Toomer's prose by looking at a few representative sentences:

> The full moon sank upward into the deep purple of the cloud-bank. An old woman brought a lighted lamp and hung it on the common well whose bulky shadow squatted in the middle of the

road, opposite Tom and Louisa. The old woman lifted the well-lid, took hold the chain, and began drawing up the heavy bucket. As she did so, she sang. Figures shifted, restlesslike, between lamp and window in the front room of the shanties. Shadows of the figures fought each other on the gray dust of the road. Figures raised the windows and joined the old woman in song. Louisa and Tom, the whole street, singing:

> Red nigger moon. Sinner!
> Blood-burning moon. Sinner!
> Come out that fact'ry door. (58)

These sentences contain words that echo earlier sentences. By the time we read the sentence, "Its yell echoed against the skeleton stone walls and sounded like a hundred yells" (67), most of the nouns are themselves echoes. This makes for a musical and visual progression. By using such words as "yell" as subjects of short sentences, Toomer also gives an energetic, imagistic quality to his descriptions, as he seems focused on a telling detail. "Fern" opens with a sentence in which "face" is the subject: "Face flowed into her eyes" (24). It makes grammatical sense, contains only familiar words, and evokes a strong image, yet is also quite mysterious.

Such a phrasing is reminiscent of Ezra Pound's "In a Station of the Metro." Toomer may, in fact, be consciously following F. S. Flint's and Ezra Pound's 1913 imagist maxims, which exhorted poets to treat the "thing" directly, use absolutely no word that does not contribute to the presentation, compose in the sequence of a musical phrase, not the sequence of a metronome and arrive at an image that presents an intellectual and emotional complex in an instant of time.[20] Toomer's images certainly are not ornaments, but they *are* the speech.

The dialectic of the accustomed familiarity of given words that make physical things visible and vivid, and the "oracular" strangeness of their precise meaning that surrounds the verbally constituted world with questions and ambiguity, is given fullest play in Toomer's descriptions such as that about Louisa: "Her skin was the color of oak leaves on young trees in fall" (51). This is a strongly visual image that makes the reader see things fresh, yet it would be hard to associate one very specific color with such a description. It is no coincidence that for Toomer such lyricism also has the function of avoiding a label. Toomer shared with imagists such as T. E. Hulme a disdain for abstractions and a desire to let fresh metaphors make the reader visualize a physical thing. Thus, Toomer does not call Karintha a "prostitute" (although reviewers such as W. E. B. Du Bois did); the narrator says only that men bring her money.[21] Yet Toomer brings to this program a particular wish that goes beyond the aesthetic.

His description of Louisa's skin color is an alternative to a racial label, a needling engagement with a reader's desire to know whether a character is black or white. Toomer's response is, "Her skin was the color of oak leaves on young trees in fall" (51). Bona, too, sees Paul in the following way: "He is a harvest moon. He is an autumn leaf. He is a nigger" (134). These are three grammatically parallel sentences, two of which offer lyrical perceptions and one of which is not just an abstraction and cliché but the worst ethnic slur as a label (though for Bona, this very abstraction is also a source of attraction). For Jean Toomer, the worst aesthetic strategy was to employ a cliché—and he saw language as complicit in racial domination.

Cane is a modernist work that has as its specific milieu the world of American race relations, polarized along the color line that divides black and white, whether in Sparta, Washington, or Chicago. Toomer's stylistic choices are an expression of his refusal to endorse this racial divide. To be sure, Cane was a book in which black life, rural and urban, was strongly thematized. But this was not all. His aesthetic was connected to a quest for unity beyond all divisions. On May 16, 1923, Toomer wrote to DuBose Heyward, "Both black and white folk come into Cane's pages. For me, this is artistically inevitable. But in no instance am I concerned primarily with race; always, I drive straight for my own spiritual reality, and for the spiritual truth of the South."[22]

This quest for wholeness and Toomer's own "spiritual reality" is related to the book's racial and historical thematic. If America is fragmented, black and white, male and female, southern and northern, rural and urban, Toomer sees his own mission, by contrast, as providing a ground for spiritual unity. His quest for union, for wholeness, for the circle is achieved precisely by thematizing the divisions that the book's author felt were so destructive and virulent in the modern world: race, sex, class, region. Toomer saw himself as a visionary who would try to redirect readers toward a wholeness—however elusive it might be—that they had lost in their differentiations by category. In other words, Toomer's aesthetic modernism was connected to an attack on false perceptions, prejudices, a priori assumptions, and labels. He was attracted to Waldo Frank, James Joyce, Eugene O'Neill (Toomer wrote a rave notice on "The Emperor Jones"), and Gertrude Stein (both Toomer and Stein contributed an homage to Alfred Stieglitz in a volume published in 1934). Toomer found that modernist forms helped to complicate facile notions about social life. Georgia O'Keeffe had painted *Birch and Pine Trees—Pink* (1925) as a modern version of a "portrait" of her friend Jean Toomer, to whom she wrote, "There is a painting I made from something of you the first time you were here." The "dancing" trees were thus a "surrogate portrait of her close friend."[23] This was, of course, also a way to deflect from portraits as realistic representations to portraits as purely *formal* expression. Toomer wrote to Georgia O'Keeffe on January 13, 1924:

> Have you come to the story "Bona and Paul" in *Cane*? Impure and imperfect as it is, I feel that you and Stieglitz will catch its essential design as no others can. Most people cannot see this story because of the inhibitory baggage they bring with them. When I say "white," they see a certain white man, when I say "black," they see a certain Negro. Just as they miss Stieglitz's intentions, achievements! Because they see "clouds." So that at the end, when Paul resolves these contrasts to a unity, my intelligent commentators wonder what its [sic] all about. Someday perhaps, with greater purity and a more perfect art, I'll do the thing. And meanwhile the gentlemen with intellect will haggle over the question as to whether or not I have expressed the "South."[24]

A philosophical spirit in a world of antagonisms, Toomer was bent on any verbal strategy that would promote the transcendence rather than the hardening of divisive categories. This included notions of racial identity, also his own, all the more so since Toomer had a modern, analytical understanding of the mechanisms of racial differentiation. Racial tension to him was not an ancient survival but a new creation. In his essay "Race Problems and Modern Society," published in 1929, he writes that

> the new Negro is much more Negro and much less American than was the old Negro of fifty years ago. From the point of view of sociological types, the types which are arising among Negroes,

such as the business man, the politician, the college student, the
writer, the propagandist, the movie enthusiast, the bootlegger, the
taxi driver, etc.—these types among Negroes are more and more
approaching the corresponding white types. But, just as certain
as it is that this increasing correspondence of types makes the
drawing of distinctions supposedly based on skin color or blood
composition appear more and more ridiculous, so it is true that
the lines are being drawn with more force between the colored
and white groups.[25]

In a posthumously published essay, "The Americans," he views America
as the place

where mankind, long dismembered into separate usually repellant
groupings, long scattered over the face of the earth, is being re-as-
sembled into one whole and undivided human race. American
will include the earth.

There is a new race here. For the present we may call it the
American race. That, to date, not many are aware of its existence,
that they do not realize that they themselves belong to it—this
does not mean it does not exist; it simply means it does not yet
exist for them because they, under the suggestion of hypnotic
labels and false beliefs, are blind to it. But these labels and beliefs
will die. They too must and will die. And the sight of people will
be freed from them, and the people will become less blind and
they will use their sight and see.

This new race is neither white nor black nor red nor brown.
These are the old terms for old races, and they must be discard-
ed. This is a new race; and though to some extent, to be sure,
white and black and red and brown strains have entered into its
formation, we should not view it as part white, part black, and so
on. . . . Water, though composed of two parts of hydrogen and
one part of oxygen, is not hydrogen and oxygen; it is *water*.[26]

The logic of racial segregation was all the more absurd to Toomer since
he perceived that the old African American culture was disappearing,
whereas the new American culture was a shared crossover culture. He
asked himself, "Was Seventh Street Negro?" and answered, "Only in the

boldness of its expression. In its healthy freedom. American. For the shows that please Seventh Street make their fortunes on Broadway."[27] Black culture, for Toomer, was an intricate part and tastemaker of American culture, and yet the mental (and social) boundaries between black and white were being reinforced rather than blurred.

What could a writer do to fight such racial blindness and ridiculousness as was prominent, for example, in the Virginia legislature, which passed the Act to Preserve Racial Purity in 1924, defining any person "in whom there is ascertainable any Negro blood" a colored person? The U.S. Census after 1920 also no longer provided a category for interracial or biracial Americans.[28] Toomer was convinced that a rethinking of the power of language in creating group divisions was in order, especially for writers. His aesthetic had to work against, and his theoretical pronouncements had to attack and transcend, facile labels. In "The Americans" he stressed in a very modern way, after having made the analogy with water, the sociological (not biological) nature of racial distinctions:

> There is only one pure race—and this is the *human* race. We all belong to it—and this is the most and the least that can be said of any of us with accuracy. For the rest, it is mere talk, mere labelling, merely a manner of speaking, merely a sociological, not a biological, thing. I myself merely talk when I speak of the blending of the bloods of the white, black, red, and brown races giving rise to a new race, to a new unique blood, when I liken the combination of these strains to the combination of hydrogen and oxygen producing water. For the blood of all the races is *human* blood. There are no differences between the blood of a Caucasian and the blood of a Negro as there are between hydrogen and oxygen. In the mixing and blending of so-called races there are mixtures and blending of the same stuff.[29]

In his post–imagist collection of aphorisms, *Essentials* (1931), he draws the consequences from such reflections and writes about himself:

> I am of no particular race. I am of the human
> race, a man at large in the human world,
> preparing a new race.
> I am of no specific region. I am of earth.

> I am of no particular class. I am of the human
> class, preparing a new class.
> I am neither male nor female nor in-between. I am
> of sex, with male differentiations.
> I am of no special field, I am of the field of being.[30]

The fourth of these "definitions" might explain the reason why in 1920 he chose the name Jean over his baptismal Nathan Eugene for publication; this choice made Toomer part of a 1920s penchant among modernists for gender ambiguity.[31]

Yet it was particularly the first maxim that remained his greatest concern. Toomer would express similar sentiments in his Whitman-inspired poem "Blue Meridian" (1936) and in his autobiographical writings. Toomer, who in this respect was also an heir to Whitman's utopian hopes for the New World, tended to see both "America" and the first person singular "I" as potentially all-inclusive. He writes in "On Being an American":

> I had lived among white people. I had lived among colored peo-
> ple. I had lived among Jews. I had met and known people of the
> various nationalistic groups. I had come into contact with my
> fellow countrymen from the bottom to the top of the American
> scene.
>
>   I had seen the divisions, the separatisms and antagonisms. I
> had observed that, if the issue came up, very few of these United
> States citizens were aware of being *Americans*. On the contrary,
> they were aware of, and put value upon, their hearsay descents,
> their groupistic affiliations.[32]
>
>   He therefore suggested to the editor of *Prairie* magazine: "It is
> stupid to call me anything other than an American."[33]

Toomer's identity choice was at odds with the way in which race is commonly defined in the United States but not with his family background. When Nathan Eugene Pinchback Toomer was born on December 26, 1894, he was born into a family with a long-standing tradition of racial ambiguity.[34] His father, Nathan Toomer, had been born in 1841 and may have been a slave or free. He was the light-skinned son of a prosperous Georgia plantation owner of English, Dutch, and Spanish descent and a "woman of mixed blood, including Negro and Indian." Nathan Toomer lived on both sides of the color line: as a white man in the South and as a Negro in Washington, DC. He was a restless man and left Jean's mother, Nina Pinchback (1868–1909), a year after Jean's birth. Nina was the daughter of Pinckney Benton Stewart Pinchback (the son of a white father, Major William Pinchback, who also had a legal white wife and family on his Virginia plantation, and a Mulatto slave mother, Eliza Benton Stewart, who, according to Toomer, was "of English, Scotch, Welsh, German, African, and Indian stock"). She bore William ten children, the first in 1829 when she was fifteen or sixteen; after the sixth childbirth, William manumitted her and the surviving children. Pinckney was born in 1837 in Macon, Georgia, when the family was journeying west after the Jacksonian Indian removals. In 1846, P. B. S. Pinchback and his brother Napoleon were sent to Hiram S. Gilmore High School in Cincinnati. After Major William Pinchback's death, no money was forthcoming. Napoleon functioned as the head of the family but went insane, and the family broke up. The twelve-year-old Pinckney was on his own and worked as a steward on riverboats, became a gambler, and moved to New Orleans, where in 1860 he married Toomer's maternal grandmother, Emily Hethorn, an Anglo-French Creole woman who was light in appearance and about whose racial background there is conflicting information. Pinchback, too, was so light-skinned that his sister Adeline advised him in 1863 to pass for white, as she was doing. Pinchback became the first African American to serve as governor of a state, when he was appointed in 1872 as acting governor of Louisiana. (At one point, Toomer declared that Pinchback had said he was black only for the political motive of being appointed governor during Reconstruction.) In addition to their daughter, Nina, the Pinchbacks had three sons: Pinckney, who was educated at Andover and the Philadelphia College of Pharmacy; Bismarck, a freethinker and lawyer; and Walter, who served in the Spanish-American War in Cuba and later became a doctor. Nina was sent to the private Riverside School in Massachusetts. After his parents' divorce in 1899, Jean Toomer lived with his mother and his grandparents in a black middle-class neighborhood in Washington, DC, until his mother remarried on August 21, 1905. Her new husband, Archibald Coombs (sometimes spelled Combes), the son of Anthony Coombs and Mary Pierce Coombs, descended from the famous Mulatto colony Gouldtown in Cumberland County, New Jersey, near Bridgeton (probably going back to Jacob Coombs and Clara Gould Coombs, a direct descendant of Gouldtown's founders), yet both Nina and Coombs were classified, or described themselves, as "white" on their marriage certificate.[35] Toomer lived with his mother and stepfather in Brooklyn and a white neighborhood in New Rochelle for more than three years when he was ten to fourteen years old. After Toomer's mother died, the death certificate, dated June 9, 1909, and signed by his uncle Walter A. Pinchback, also described her as white.[36] Jean Toomer returned to Washington, DC, to live with his maternal grandparents, and he graduated from the famous black Dunbar (then still called M Street) High School.

Obviously, his mysterious father's background in Georgia and the birth in Georgia of his overpowering maternal grandfather made Toomer's teaching experience in Sparta a much deeper quest. "When one is on the soil of one's ancestors, most anything can come to one" (31), he writes in *Cane*, and in "Song of the Son" it is hard not to think of an autobiographical significance to the lines of the son who comes to the soil "to catch thy plaintive soul":

> Thy son, in time, I have returned to thee,
> Thy son, I have in time returned to thee. (21)[37]

Toomer's project in *Cane* was thus an aesthetic experiment, a study of a vanishing rural folk culture, a quest for the meaning of modern "America" and his own Americanness, and the expression of a profoundly personal and deeply felt genealogical engagement. He described his background in a famous letter to Max Eastman and Claude McKay, the editors of the radical *Liberator* in 1922, to explain *Cane*:

> Racially, I seem to have (who knows for sure) seven blood mixtures: French, Dutch, Welsh, Negro, German, Jewish, and Indian. Because of these, my position in America has been a curious one. I have lived equally amid the two race groups. Now white, now colored. From my own point of view I am naturally and inevitably an American. . . . Within the last two or three years, however, my growing need for artistic expression has pulled me deeper and deeper into the Negro group. And as my powers of receptivity increased, I found myself loving it in a way that I

could never love the other. It has stimulated and fertilized whatever creative talent I may contain within me. A visit to Georgia
last fall was the starting point of almost everything of worth that
I have done. I heard folk-songs come from the lips of Negro
peasants. I saw the rich dusk beauty that I had heard many false
accents about, and of which till then, I was somewhat skeptical.
And a deep part of my nature, a part I had repressed, sprang suddenly to life and responded to them. Now, I cannot conceive of
myself as aloof and separated.[38]

"American" as an ideal self-description meant for Toomer an identification for people of all backgrounds who could acknowledge their shared
and mixed characteristics—in opposition to the silent usurpation of the
term "American" to stand for "white American."[39] The United States
as a reality, however, was characterized by an emphasis on "groupistic"
descents, which drew Toomer at the time of *Cane* both closer to a deeper
experience of black life and to a more profound claim on his Americanness. Like many nineteenth-century New Orleans Creoles, Toomer
lived—and responded intellectually and aesthetically to—the paradox of
American racial construction that simply defined him as "colored," all his
other "ascertainable" ancestry notwithstanding. When he and the novelist
Margery Latimer, a descendant of Anne Bradstreet, got married in March
1931 (after the group psychology experiment at Portage), he issued the following, familiar-sounding statement, entitled "A New Race in America":

There is a new race in America. I am a member of this new race.
It is neither white nor black nor in-between. It is the American race, differing as much from white and black as white and
black differ from each other. It is possible that there are Negro
and Indian bloods in my descent along with English, Spanish,
Welsh, Scotch, French, Dutch, and German. This is common in
America, and it is from all these strains that the American race is
being born. But the old divisions into white, black, brown, red,
are outworn in this country. They have had their day. Now is
the time of the birth of a new order, a new vision, a new ideal of
man. I proclaim this order. My marriage to Margery Latimer is
the marriage of two Americans.[40]

The *World Telegram* headline read, "NEGRO WHO WED WHITE NOVELIST
SEES NEW RACE." Whatever Toomer saw, the newspaper failed to see—
and the headline seems like a translation of one of Toomer's *Essentials*
into a journalistic cliché.[41]

Toomer would not only deplore such sensationalist and hostile label-
ing at a time that interracial marriage was prohibited in the majority of
the United States. Upon the completion of *Cane* he also came to reject
the label "Negro writer." He received largely favorable reviews and comments from black intellectuals—for example, the authoritative Du Bois
praised Toomer for daring to "hurl his pen across the very face of our
sex conventionality," noted that he painted things "with an impression-
ist's sweep of color," and admired the book's "strange flashes of power"
even when it was difficult to understand it. And the aesthete Alain Locke
thought that *Cane* was, with Richard Wright's *Native Son* and Ralph
Ellison's *Invisible Man*, one of the three best works of the modern period
and found that in Toomer's text "the emotional essences of the Southland
were hauntingly evoked in an impressionistic poetic sort of realism."[42]
Yet Toomer questioned—as we saw in his letter to O'Keeffe—his role
as a representative of "the South," and more controversially, he did not
wish to be included in anthologies such as Nancy Cunard's *Negro*.[43] He
did, however, contribute to Sterling Brown, Arthur P. Davis, and Ulysses
Lee's *Negro Caravan* (1941).[44] He was also apprehensive of friendly writers
who, like Sherwood Anderson, saw him too exclusively as "Negro." He
wrote to Waldo Frank (around March 1923), "Sherwood limits me to
Negro. As an approach, as a constant element (part of a larger whole) of
interest, Negro is good. But try to tie me to one of my parts is surely to
[lose] me. My own letters have taken Negro as a point, and from there
have circled out. Sherwood, for the most part, ignores the circles."[45] Conversely, Toomer would also question Frank's failure to include the Negro
more fully in *Our America*: "No picture of a southern person is complete
without its bit of Negro-determined psychology."[46]

For Toomer, black and white were linked together like twins, like
yin and yang, but racist labels, lazy thinking, and faith in clichés pre-
vented this reality from finding universal creative expression. And it is
here that Toomer perceived his own avant-garde position. In the ideal
American world of racial reciprocity, Toomer conceived of his art as a
spiritual sort of racial amalgamation, which he explained in his letter to
McKay and Eastman:

I have strived for a spiritual fusion analogous to the fact of racial intermingling. Without denying a single element in me, with no desire to subdue one to the other, I have sought to let them function as complements. I have tried to let them live in harmony.[47]

A few days earlier, he had written similarly to John McClure:

I alone, as far as I know, have striven for a spiritual fusion, analogous to the fact of racial intermingling. It has been rough riding. Nor am I through. Have just begun, in fact. This, however, has neither social nor political implications. My concern is solely with art. What am I? From my own point of view, naturally and inevitably an American.[48]

Toomer thought that *Cane* was only the beginning of a long road. Although, indeed, many projects and fragments, long manuscripts, a few literary publications, and published essays and aphorisms followed, no second book by Toomer to equal the brilliance of *Cane* ever appeared. *Cane* united aesthetic experimentation; the contemplation of African American folk culture in modern America; and the themes of genealogical origins, migration, and interracialism while it challenged easy labels and insisted on the need for a new spiritual wholeness. It remains Toomer's outstanding contribution to modern literature.

Figure 5.1. Claude McKay speaking in the Throne Room of the Kremlin. (Unidentified photographer, *The Crisis*, November 1923, Widener Library, Harvard University.)

CHAPTER 5

African American Intellectuals and Europe between the Two World Wars

1923: In Negri v Amerike (Негры в Америке), *Claude McKay responds to Leon Trotsky's offer to train a group of Negroes as officers in the Red Army.*

BLACK AMERICAN intellectuals' European adventure stories have been traced as far back as Phillis Wheatley. Another rarely mentioned eighteenth-century African American who spent significant time in Paris was Sally Hemings, whose relationship with her travel companion, lover, and *uncle* Thomas Jefferson may be the reason that she is not typically included in discussions of blacks in Europe. William Wells Brown, Frederick Douglass, Frank Webb, and James Weldon Johnson spent significant time in Europe and wrote about it. Douglass's German companion and translator Ottilie Assing has recently been made the subject of a biography, and her essays have been republished.[1]

A "European theme" is pervasive in black American writing, in which Europe is typically stylized as the haven for black and mixed-race Americans, where there are whites who do not share white American

SOURCE: Werner Sollors, "African American Intellectuals and Europe between the Two World Wars," in *Regards Croisés sur les Afro-Américains: Hommage à Michel Fabre*, ed. Claude Julien (GRAAT No. 27) (Tours, France: Presses Universitaires François Rabelais, 2003), 41–57. Copyright © 2003 by Werner Sollors.

prejudices, and where interracial couples and their descendants can live happily ever after. Jessie Fauset's novel *Plum Bun* offers this typical possibility for Angela Murray:

> She asked for nothing better than to put all the problems of colour and their attendant difficulties behind her. She could not meet those problems in their present form in Europe; literally in every sense she would begin life all over. In France or Italy she would speak of her strain of Negro blood and abide by whatever consequences such exposition would entail. But the consequences could not engender the pain and difficulties attendant upon them here.[2]

In other texts, Spain, Italy, Switzerland, Austria, Germany, the Netherlands, England, the Scandinavian countries, and Russia were offered as alternatives to America, articulating what one could even call the "European dream." Here I focus on African American intellectuals and Europe between the two world wars.

The interstitial moment between World War I and World War II was a cease-fire during the Great European Civil War, a war that started with shots in the Balkans and ended thirty-one years later, leaving sixty-five million casualties and a degraded, bombed-out continent behind. This second thirty years' war also took a severe toll among oppositional intellectuals. The "interwar period" saw the rise of communism and its transformation into Stalinism; the emergence of fascism; and two momentous "interwar wars," the Italian war against Ethiopia and the Spanish Civil War, in which Italian and German forces, as well as African colonials, helped Franco's fascists to defeat the elected Republican government.

It was uncertain which American response to fascism would prevail. One need only remember that in 1928 Benito Mussolini's autobiography was ghostwritten by the anti-immigration and pro-deportation writer Richard Washburn Child, who had been the U.S. ambassador to Italy during the march on Rome, and it was serialized prominently in the *Saturday Evening Post*.[3]

By the mid-1930s, the American decision had been made, and it affected race relations in the United States. When Joe Louis defeated Max Schmeling on June 22, 1938, at Yankee Stadium, this marked the victory not of a black boxer over a white man, but of a hero of American democracy over a foreign fascist.[4] Similarly, Jesse Owens was sometimes seen as an American national representative at the Berlin Olympics in 1936. In the interwar period, then, black American men for the first time could serve as symbols of the United States. I relate a few Afro-European encounters (with an aside on fascist and Stalinist aesthetics) below and leave it up to the reader to draw conclusions. My essay focuses on black men, although many African American women—Augusta Savage and Jessie Fauset, for example—also went to Europe in the period and could be presented in a similar way. This chapter later touches on Nella Larsen's pre–World War I stay in Denmark.

Black American soldiers went to Europe in World War I and brought back not only the expressions "boo coos" (from the word *beaucoup*) and "toot sweets" but also a new militancy against injustice at home after having helped to make the world safe for democracy. Black American writers represented World War I with the plotline that Frantz Fanon was later to consider the typical Third World story: the veteran who has fought and been ready to die for a country that, when he returned, denies him his right to live.[5] W. E. B. Du Bois expressed the mood in the formula, "We return. / We return from fighting. / We return fighting."[6]

Countée Cullen and Claire Goll

Many individual and civilian European encounters that followed raise issues of transnational intimacy, colonialist practices, and human misunderstandings. There is, for example, the case of the prototypical Harlem Renaissance poet Countée Cullen, who wrote chain letters during his European year, 1928–1929. These letters, published in *The Crisis*, conform to the chatty genre that has accompanied the European tour and that Anita Loos parodied in *Gentlemen Prefer Blondes* (1925):

> Then Paris en route to Algiers. It was July 13th; tomorrow Paris would celebrate her Independence Day and the Fall of the Bastille. We must stay over for the parade. We . . . hankered for a sight of the strapping black French colonial who, we had been told, led the parade with twirling baton, glistening face, and the gayest of martial strides. But, alas, though in Paris, we fell asleep as New Yorkers; consequently we arose at eleven to view a parade that had already passed at nine.[7]

Cullen may have been particularly curious about, and proud of, the presence of black French colonials in Europe, but otherwise he sounds like any American traveler. After passing through Oberammergau for the Passion Play, he reports on the German capital:

> Berlin, an orderly, clean, regimented city, as if on dress parade; the Germans shaped for joviality but in the main serious-miened. Remembered incidents: Crab-soup at Kempinsky's; a chance encounter on the street with the Marcus Garveys. . . . Drinking coffee in a Berlin cafe and suddenly hearing the strains of "Nobody Knows the Trouble I've Seen" being softly wafted to us from a distant corner of the room; looking up gratefully to see the pianist watching us, his expression conveying the wish to make a stranger welcome with some remembrance of his own people.[8]

Social and political issues do not pass him by. In "The Street Called Crooked," Cullen empathizes with prostitutes in Le Havre, and he has friends in the socialist city government of Vienna and there visits a cooperative apartment house for impoverished people: "a one-room, kitchenette and bathroom arrangement for which the occupant pays less than one dollar per week."[9] The socialist *Arbeiter-Zeitung* also published some of Cullen's poems in German.[10] Yet his oppositional passions get aroused most by American issues.

After an encounter with the writer Claire Goll, Cullen describes her as "slight, blond, and pretty; born of French parents and educated in Germany, she can write her books in either language and translate them herself for publication in the other."[11] Born in Nuremberg, Goll had fled Germany in protest against World War I, had married and divorced young, and lived in a radical circle in Switzerland that included Romain Rolland and V. I. Lenin.[12] There she met and married the French pacifist and avant-garde poet Yvan Goll. She wrote feminist essays, published a sharp critique of the genocide of the Armenians, and was the author of the odd interracial novel *Der Neger Jupiter raubt Europa* (1926).[13] She translated American poetry (including Fenton Johnson and other Negro poets, as well as Native American poems) for her anthology *Die neue Welt* (1921) and praised Carl Sandburg for protesting against both "the civilized bestiality of war" and "the enslavement and dehumanization of the

Negro."[14] In 1939, Goll fled to the United States; her last French home was ransacked by German troops when they occupied Paris.[15]

Cullen calls this firebrand radical "Madame" and faults her for what one could call Negrophilia. "When Madame speaks of the Negro's artistic endeavors today," Cullen comments, "she is well nigh irresistible if one does not hold himself in check against the enormity of her enthusiasm."[16] Cullen defends white American writers such as Edna St. Vincent Millay, Willa Cather, and Eugene O'Neill against Goll's view that "little of artistic merit is now being produced in America except that which is being done by Negroes." He claims a universalist aesthetic against the radical European's preference for black art. "Must we," Cullen asks after the encounter,

> willy-nilly, be forced into writing of nothing but the old atavistic urges, the more savage and none too beautiful aspects of our lives? May we not . . . create a bit of phantasy in which not a spiritual or blues appears, write a tract defending Christianity though its practitioners aid us so little in our argument?[17]

Cullen demanded freedom for black artists from the well-intentioned expectation that they produce *black* writing. He did not see a connection between the socialists he had visited in Vienna and Goll's enthusiasm for revolution, pacifism, and the Negro.

Claude McKay, Alain Locke, and George Grosz

Unlike Cullen, the Jamaican-born and Jamaican-educated poet and novelist Claude McKay was in search of a political aesthetic.[18] McKay had submitted poetry to the radical *Masses*, a journal banned in November 1917 for its critique of America's entry into the war. McKay took interest in the fates of prostitutes, in Irish independence, in working-class movements, and in the effects of the inflation in Germany of the 1920s. He engaged in dialogues with the likes of Leon Trotsky and Vladimir Mayakovsky.

One such confrontation took place between McKay and the New Negro philosopher Alain Locke when they met for the first time in Berlin in 1923. McKay triangulates his encounter with Locke by using the German political radical and post-Dadaist George Grosz as a touchstone.

For McKay, Grosz's *Ecce Homo* (1923) rendered "perfectly the atmo-
sphere, temper and tempo of the Berlin of that period." McKay added,
"For me that book of drawings is a rare and iconoclastic monument of
this closing era even as Rabelais is of the Renaissance."

Grosz attacked and unmasked the hypocrisy of the "pillars" of Ger-
man society, ranging from military officers and bribed politicians to
pimps, prostitutes, academics, and industrialists. (In the preceding year,
Grosz had also produced an image of a student for a play by Yvan Goll).
As fellow radical spirits, McKay and Grosz had met in Moscow after both
had appeared in a special pictorial section of *Pravda*. "It was the first time
I had seen any of Grosz's drawings. They gripped me," McKay writes.
And Grosz continued to fascinate McKay, who reports:

> When I returned to Berlin I hunted him up to ask him to sign
> a copy of *Ecce Homo*, which I had bought privately. The book
> was banned by the government of the Social Democracy. Grosz's
> remarkable personality gave not the slightest hint of the artistic
> type. And in his little apartment, his pretty and pleasant *frau* had
> surrounded him with the neatest of bourgeois comforts. He fitted
> respectably into the frame, and if you did not know he was an
> artist, you might have taken him for a responsible bank clerk. Yet
> there was a charming felicity and harmony in the *ménage*. It gave
> the impression that Grosz needed just that kind of domestic back-
> ground from which he could swing up and out with his powerful
> artistic punches.[19]

It is against his rapport with Grosz (who fled to America in 1933) that
McKay describes his encounter with Locke:

> When we met for the first time in Berlin in 1923, [Locke] took
> me for a promenade in the Tiergarten. And walking down the
> row, with the statues of the Prussian kings supported by the
> famous philosophers and poets and composers on either side, he
> remarked to me that he thought those statues the finest ideal and
> expression of the plastic arts in the world.

Locke had been a student in Berlin in 1910–1911, so this walk may have had
nostalgic meaning for him. But now McKay contrasts Locke with Grosz:

[Locke's] remark was amusing, for it was just a short while before that I had walked through the same row with George Grosz, who had described the statues as "the sugar-candy art of Germany." When I showed Dr. Locke George Grosz's book of drawings, *Ecce Homo*, he recoiled from their brutal realism. (Dr. Locke is a Philadelphia blue-black blood, a Rhodes scholar and a graduate of Oxford University, and I have heard him described as the most refined Negro in America).

So it was interesting now to discover that Dr. Locke had become the leading authority on African Negro sculpture. I felt that there was so much more affinity between the art of George Grosz and African sculpture than between the Tiergarten insipid idealization of Nordic kings and artists and the transcending realism of the African artists.

In McKay's eyes, "Dr. Locke seemed a perfect symbol for Aframerican rococo in his personality as much as in his prose style," and McKay deplored the "effete European academic quality" of "Dr. Locke's artistic outlook."[20] When Locke reviewed McKay's autobiography he took revenge and called McKay a "spiritual truant" who lacked "common loyalty" and was nothing but the "*enfant terrible* of the Negro Renaissance."[21]

McKay, Vladimir Mayakovsky, and Leon Trotsky

In an encounter between McKay and the second-generation Jewish American proletarian writer Mike Gold (born Itzok Isaac Granich), who was not only a World War I pacifist who had dodged the draft and left the United States for Mexico during the war, but also a spit-on-the-bourgeois-Persian-rug-style proletarian, McKay insisted on the importance of aesthetic standards:

I preferred to think that there were bad and mediocre, and good and great, literature and art, and that the class labels were incidental. . . . I believe that whenever literature and art are good and great they leap over narrow group barriers and periods to make a universal appeal.[22]

His Russian encounter with Vladimir Mayakovsky similarly made McKay defend his poetry against the Russian proletarian poet: "He recited one of his poems for me. It sounded like the prolonged bellow of a bull. He very kindly presented me with a signed copy of his latest book. Also he presented me to his wife, and said that she desired to dance a jazz [*sic*] with me." McKay did dance with her but feared the he did not "live up to the standard of Aframerican choreography."[23]

Another encounter took place between McKay and Leon Trotsky. Trotsky sounded like Booker T. Washington and spoke of Negroes as a "backward" people who needed to "lift themselves up as a group to a level of equality with the whites." McKay specifically remembered that Trotsky "used the word 'lift' or 'uplift.' And he urged that Negroes should be educated about the labor movement."[24] Trotsky also worried about France's use of colonial troops (in the German Rhineland, for example) as a wedge between working-class interests in different countries and colonies: "It is necessary to set the blacks themselves against this. It is necessary to open their eyes to the fact that, by aiding French imperialism to enslave Europe, the blacks are enslaving themselves by supporting the dominion of French capital in Africa and other colonies."[25] Trotsky told McKay that "he would like to set a practical example in his own department and proposed the training of a group of Negroes as officers in the Red army."[26] In his response, published in *Pravda* and *Izvestia* and as the separate pamphlet *Negri v Amerike* (1923), McKay referred "Comrade Trotsky" to the growing Pan-Africanist movement as a sign of hope, but he shared Trotsky's worries about the use of colonial troops. The effect was absurd:

> Progressive Negro radicals found themselves in the same camp with American officers, . . . and the capitalist newspaper[s] . . . in defending the morality of the Negro race and the presence of black troops in Germany before German nationalists and the leaders of the Second International.[27]

Horace Cayton and Nancy Cunard

In *Long Old Road*, the sociologist Horace Cayton offered a retrospective account of a trip he took to Europe in 1933 in the company of a Swedish student whom he simply calls Torstein (perhaps with a nod to Veblen).

At the time, Cayton was what personal ads would now describe as an "interracially divorced black male," and he was looking for a sense of "at-homeness in Sweden or France."[28] In Paris, then threatened by a coup of the fascist Croix-de-Feu, Cayton saw Mike Gold at a left-wing In Defense of Culture meeting:

> I sent Gold a note stating that we had many friends in common and that I would like to meet him. . . . Hastily Gold scribbled a reply on the bottom of the note I had sent him, which the usher brought back to me. It read, "Come on up to the stage. We need a Negro badly." (212)

Although he had "published but one short article in *The Nation*," Cayton was introduced to the audience as "the celebrated American Negro author" and met Aldous Huxley, André Gide, John Dos Passos, André Malraux, and, perhaps more fateful, the Anglo-American shipping line owner's daughter, modernist, and risk-taking femme fatale Nancy Cunard, who without much ado took Cayton to a "circus"—"a sexual performance involving men, women, and animals." There Cunard said to Cayton, "This is a bore. Let's go where we can drink and talk" (214). Starting on a serious absinthe-drinking binge, she abruptly began railing against America, "I hate your country for what it is doing to your people." As Cullen had responded to Claire Goll, Cayton finds himself defending America. Cayton adds an attack on Cunard's England for having "abused and repressed more black people than America ever has" (214). Although he is initially "attracted to this woman intellectually and physically" (as he puts it), Cayton is turned off by her maudlin conduct and takes her home to get the evening over with.

In her apartment, however, he is truly impressed by her library, writing, "There was more material about the Negro than I had ever before seen assembled in one place" (216). Cunard returns with coffee. Now dressed in "an attractive dressing gown," she acts completely sober. Cayton writes:

> She handed me an enormous binder across the front of which was printed "NEGRO/BY NANCY CUNARD." It was an anthology of Negro writings and writings about Negroes from contributors throughout the world. I hastily skimmed the table of contents,

and saw that every prominent Negro scholar I knew or had ever heard of in the United States was represented as were a number of foreign writers I was not familiar with. Altogether, it was the most complete collection of its kind that I had ever encountered. I was more impressed than I cared to admit, for I had fancied myself an expert in the field to which this exiled, alcoholic English noblewoman had devoted her life. (216–217)

Yet just as his opinion of her has risen, she proclaims that she "loves Negroes," tells him to move to Paris, and offers him her support. Cayton is again completely taken aback:

There was such superiority about her manner, as if she were dealing with a child. Underneath this preoccupation with Negroes, she was still the haughty upper-class English woman telling an inferior what he should do. (217)

When he prepares to leave, she looks up at him "lazily." "Don't go," she says. "I feel so comfortable and relaxed." But Cayton's mind has been made up, and he is tough:

"Do you usually get what you want from Negroes, Lady Nancy?" I asked.
"What do you mean?"
"I mean, do all Negro men oblige?" (217)

Before he manages to leave her, she still accuses him, "You are afraid, . . . afraid of white women. I should have realized that." Cayton fumes as he walks home, thinking that he will never understand people like her.[29] World politics reenters Cayton's narrative when he goes to Germany, then "filled with men in storm trooper uniforms," with arms always snapping "into the air with the cry, 'Heil Hitler!'" (228). When Cayton sits on a park bench in Hamburg, he is approached by an officer who asks him whether he is a Jew. His answer is unambiguous: "No, I am an American." Cayton is told, "If you are not a Jew you don't have to sit on this bench. It is for Jews only." He replies, "I like it here. . . . Is there any law that says I can't sit here?" This potentially quite dangerous encounter makes Cayton reflect:

I had, of course, heard of the persecution of Jews, but this was the first time I had actually encountered it. It seemed to me even sillier than Mississippi, where discrimination was at least based on color difference. Here they couldn't even be sure what a Jew looked like. (230)

Cayton interprets his action as a "broad gesture of protest against prejudice in any form." Torstein realizes the danger, tells Cayton that the "Nazis are as much against Negroes as they are against Jews," and mentions the terrible treatment of the mixed-race children who had been fathered by French colonial soldiers in the Rhineland.[30]

Alain Locke and "The Black Watch on the Rhine"

African American responses to the French African troops on the Rhine have emerged as a theme. Alain Locke was commissioned to write a report on German complaints about French-African soldiers. In 1924, he published the article "The Black Watch on the Rhine," illustrated with photographs of African soldiers in the Rhineland.[31] Locke marvels at the variety of human types: "Among colored audiences of America I have seen many varieties of color and feature, but I have never seen a group of its size with more varieties of human countenance or figure." He finds that French comradeship of arms really welds a brotherhood of soldiers. "Not only do black and white, straight national and colonial fraternize successfully, but black Christians with black Mohammedans, full-blood with half-caste and hybrid, men from Africa with men of the Indies, races that in Africa speak very different tongues and have traditional feuds; and more significant still, men of very diverse grades of culture" (8). Specifically addressing rape charges, Locke reports that in Königstein, for example, "respectable women" were "walking unescorted as far as two kilometers from the town, through the wooded lanes, as late as ten o'clock . . . obviously safe in mind and body." His conclusion about the rape reports was to defend the African soldiers and blame German women by returning to "the fundamental equation": "the attitude and bearing of the women themselves" (7).

The francophone Martinique-born writer and Goncourt Prize–winner René Maran criticized Locke sharply for his rosy view of France's use of colonial troops. Maran told Locke that he had "been the victim of a conjurer's mirage," for "the benevolence of France toward subject races is a matter of theory and official pretense." He reminded Locke of French colonial coercion and told him that "the black, brown and yellow soldiers did not come to the French colors as the little children came to Jesus." Locke, who had just been elected foreign corresponding member of the French Colonial Academy defended himself by saying that he had been "primarily concerned with contrasting [the] treatment of the man of color in the armies of France with that of our own American army, and with reporting . . . facts that would help to vindicate black soldiers in Europe from libelous reports as to their conduct."[32] (One is reminded of Trotsky's and McKay's worries.) The German right wing exploited France's use of African soldiers in propaganda; in 1920, the official Bavarian mint went as far as to represent a black phallus as a threat to white womanhood, following a design by Karl Goetz.[33] This was probably the only time the Bavarian mint focused on this detail of the male anatomy.

Stalinist Aesthetics and Paul Robeson/National Socialist Aesthetics and Emil Nolde (and Nella Larsen?)

In the course of the 1930s, the official aesthetic of the Soviet Union turned from the avant-garde orientation of the postrevolutionary period that McKay had witnessed to the official propagation of socialist realism and the banning of jazz—both inspired by Maxim Gorky, whose essay "O muzyke tol'stych" ("On the Music of the Gross"—or perhaps, "Fat," or "Degenerate," as the official English translator put it), was published in 1928 in *Pravda* and soon became the backbone of Stalinist repression of black music as exploitative, vulgar, sexualized, animalistic, threatening, and degenerate. Gorky particularly loathed the saxophone, which he thought emitted a "quacking nasal sound." He heard the music, a foxtrot really, this way:

> One, two, three, ten, twenty strokes, and after them, like a mud ball splashing into clear water, a wild whistle screeches; and then there are rumblings, wails and howls like the smarting of a metal pig, the shriek of a donkey, or the amorous croaking of a monstrous frog. This insulting chaos of insanity pulses to a throbbing

rhythm. Listening for a few minutes to these wails, one involuntarily imagines an orchestra of sexually driven madmen conducted by a man-stallion brandishing a huge genital member.[34]

Gorky believed that oppressed Negroes had turned *away* from jazz and
were only laughing at the twin effects that such music radio broadcasts
were having on white middle-class listeners: obesity (or "gross"-ness) and
epidemic homosexuality. Somewhat surprisingly, Gorky's essay became
the theoretical backbone of Soviet bans of jazz and black musical entertainment that would extend to the whole communist world.

It had a direct impact on the career of Paul Robeson, whose singing
repertoire now had to emphasize serious and political songs. As Martin
Duberman has shown, Robeson also witnessed the change brought about
by the rise of National Socialism in Berlin, which he visited twice in the
period. In 1930, Robeson starred for two performances of *The Emperor
Jones* at the Berlin Deutsches Künstlertheater, in which Oskar Homolka
otherwise had the leading part. Robeson and his wife, Essie, then loved
Berlin and were enchanted by the aesthetic vitality of Weimar culture.
They heard Sam Wooding's Negro Band at the Zoo roof garden. Robeson commented that "Germany is the gateway now of all of Europe" and
that "on the Continent the colour bar does not exist"—the European
dream, one could say. He seemed to be so little worried about fascism
that in 1932 he was quoted by a reporter from Jamaica as having said, "If
the real great man of the Negro race will be born, he will spring from
North America. The Negro Gandhi or Mussolini cannot be begotten
but in the land of ancient oppression and revolutionary emancipation."[35]

During a second visit in 1934, however, Robeson saw a different
Berlin. Duberman reports: "On the walk from Friedrichstrasse Station
to the hotel, his dark skin drew instant attention—surreptitious glances
from passers-by, contemptuous stares from storm troopers." A Jewish
friend the Robesons called came "by the hotel, furtive and frightened,
and told them of the horrors of the mounting persecution. He looked like
'a living corpse, skeleton head, haggard eyes,' Essie wrote in her diary; he
was 'terrified.'" At the station (they were leaving for Moscow), an "older
woman stared in angry disbelief at the sight of a black man and a white
woman together." She reported them to three uniformed men who had
"hatred in their eyes."[36] The Robesons managed to board the train and
leave this threatening situation.

The vulgar racist theme of a black threat was interwoven into the anti-Semitic propaganda of the Nazi movement, culminating in a racially sanctioned ban of jazz and of modernist art and literature as the defining act of the official Nazi aesthetic. The "Degenerate Art" show in Munich in 1937 used a reproduction of the African-inspired sculpture *The New Man* (1912) by Otto Freundlich as cover art. Freundlich was also featured in a special room devoted exclusively to Jewish art. In 1938, he painted an abstract work dedicated to the colored peoples (*Widmung an die farbigen Völker*). He was arrested in his French exile in February 1943, deported, and murdered at Majdanek.

The "Degenerate Music" show in Düsseldorf in 1938 featured a specially designed catalogue cover on which a stereotyped saxophone-playing black figure appears wearing a Jewish Star of David. One of the dramatic installations of the exhibition was devoted to "Niggerjazz," the official term for the kind of swing that was banned. It was explicitly not permitted to be broadcast, for it was a music enjoyable only to "snobs aloof from the people," and it was characterized by the

> prominence of the saxophone, which alone carries the tune obtrusively while all other instruments only emphasize the rhythm and hasten onward. Such an orchestration turns the manner of dancing into grimacing. It insinuates itself through its hammering rhythm, systematically blunting any sense of euphony.[37]

Thus, both Stalinist and National Socialist music policies were worried about the saxophone most particularly.

Installation views of the "Degenerate Art" exhibition focus on Göring and Hitler examining the artwork, and newspapers covered "The Horror Chamber of Art." One image shows men in uniforms inspecting expressionist paintings such as Emil Nolde's *Mulattin* (The Mulatto, 1913) and Karl Schmidt-Rottluff's *Portrait of B. R.* under a banner that reads, "The niggerizing of music and theater as well as the niggerizing of the visual arts was intended to uproot the racial instinct of the people and to tear down blood barriers." All Jews were considered *inherently* producers of degenerate art, but non-Jews and even Nazis could succumb to the temptation to be the same. Thus, Nolde, who had joined the Nazi Party as early as 1920, simply could not understand why he was expelled from the Prussian Academy of Arts in 1933, was exhibited as "degenerate" in

1937, and was prohibited to paint after 1941. Nolde's *Mulattin*, now at Harvard University, was considered *entartet* for its modernist style, as well as for its tabooed subject of racial mingling.

As George Hutchinson has shown, Nella Larsen visited Denmark from 1908 to 1912 and fictionalized aspects of her visit in her novel *Quicksand* (1928), portraying among other scenes an encounter of her heroine Helga Crane with a Danish painter, Axel Olsen, to whom she is initially quite attracted.[38] He takes her to a vaudeville circus in Copenhagen, where they see an American Negro ragtime act; then he makes advances to her that she finds repugnant, giving her "a stripped, naked feeling under his direct glance." Finally he proposes marriage to her, saying that he "cannot hold out against the deliberate lure of" her, kissing her hand, and adding that with her as his wife he might "become great. Immortal."

She shrinks back and firmly turns down his proposal, so that what remains of their non-relationship is a portrait he has painted of her and that she has always found upsetting:

> The picture—she had never quite, in spite of her deep interest in him, and her desire for his admiration and approval, forgiven Olsen for that portrait. It wasn't, she contended, herself at all, but some disgusting sensual creature with her features. . . . [C]ollectors, artists and critics had been unanimous in their praise and it had been hung on the line at an annual exhibition, where it had attracted much flattering attention and many tempting offers.

Axel considers her decision "a tragedy" and insists that his portrait of her "is, after all, the true Helga Crane. . . . It isn't, it isn't at all, she said aloud."[39]

Hutchinson suggested that Larsen might have modeled Olsen partially on Nolde, who came from the German-Danish border region. In 1911, Nolde was fascinated by African masks and figures in Berlin's ethnological museum, planned to write a book on artistic expressions of natural people, and painted subjects of African descent in the period. Might Larsen have met Nolde a decade before he joined the Nazi Party? Might his *Mulattin* of 1913, the painting that turned out to be so scandalous to the Nazi aesthetic, have been inspired by Larsen?[40]

Nolde was in good company at the Nazi art show, for among many other artists, George Grosz (who had effectively caricatured Hitler as an operetta Siegfried and who had produced a portrait entitled *Black Lady*) was exhibited as an example of "degenerate loathsomeness."

Langston Hughes, James Yates, and the Spanish Civil War

Langston Hughes, who spent some time in the Stalinist Soviet Union, where he also witnessed show trials, reports that his friend Sylvia Chen had to sing American spirituals and hymns on the Russian radio without any reference to God (replacing the word "God" actually with "dog," as in "Rise and shine, and give dog glory"), but he seems unaware of Gorky's role in cultural politics.[41] Hughes writes cheerily how he participated during his train travels through Kazakhstan in a celebration in 1932 honoring the fortieth anniversary of Gorky's literary career, giving a speech, hearing it translated into Russian and the Kazakh tongue, and sending "a telegram to Comrade Gorky."[42] Hughes may simply not have known Gorky's position on jazz, although Gorky's diatribe was published in English in the December 1928 issue of *Dial*, a few pages after a contribution by Jean Toomer and in the same volume with reviews of Cullen and Locke.[43]

Hughes also was among the leftist African Americans who went to Spain during the Civil War, and in his reports for the *Afro-American*, even war-torn Spain became a meeting ground for black people. In Spain, Hughes felt, "there is no color prejudice." After the Battle of Brunete in July 1937, he visited wounded prisoners in a Madrid hospital, but he wrote: "I was most interested in the Moors, who are my own color."[44] Talking with a thirteen-year-old Moroccan boy whose mother has been killed, Hughes learns that Franco had brought Moorish women and men in to support the troops: "Thus the Moors die in Spain, men, women, and children, victims of Fascism, fighting . . . against freedom—under a banner that holds only terror and segregation for all the darker people of the earth."[45]

In Spain, Hughes met James Yates, who later published his own memoir of the black members of the Abraham Lincoln Brigade.[46] Incidentally, Yates mentions that when he left for Spain, he took along three paperbacks—by McKay, Gorky, and Hughes—but found them too heavy and ended up keeping only Hughes.[47] One of Yates's encounters in the Lincoln Brigade was with the black World War I veteran and strike organizer Oliver Law, who died in the Spanish Civil War. Here Yates draws a circle that unites the interwar period as a struggle against racism:

> "Hey, Oliver is dead. They killed Oliver Law." . . . I was very quiet. My thoughts were with Oliver Law. . . . He had made history on the battlefields of Spain and now he was dead. He was the first Black man in US history to become commander of a mostly white unit.[48]

For Yates, Law's death held the hope of a victory over fascism and racism. At the time of the Spanish Civil War, McKay had adopted an anti-Stalinist leftist position and attacked, in print, "Russia's role, along with the Nazis and Fascists, in helping to destroy Democracy in Spain."[49] By then, McKay's conversation partner Mayakovsky was dead, and Trotsky was in exile in Mexico, where he would soon be murdered.[50]

As I stated, I wanted to present a series of black intellectuals' European encounters and an aside on totalitarian aesthetics without offering a conclusion. If any trends appear beyond individual idiosyncrasies, they might show more overarching political views among Europeans who tended to be pacifists with great frequency, and more concern with issues of race—especially the colored races—among African Americans, for whom World War I had presented a sense of entitlement to fuller citizenship. These episodes also add up to a dance on the volcano, as these freewheeling encounters and comedies of errors took place against the looming rise of fascism and the hardening of communism into Stalinism. I hope, in any event, that this brief foray will be only a beginning of more internationally oriented research at the crossroads of African American studies and European studies, spanning the black-and-white Atlantic.[51]

Figure 6.1. Winold Reiss, *W. E. B. Du Bois*. Pastel on artist board, ca. 1925. (National Portrait Gallery, Smithsonian Institution/Art Resource, New York. Courtesy of Renate Reiss.)

CHAPTER 6

W. E. B. Du Bois
in Nazi Germany, 1936

June 5, 1936: At age sixty-eight, W. E. B. Du Bois boards the S.S. St. Louis in New York for a six-month trip.

W. E. B. Du Bois is usually assigned a subordinate role in discussions of Americans who spent significant amounts of time in Europe in the interwar period. Although he was proud of his many trips to Europe, scholars have focused mostly on his years as a student in Berlin from 1892 to 1894 and, to a lesser extent, on his work for Pan-African Congresses in 1921 and 1923 or on his trips to the Soviet Union. Du Bois's posthumous *Autobiography* (1968) contains a calendar of his public life, which mentions a "trip around the world" as the single event of 1936, but the book's text contains virtually no information about this journey, and the bibliography includes no writings related to it.[1] In *Dusk of Dawn: An Essay toward an Autobiography of a Race Concept* (1940), Du Bois said little about that year:

> In 1936, my reapplication to the Oberlaender Trust for a chance to restudy Germany was granted. I spent five months in Germany, and some time in England, France, and Austria, interviewing scholars. . . . I then took a two months' trip around the world.[2]

SOURCE: Werner Sollors, "W. E. B. Du Bois in Nazi Germany, 1936," *Amerikastudien/American Studies* 44, no. 2 (1999): 207–222.

Du Bois's long presence in Germany in the year of the Nazi Olympics is intriguing, and although Kathryne Lindberg and Russell Berman have briefly mentioned it, I am not aware of any detailed discussions of this subject.[3]

There are many questions: Why exactly did the sixty-eight-year-old champion of racial equality go to a country in which anti-Jewish notice boards were proliferating? What did he find out when he went? What were his comments on the trip at the time? The first source one turns to is the published correspondence. In several published letters dated 1936, the German American anthropologist Franz Boas invited Du Bois to join the American Committee for Anti-Nazi Literature. When Du Bois declined, citing his impending six-month investigative trip to Germany, Boas warned him that he might have difficulties there with "the officially stimulated race prejudice" but that the Nazis might also "try to be particularly courteous to you and show you Potemkin villages." Boas wished only that he could direct Du Bois to "some people who might allow you to look behind the scenes." Du Bois thanked him, realizing that "it's going to be a little difficult for me to see and know anything in Germany, but the offer was made and it is too good an offer not to take advantage of."[4]

The microfilmed collection of *The Papers of W. E. B. Du Bois* yields more material that throws a little light on Du Bois's 1936 trip. Du Bois's grant proposal of 1935 (preserved in *The Papers*) amazingly indicated his purpose to help update Tuskegee's and Hampton's system of industrial education by studying "the way in which popular education for youth and adults in Germany has been made to minister to industrial organization and advance; and how this German experience can be applied so as to help in the re-organization of the American Negro industrial school, and the establishment of other social institutions."[5] That this application was granted was all the more remarkable since the German American donor Gustav Oberlaender was one of the world's richest stocking manufacturers, an opponent to labor organization and strikes, and a known Nazi sympathizer who had received an award from Hitler and had dined with Goebbels. In Oberlaender's lifetime, the trust that he established in his name seems to have been used mostly to train foresters in Oberlaender's new home of Pennsylvania in German forestry skills, and if they came back from a year in Germany as Nazi Bund supporters, that was alright with him. (Although most materials from 1933 to 1945 have been "lost" in the Schurz archives, sufficient evidence remains in the folders that are now housed in the Balch Institute.)[6] Du Bois went on his journey aboard the Hamburg-Amerika Line's *St. Louis*,[7] leaving New York on June 5, and, after some traveling, staying in Germany for five months. He arrived in Germany well in advance of the Olympics, which started in August.[8] He received a letter of recommendation from Dr. Georg Kartzke in Berlin, dated July 17, 1936, which mentioned that Du Bois had already received support for his project from Dr. Leitner, Auswärtiges Amt; Dr. Handrick, Reichsanstalt für Arbeitsvermittlung und Arbeitslosenversicherung; and Dr. Studders of the Reichgsruppe Industrie.

In an interview that Du Bois gave the *New York Staats-Zeitung und Herold* on January 29, 1937, shortly after his return to the United States on December 30, 1936, he is quoted as saying that he found the attitude of the German press toward the colored Olympic athletes "quite fair, even friendly." The anonymous journalist praises Du Bois's German pronunciation; mentions that Du Bois had studied in Germany thirty years (in fact, more than forty years) earlier, with Treitschke, Schmoller, and Adolf Wagner; and finds his observations particularly interesting, since Du Bois, as a member of a race persecuted in America, was uniquely qualified to make comparative observations on Germany. Du Bois also commented on a rally in Nuremberg and found what was said there quite terrible; it was the sort of thing that would have caused a war in the past. Rudolf Hess made a good impression on him, although Du Bois believed that Hess's influence was waning. He praised the Nazi government's program to construct apartments (unmatched in Europe) and highways but found the national mood depressed, lacking *Gemütlichkeit*, that untranslatable German sense of ease. He noticed food shortages and the publicized winter aid collections, but he observed an unconditional trust in National Socialism and in Hitler personally, as well as much gratitude for what Hitler had done in the few years of his rule.

Speaking directly to the issue of race, Du Bois also observed that the treatment of Negroes in Germany did not yet show any traces of racial hatred, although he "simply could not comprehend" the German attitude toward Jews. The situation of the Jews, he said, was very regrettable, but it could not be compared with that of the Negroes in the United States. What happened in Germany took place quite legally, even if it was cruel and unjust; in the United States, by contrast, the Negroes were discriminated against and persecuted in glaring violation of the law. The reactions of blacks and Jews were similar: they tried to remain unnoticed.

Both races were stereotyped as lascivious, and Du Bois compared the tone and content of Streicher's violently anti-Semitic paper *Der Stürmer* with similar Negrophobic propaganda in the South. Apart from that, the situation was not comparable. The interview ended with Du Bois's declaration that he had been received very cordially in Germany and had not suffered from any racial prejudice whatsoever.[9]

Du Bois's position may, of course, have been misrepresented by the German-language journalist from New York. We do have, however, at least a bit of correspondence surrounding the interview: an officer of the American Jewish Committee (AJC) wrote to the National Association for the Advancement of Colored People (NAACP) for the full text of the interview, and when Du Bois answered that he had not seen it, he sent Du Bois a copy of the printed article for confirmation. Du Bois answered on March 10, 1937, with the statement

It is extremely difficult to express an opinion about Germany today which is true in all respects without numerous modifications and explanations. In the first place what I said . . . was strictly confined to my experience and to what was apparently happening while I was there. I am convinced that without doubt the mob rule and illegal aggression practiced upon Jews in the earlier days of the Nazi Movement was very grave and equaled in some cases the aggression upon Negroes in the United States. But the point I was trying to make in my interview in New York was that while I was in Germany the Nazi[s] had so changed the laws that practically anything they did to Jews was legal, and what you had was legal oppression rather than the illegal cast[e] and lynching of Negroes in the United States. On the other hand, the difference between these two methods is not essential, but it does make direct comparison between the plight of the Negroes in America and the Jews in Germany difficult and in many respects misleading. Of course I was not at all deceived by the attitude of Germany toward me and the very few Negroes who happened to be visiting there. Theoretically, their attitude toward Negroes is just as bad as toward Jews, and if there were any number of Negroes in Germany would be expressed in the same way. But the point that interested me was that while this is the theoretical attitude, there was on the part of the populace no natural reaction of prejudice toward Negroes while there was such reaction toward Jews. This arose naturally from the frightful anti–Semitic propaganda.[10]

As one goes through Du Bois's papers, with his passport application and correspondence about travel arrangements; with the postcards he kept of the Rothschildhaus and the Judengasse in Frankfurt; with an address list of possible contacts, including Africanists and ethnologists, one yearns for a fuller account of the encounters Du Bois must have had in Germany and other European countries in 1936.[11] Fortunately, Nathan Huggins pointed out that Du Bois covered his trip in articles for the *Pittsburgh Courier*, then edited by George S. Schuyler, who only five years earlier had satirized Du Bois in the novel *Black No More* (1931) as "Shakespeare Agamemnon Beard," alias "Dr. Karl von Berde." Du Bois's opinion pieces appeared on the editorial pages, under the heading "Forum of Fact and Opinion," and covered a wide range of subjects.[12] In one of those pieces, Du Bois gave a detailed account of the extent of his travels in Germany:

> I have been in all parts of Germany: in Prussia, including Meckl[e]nburg, Brandenburg, Hanover, and Schlesien; I have seen the Hansa cities of the northwest and East Prussia; I have looked on the North Sea and the Alps, and traveled through Saxony, Thuringia, Westphalia, W[ürtt]emberg and Bavaria. I have seen the waters of the Rhine, Elbe, Weser[,] Oder and Danube. I have seen all the great German cities: Berlin, Hamburg, L[ü]beck, Bremen, both Frankforts, Cologne, Mayence, Stuttgart, Breslau and Munich, not to mention Vienna and Strassburg. I have seen Germany; and not in the mists of a tourist's rush, but in slow and thoughtful leisure. I have read German newspapers of all sorts and places; I have read books, listened to lectures, gone to operas, plays and movies, and watched a nation at work and play. I have talked with a half dozen officials. (*Pittsburgh Courier*, December 5, 1936)

In other essays, Du Bois reflected on the Berlin Olympics, including the significance of the colored athletes (October 17, 1936), the changing role of amateur sports (September 19, 1936), and the political contexts of the Olympics (December 5, 1936, December 19, 1936, and January 2, 1937); he wrote on opera in Bayreuth (October 17, 1936), in Munich, where he took in a heavy dose of Wagner (October 31, 1936), and in Hanover, where he saw *La forza del destino* (January 9, 1937); he gave a detailed account of the Deutsches Museum München (October 10, 1936); and he noted the similarities of fascist, socialist, and democratic laws of the period in their shared focus in "furnishing individual citizens with recreation, insurance, pension, education, public expositions, lectures and theaters" (September 19, 1936). The moment he left Nazi Germany, he commented openly on censorship (December 5, 1936) and the curtailment of free speech (January 9, 1937), on the nature of Nazi propaganda (December 12, 1936), and, in great detail, on race prejudice, anti-Semitism, and "The Present Plight of the German Jew" (December 19, 1936). He asked "How Long Will Hitler Last?" drew charts comparing Hitlerism and communism (December 26, 1936), and wondered whether the *Anschluß* of Austria was inevitable (January 9, 1937). Although a complete reprinting and full examination of these opinion pieces would be ideal, here I can only excerpt a few representative examples concerning industrial education, opera, and race relations.

Industrial Education

Closely related to the official purpose of his visit, Du Bois examined and admired Siemensstadt (Siemens's City) in Berlin, which "represents a capital of a hundred million dollars and employs over 60,000 of the most highly skilled workers of Europe" and meant "what General Electric, Westinghouse, Baldwin, and several such names mean in American industry":

> I came to Germany to learn, among other things, something of industrial education as carried on in a country where the industrial and technical development has been greater in the last fifty years than in any other land on earth. I hoped by what I might see to be able to see just what is wrong with industrial training among American Negroes. My first tentative conclusions . . . may be expressed in this aphorism: What Germany has is not Industrial Education, but Educational Industry. Or, in other words, Germany in general is not seeking to use industry and industrial processes as a means of education, but on the contrary is using education as a means of carrying on and perfecting industry. (November 7, 1936)

Du Bois seems enamored with the apprentice system: each year, Siemens offers 150 twelve- to fifteen-year-old pupils a four-year training program that starts, after an entrance examination, with a "general year of seeking the ability of the student and his fitness for the various branches of work":

> Then three years of work, hard and exacting. The spirit is remark-
> able, and no wonder: these students do not pay, they are paid
> to study—not much, to be sure, but an increasing part of their
> livelihood as they progress. They are entering on a life work and
> will live and be pensioned and die at this job. The competition is
> severe and they must keep up and excel if they would win success.
> They are encouraged and enthused in every way: a clubhouse,
> fields for games, evening entertainments for their families and
> friends, the mid-day meal is served free, etc. (November 7, 1936)[13]

One could easily presume that Du Bois would have loved to see features of this system adopted for the failing method of industrial education
for American Negroes. Yet he is also politically astute and emphasizes
that although Siemensstadt may be a case of industry controlling education, it is actually the state that controls industry. He asks pointedly,
"Who now controls the State?" and concludes with the sentence, "And
this crucial question I will discuss in my next letter and with more clarity
and frankness than I have hitherto allowed myself" (November 7, 1936).
As we shall see, Du Bois kept this promise.

Opera

It is interesting to see Du Bois return to the "Song of the Bride" from
Wagner's *Lohengrin* in 1936, which he had cited in *The Souls of Black Folk*
(1903). In fact, Du Bois pays quite a bit of attention to opera in general,
and to Wagner in particular, in his *Pittsburgh Courier* pieces. As he did
in "The Coming of John," in *The Souls of Black Folk,* he tries to make
Wagner particularly meaningful to black American readers. He does so
in 1936 by stressing Wagner's long exile, the fact that he had a "hard time
getting an education and at last had to give it up. . . . The musical dramas
of Wagner tell of human life as he lived it, and no human being, white
or black, can afford not to know them, if he would know life" (October
31, 1936). He finds that *Die Meistersinger* "tells of the efforts of a natural
untaught singer to triumph over the jealous and petty rules of a labor
union" and sees in *Parsifal* "the story of the Crucifixion, told neither by

the mediaeval Church nor by modern science, but by a genius who knew
and sought to interpret the suffering and sacrifice of the human spirit"
(October 31, 1936). He comments on *Der Ring des Nibelungen* and on
Lohengrin (October 31, 1936), again misquoting, as he did in 1903, the
"Song of the Bride" as "Freudig geführt, ziehet dahin," instead of "Treulich geführt" (October 31, 1936).[14] Yet he not only makes connections
between the composer-genius and all those "who wish in truth to know
Life" (October 31, 1936); he also looks at the economy of operagoing,
which he differentiates from the Oberammergau folk festival, "done by
peasants with something of a mediaeval simplicity, despite evident com-
mercialization" (October 17, 1936). By contrast, "only the rich or the
well-to-do can enjoy the experiment of Bayreuth," for "so few people in
any land can afford the price," and he takes this opportunity to complain
about boastful Americans in Bayreuth (October 17, 1936). Fortunately,
however, "no German city of any size is without a theater and opera
house, where from October to May citizens may hear the best in music
and drama for the cost of a woman's spring hat" (January 9, 1936). Correspondingly, the list of operas Du Bois saw after Bayreuth and Munich,
in affordable productions, is impressive: *Carmen, The Barber of Seville, The
Marriage of Figaro, The Magic Flute, The Flying Dutchman, Tristan and Isolde,
Rigoletto, La Traviata,* and *Manon* (January 9, 1936).

Du Bois fails to comment on the exploitation of the Wagner cult by
the Nazis and the anti-Semitic use that was made of it, although he does
mention the English anti-Semite Houston Stewart Chamberlain:

> At the corner of Wahnfried street, where I daily turn toward
> town, I pass the former home of H. S. Chamberlain . . . , who,
> writing in German, did perhaps more than any one to establish
> in Germany the theory of Nordic superiority. (October 17, 1936)

However, he does connect one opera experience with the theme of
"race" in the American sense of the word. When he goes to the opera in
Hanover, he realizes that the title of Verdi's opera *La forza del destino* is
"quite new" to him and wonders: "Singular I thought that I should not
even have heard the title before of this work of the master." The answer
comes quickly: "As I read the libretto, however, I began to understand
why. It was a music drama of the color line" (January 9, 1937). Reading
the story of the Mulatto Alvaro and his Leonore, tragically star-crossed

lovers, Du Bois worries "how the Nordic audience would take the presence in the orchestra of a very brown listener, to a race play. . . . But all difficulty was surmounted just as we arrange the black Othello for Atlanta: Alvaro was blonde and actually lighter than the brother! Race was eliminated neatly, unless one listened too closely to the words. Am I quite alone? Who ever heard of this colored hero of Verdi?" (January 9, 1937). In his predilection for Wagner and Verdi, as well as in his avoidance of any of the new Nazi operas, Du Bois was representative of German audience preferences and repertory offerings in the 1930s.[15]

Race Relations

Du Bois addresses race relations also directly and perceptively, and not only through the indirection of operagoing. For example, he intersperses his pieces with comments on American race relations. On one occasion, he makes the remarkably up-to-date argument that the concept of race has "fallen before scientific investigation" because "there are no innate unchanging racial differences between the groups of men," and the last word of science has prompted some to argue that "what we are to do in this new century is to give up thinking of race and to begin thinking of work and wage and of the social classes which these problems of labor give rise to" (November 14, 1936). He continues:

> This, however, is a mistake. Whatever the scientific dicta are concerning race, the fact remains that the colored people of the world, compared with other people, are poor, ignorant, and disorganized; and against such facts no theories can for a moment maintain themselves. . . . We may and must, therefore, re-word our problem, but it is still a problem. It is still a problem of a group which we must by the necessity of language call a race, and which is "Negro" by historical wording. . . . One must think hereafter, therefore, not of the Negro, the Chinaman, and the Indian as part of the labor problem, but rather as the labor problem being primarily a problem of the colored masses of men, and insoluble save as their economic and cultural future is assured. (November 14, 1936)

Du Bois here not only anticipates notions of the social construction of race and of "strategic essentialism" but also places issues of race in the context of issues of labor, and on a global scale. This does not at all blind him to, or make him less sensitive toward, the "white-on-white" racism that Nazi anti-Semitism represented.

Du Bois's first report mailed to the *Pittsburgh Courier* from outside of Germany states unambiguously, "There is a campaign of race prejudice carried on, openly, continuously and determinedly against all non-Nordic races, but specifically against the Jews, which surpasses in vindictive cruelty and public insult anything I have ever seen; and I have seen much" (December 5, 1936). While giving a careful historical account to offer explanations for the rise of Nazism, Du Bois excoriates the Hitler state as tyranny: "a state with a mighty police force, a growing army, a host of spies and informers, a secret espionage, backed by swift and cruel punishment, which might vary from loss of job to imprisonment, incommunicado, and without trial, to cold murder" (December 12, 1936). And he stresses that propaganda, the "greatest single invention of" World War I, makes the mass of people believe that "the thing works":

> Newspapers, public speakers, the radio, expositions, celebrations, books and periodicals, every possible vehicle of information and training, including schools, is being used today on German people to teach them that they are the most remarkable people on earth; that the national socialist government is the best government for Germany, if not for the world; that other countries, especially Russia, are in the depths of misery, and that Jews are responsible for all criticism heaped on Germany and for most of the other ills of modern countries. (December 12, 1936)

For this reason Du Bois sees that there is "race prejudice in Germany, and a regular, planned propaganda to increase it. . . . But it is not instinctive prejudice, except in the case of the Jews, and not altogether there" (December 19, 1936). As a black person, Du Bois feels that he has "complete civic freedom and public courtesy," although "no German woman of good standing would think of marrying a Negro under ordinary circumstances; nor could she do so legally. It is a question if she could legally marry a Japanese" (December 19, 1936). This is an excellent observation, as it suggests the tension that existed between foreign policy goals and racial ideology under Nazi rule. He also notes that in

public dance halls and in the half-world [Du Bois uses a loan translation of the German *Halbwelt* and French *demi-monde* to name
the semicriminal underworld of nightclubs and disreputable bars]
Negroes must be welcomed with care and secretly; police spies
would quickly suppress any open commerce. (December 19, 1936)

It is against this background that Du Bois turns toward a discussion of
anti–Semitism: "In the case of the Jews, one meets something different,
which an American Negro does not readily understand. Prejudice against
Jews in Germany comes nearer being instinctive than color prejudice"
(December 19, 1936). He gives a historical rundown and states that the
prejudice goes back to "economic reasons, built on a foundation of religion and clan solidarity," reasons that are "not at all analogous to the
white dislike of blacks in America" (December 19, 1936). The Jews'
"success in professions and in the competitive civil service brought all
the envy and jealousy of the wretched to bear on them, and Adolf Hitler,
born to dislike of Jews, was the appropriate instrument for the undoing
of the Jew in Germany" (December 19, 1936).

Unlike other travelers and observers, Du Bois was unambiguous in
his assessment and pessimistic in his prognosis. In the remarkable piece
"The Present Plight of the German Jew," he writes:

There has been no tragedy in modern times equal in its awful effects
to the fight on the Jew in Germany. It is an attack on civilization,
comparable only to such horrors as the Spanish Inquisition and the
African slave trade. It has set civilization back a hundred years, and
in particular has it made the settlement and understanding of race
problems more difficult and more doubtful. It is widely believed
by many that the Jewish problem in Germany was episodic, and is
already passing. Visitors to the Olympic Games are apt to have gotten
that impression. They saw no Jewish oppression. Just as Northern
visitors to Mississippi see no Negro oppression. (December 19, 1936)

Du Bois reminds the optimists that Germany is now in the hands of
the Nazis—of Hitler, his "coadjutors and backers"—and that an integral
part of their policy "just as prominent now as earlier and perhaps growing in prominence, is world war on Jews. The proof of this is incontro-
vertible, and must comfort all those in any part of the world who depend
on race hate as the salvation of men":

Adolf Hitler hardly ever makes a speech today—and his speeches reach every corner of Germany, by radio, newspaper, placard, movie and public announcement—without belittling, blaming or cursing Jews. From my window as I write I see a great red poster, seven feet high, asking the German people to contribute to winter relief of the poor, so that Germany will not sink to the level of the "Jewish-Bolshevist countries of the rest of the world." At Nuremberg recently he accused the "foreign Jewish element" of causing the rotting of the Aryan world. His propaganda minister was more insulting, and said that the whole oppression of Germany by the world was caused by Jewish emigrants. Every misfortune of the world is in the whole or in part blamed on Jews—the Spanish rebellion, the obstruction to world trade, etc. One finds cases in the papers: Jews jailed for sex relations with German women; a marriage disallowed because a Jewish justice of the peace witnessed it; Masons excluded from office in the National Socialist Party, because Jews are Masons; advertisements excluding Jews; the total disfranchisement of all Jews; deprivation of civil rights and inability to remain or become German citizens; limited rights of education, and narrowly limited right to work in trades, professions and the civil service; the threat of boycott, loss of work and even mob violence, for any German who trades with a Jew; and, above all, the continued circulation of Julius Streicher's [*Stürmer*], the most shameless, lying advocate of race hate in the world, not excluding Florida. It could not sell a copy without Hitler's consent. (December 19, 1936)

There are many more remarkable points that Du Bois made in these columns than I can relate. Perhaps no point is as significant as the fact that he unambiguously condemned the Nazi political system while he remained distinctly fond of Germany—of German culture, people, and, as we saw, Wagner's oeuvre—and of Europe in general. Even in the midst of the serious international political crises on which he commented—the Balkans and Spain, for example (October 17, 1936)—Du Bois stressed the centrality of Europe for an understanding of modern culture and pointed out that "civilization does not center in the United States or in Australia. . . . Despite all our boasting and national pride, we turn continually and repeatedly toward Europe to know and understand the last word of human culture in matters of vital and everyday interest to us" (September 26, 1936). He was happy about the greater possibility of human contacts across the color line that Europe provided in the 1930s. "I have not especially sought such contacts, but they have been all the more welcome and valuable because they have come naturally. Even on this trip it was a great source of knowledge and understanding to dine with [Bronisław] Malinowsk[i], the great English anthropologist; to have a visit from [N. P. M.] De Cleene, the colonial expert, in Belgium; to meet in Germany, [Diedrich Hermann] Westerma[nn], who knows more African tongues that any man, and to lunch with H. G. Wells in London." He concluded that "more is being done today in the scientific study of races and race relations in Europe than elsewhere in the world. And this is the primary reason why I am here" (September 26, 1936). And even after he had left Germany and felt more at liberty to be critical of its racial politics he reiterated that he had been "treated with uniform courtesy and consideration" in Germany and added pointedly, "It would have been impossible for me to have spent a similarly long time in any part of the United States, without some, if not frequent cases of personal insult or discrimination. I cannot record a single instance here" (December 5, 1936). His perceptive critique of Nazi Germany did not induce him for a moment to idealize race relations in the United States, and it is suggestive of his balanced vision that he mentioned Florida in the same breath as Nuremberg and called attention to German anti-Semitism as well as to American racism.

Du Bois's visit to Nazi Germany constitutes an interesting intersection of African American and European history. It is also an undoubtedly rare case of an early examination of Nazi rule and of the nature of its anti-Semitism by a German-speaking, Harvard- and Berlin-trained African American historian and sociologist whose lifelong specialty was the field of race relations. And it is an unexamined case of black-Jewish relations, for Du Bois approached the danger of the impending Holocaust with remarkable insight and caring, combining sharp political antiracism with pronounced cultural Eurocentrism. This trip is thus a chapter both in the history of memorable democratic critiques of racial prejudice and in the history of opera loving. It would therefore seem desirable to unearth more evidence that must exist about his long visit in Germany, ranging from police reports and party documents to the full Oberlaender Trust archives and possible memoirs of some of Du Bois's former contacts.[16] It is remarkable that this momentous half-year in Du Bois's life, accompanied by many interesting sources, has not received more attention.

Figure 7.1. Carl Van Vechten, *Richard Wright,* June 23, 1939. (Photo by Carl Van Vechten. Used with permission of the Van Vechten Trust, Beinecke Library, Yale University.)

CHAPTER 7

Modernization as Adultery

Richard Wright, Zora Neale Hurston,
and American Culture of the 1930s and 1940s

April 2, 1938: Zora Neale Hurston pans Richard Wright's first book in the high-circulation Saturday Review.

THE PERIOD FROM 1930 TO 1950 marks the transition made by American authors of non-English stock from the outskirts in American writing (the precarious positions held, for example, by Charles W. Chesnutt and Abraham Cahan) to the center (where writers such as Ralph Ellison and Saul Bellow were firmly positioned in the 1950s). It was in the Roosevelt and Truman eras—in which mass-produced popular culture, from radio serials and phonograph records to comic books, also proliferated to an unheard-of extent—that the new and now dominant American story was fabricated, the story that incorporated immigrants and minorities as prototypical Americans because Puritans, foreign immigrants, and urban migrants were now *all* considered pioneers.

SOURCE: Werner Sollors, "Modernization as Adultery: Richard Wright, Zora Neale Hurston, and American Culture of the 1930s and 1940s," *Hebrew University Studies in Literature and the Arts* ("Women and American Ideology," special issue, ed. Emily Budick) 18 (1990): 109–155. A similar version was published as Werner Sollors, "Anthropological and Sociological Tendencies in American Literature of the 1930s and 1940s: Richard Wright, Zora Neale Hurston, and American Culture," in *Looking Inward, Looking Outward: From the 1930s through the 1940s*, ed. Steven Ickringill, vol. 18 of *European Contributions to American Studies* (Amsterdam: VU Press, 1990), 22–66.

During World War I, when the immigrant Mary Antin spoke of the founding fathers as her ancestors, the Boston Brahmins' eyebrows were raised aggressively, because the term "American" was then used as synonym for "white native-born citizen, typically of English stock." When the immigrant author Louis Adamic advocated the equation of Ellis Island and Plymouth Rock shortly before and during World War II, his vision began to take hold in an ever more rapidly urbanizing America and initiated a reinterpretation of the United States as Walt Whitman's "nation of nations."

The opposition to Stalinism, on the one hand, and to fascism, on the other, made many writers eager participants in the search for a shared cultural center of the United States. The need to define American culture *against* what became called "totalitarianism" (or according to what was banned in the Soviet Union or in Nazi Germany) led to an almost official revalidation of modernism, less sexual prudishness in writing, a new stress on the black dimensions of American music, and an altogether intensified interest in ethnic diversity as America's new trademark. The journal *Common Ground* and the *Cross Section* anthologies that aimed for a polyethnic cultural space in the nation of nations, the ethnically heterogeneous platoon stories in the commercial culture during and after the war, and the founding of American studies (to a considerable extent, a field for children of immigrants who were then still excluded from teaching English) were symptomatic of the cultural changes that took place during those years. Whit Burnett and Martha Foley's *Story Magazine* published and awarded such "new" writers as the Armenian American William Saroyan, the southerners William Faulkner and Erskine Caldwell, the American Jewish author Tess Slesinger, the Chicago ethnic Nelson Algren, and the Afro-Americans Zora Neale Hurston and Richard Wright. Most important, the Federal Writers Project helped to employ writers of diverse background, created a wide forum for exchanges of opinions (such as theaters, journals, and conventions), and involved authors in often interesting historical and social science research projects that ranged from the background work for the famous Writers' Guide Series to the collecting of folklore. The fact that on June 14, 1939, during his work on the Federal Writers Project in Harlem, Ralph Ellison heard and recorded the black tale of Sweet-the-monkey who "could make hisself invisible" is suggestive of the importance of the Work Projects Administration (WPA) in the development of American literature.

While the foundations for a more consciously polyethnic society were being laid in the period, the contradictions were extraordinary. Immigrants became the typical Americans in war effort-sponsored work such as Margaret Mead's national character study *And Keep Your Powder Dry* (1942) and Geoffrey Gorer's *The American People* (1948), yet the legislation restricting immigration that was enacted in the 1920s remained in full force during much of the period and prohibited European refugees (especially Jews) from entering the United States in the numbers that would have been necessary to save them from the Holocaust. And while Victory Records and the American Forces Network used swing—black and white—as if it were the national music, blood banks of the American Red Cross carried separate blood for black soldiers during World War II.

It was in this time that writers from the fringes vied for a space in the center, and perhaps more often (or more noticeably) than before or after they incorporated perspectives derived from the recently expanding social sciences into their works, among them anthropological and sociological tendencies. This strategy helped them in their attempts to generalize their stories, to give a *representative* character to their tales, and to write the ethnic and racial groups to which they belonged *into* the American story.

I focus on a few texts, mostly by Richard Wright and Zora Neale Hurston, to suggest the relationship of social science concerns with writing in the period. Wright and Hurston perceived their divergent trajectories not merely as antithetical to each other but as mutually exclusive, and their strategies are representative of the choices a great many writers made.

"Brrrrrrriiiiiiiiiiiiiiiiiiiiinng!"

Few readers of Richard Wright's novel *Native Son* (1940) are likely to forget its beginning. The startling sound of this alarm clock forms the opening of a novel that has been translated into many languages (among them, most European languages, as well as Japanese, Turkish, Hebrew, and Chinese). It is a dramatic first line that is intelligible to readers around the globe as it embodies the intrusion of the most familiar instrument of modern time into the natural world of sleepers—a small, capsule version of *the* story of modernization. The topic of time was in the air in the 1930s and 1940s, especially since the publication of Robert Redfield's influential study of a Mexican village, *Tepoztlán* (1930), which theorized about the modernism that transformed natural into clocked time; traditional, sacred, primitive life into modern, secular, industrial life; "folk" into people and orally transmitted folklore into mechanically reproduced popular arts; *Gemeinschaft* into *Gesellschaft*; and local cultures into a widely shared civilization.[1]

Many writers around the world fictionalized this development. What makes Wright's version of the story of the rupture brought about by modern time so powerful is the fact that the beginning of *Native Son* eradicates any sense of a "sacred" folk existence prior to the alarming intrusion of clocked time. In the novel, there is literally no *word* before the sound of the alarm clock, and the clock is also the subject of the first full sentence after the *"Brrrrrriiiiiiiiiiiiiiiiiiiiiinng!"*: "An alarm clock clanged in the dark and silent room." After that opening, and for the rest of the book, characters are thrown into, and live and die in, the modern world of Chicago.

The first few sentences of *Native Son* may illustrate how Wright lets the reader enter into this world:

> A bed spring creaked. A woman's voice sang out impatiently: "Bigger, shut that thing off!"
>
> A surly grunt sounded above the tinny ring of metal. Naked feet swished dryly across the planks in the wooden floor and the clang ceased abruptly.
>
> "Turn on the light, Bigger."
>
> "Awright," came a sleepy mumble.
>
> Light flooded the room and revealed a black boy standing in a narrow space between two iron beds, rubbing his eyes with the backs of his hands. (7)

It is not the characters that are the subjects of the sentences. Instead, a bed spring, a surly grunt, the ring, the clang, and light dominate the grammatical constructions after the alarm clock. People are crowded into a dark and narrow space filled with metallic sounds and iron structures. Human beings seem to be little but objects of modernization. Their first appearance is consciously reified: they make themselves felt simply as "a woman's voice," "a surly grunt," "naked feet," or "a sleepy mumble," as if they were parts rather than a whole. The hero's, or antihero's, name is Bigger Thomas (his last name probably an allusion to Harriet Beecher Stowe's *Uncle Tom's Cabin*). The first direct reference to him—other than by maternal address in the imperative—is in a generic way as a "black boy" (the same words, of course, that Wright ultimately used as the title of his autobiography). The characters are not beetles after a Kafkaesque metamorphosis, although—as careful readers such as Keneth Kinnamon have pointed out[2]—in the famous scene of Bigger's killing of the rat with a kitchen skillet that comes a couple of pages later, the animal image seems like an allegory of the protagonist himself: both are killed in metallic environments. Significantly, the novel ends as Bigger Thomas, sentenced to death, "heard the ring of steel against steel as a far door clanged shut" (392). Bigger's life in *Native Son* is thus framed by two clangs.

The beginning and ending of *Native Son* form a microcosm of Wright's enterprise as a writer, which always places an individual occurrence into a larger social context through the use of socially charged imagery. The plea by Bigger Thomas's lawyer Boris Max is thus representative of the strategy that led Wright from the publication of *Native Son* to that of the nonfictional *12 Million Black Voices*: "Multiply Bigger Thomas twelve million times, allowing for environmental and temperamental variations, and for those Negroes who are completely under the influence of the church, and you have the psychology of the Negro people" (364).[3]

Zora Neale Hurston defined herself openly against being a representative of millions. "I know," she writes in a chapter intended for her autobiography, "that I cannot accept responsibility for thirteen million people. Every tub must sit on its own bottom regardless."[4] Yet her work, too, is informed by the drama of modern time, as experienced, however, by a more forceful traditional people. Her characters are not overwhelmed and reified by this drama; they would much rather incorporate it into their creative mode of being. Thus, Hurston renders a song poem in which the clock has become part of a courtship story that goes around the clock and of which two stanzas may here suffice:

When the clock struck ten I was in the bin, in the bin with Sue,
in the bin with Sal, in the bin with that pretty Johnson gal.
When the clock struck eleven, I was in heaven, in heaven with Sue,
in heaven with Sal, in heaven with that pretty Johnson gal.[5]

Even where the concept of punctuality collides with an older folk ethos of "natural" time, Hurston relies on an ironic self-consciousness that makes this disparity humorous rather than lethal. Thus, she prints the story of how blacks got their color in *Mules and Men*, according to which blacks came late when God gave out color and when they finally arrived at the throne, they started pushing and shoving until God said, "Git back! Git back!" which they misunderstood as "Git black," and, the tale concludes, "they been black ever since."[6]

"Long Black Song"

If Bigger Thomas was really meant as a representative character,[7] *Native Son*'s radical elision of any life before modernity was not the only solution Wright sought in his fiction. In the story "Long Black Song," published two years before *Native Son* in the short story collection significantly titled *Uncle Tom's Children*, he uses an isolated black southern rural setting to stage the cataclysmic intrusion of modernism. It is no coincidence that in the story, the intruder is a white *clock* salesman who wants to make money to study science in Chicago.[8]

The four-part story is told from the point of view of a female protagonist, Sarah, whom Wright once described as "a very simple Negro woman living in the northern hills of Mississippi."[9] Sarah, waiting for her husband, Silas, to return from Coldwater, sings a lullaby to her baby Ruth, who is crying until she starts banging a stick against an old clock (which she keeps doing throughout the first section). Sarah remembers the past, her first love, Tom, who was sent, almost a year earlier, to Europe to fight in World War I and for whom she still yearns. Soon a white salesman comes with a thudding car and stops at Sarah's shack. Addressing her as "auntie," he demonstrates a gilt-edged and shiny $50 clock-phonograph, playing a religious recording of a song about Judgment Day.[10] He makes sexual advances to her. While she keeps saying no to him, the appearance of the salesman is clearly connected in Sarah's imagination with Tom, and finally the salesman succeeds in making love to her.

He leaves the clock-phonograph behind and offers it to Sarah, now for the reduced price of $40, promising to return the next morning to pick up a down payment or the merchandise. Later that night, Silas comes home and brings Sarah shoes, as well as the good news that Tom has returned from the war. Silas is happy because he has sold the cotton for $250, made a down payment for more land, and now intends to hire a helper. His mood changes, however, when he discovers first the graphophone outside the shack, then the white salesman's hat on the mantel, his pencil on the crumpled quilt, and, finally, a strange handkerchief inside the bed. When Sarah says that the salesman wants $40 for the phonograph although the price tag is $10 higher, Silas's jealousy of the white man (merging with his jealousy of Sarah's past with Tom) explodes. He has already broken the phonograph; now he starts whipping his disloyal wife, who manages to escape with Ruth into the hills.

The next morning Sarah sees from her distance—like in a puppet theater—the arrival of the salesman's car; Silas's whipping of the white man; and the ensuing struggle among Silas, the salesman, and the salesman's buddy. Then Silas runs to the shack, and while Sarah is running toward the scene shouting, Silas shoots one of the white men, while the second one drives off with the car.

Sarah falls at Silas's feet, but he drags the white man's body into the street and throws her belongings, including the baby's cradle, out of the house. Cursing all white men, he bitterly accepts his fate—certain death, no matter what he does. Sarah runs back into the hills with the baby and sees a long line of cars full of white men arriving. She watches Silas shoot some of them until they set fire to the house in which Silas dies without a murmur. Sarah runs away from the scene crying, "Naw, Gawd!"

The manuscript of "Long Black Song" included a fifth section, a last act that did not become part of the version published in *Uncle Tom's Children*. In the manuscript, Sarah's old lover, Tom, reappears in a car together with her brothers Bill and Leroy. (It was about her brothers' return from the war that Sarah had asked Silas, which is more plausible than the published dialogue.)[11] All of the men, uniformed veterans who have just come back from World War I, die fighting at Silas's burning house, and Sarah is again left alone with her baby. The section is formally distinguished by rendering much direct speech by the men in indirect discourse, as if Sarah heard the words of others only in a swimming blur.[12]

In "Long Black Song," Wright clearly describes both: the natural and the technical-commercial worlds; the realm of "Gawd," the sun and the seasons, and the sphere of the clock; the world of primal pleasures and the world of organized modern leisure that lures and seduces (some readers, such as Margaret Walker, say, "rapes") the peasant woman.[13] The salesman literally offers Sarah a $10 rebate for sex, which has become a commodity. It thus seems an allegory of the transformation of rural folk culture into modern urban civilization where human contacts are dominated by reified desires and sales contracts, and where catastrophes are never far away.

It is the story of the disappearance of feudal remnants under the onslaught of the capitalist ethos (which is associated with a clock or a watch and Benjamin Franklin's equation of time and money that Max Weber placed at the center of his analysis of the rise of capitalism).[14] That technological modernity appealed to sexuality was apparent in other cultural expressions of the period. Thus, Robert Johnson recorded a "Phonograph Blues" on November 23, 1936, with such telling lines as, "I'm gonna wind your little phonograph, just to hear your little engine moan."[15]

For Wright, the modernizing process seems to be seductive but ruthless, irresistible but catastrophic. It is imagined as the inevitable clash of two worlds. The confrontation reaches its deadly cataclysm when Silas and a number of white men go under (among them probably—although Wright does not explicitly say so—the salesman; the battle, after all, has become transformed into an abstract fight of what Sarah perceives as black and white dolls).[16]

Yet Wright also explores, in dialogue as well as in narrated prose, the absurdly incongruous potential in the encounter between the salesman and Sarah:

> "Mistah, we don need no clock!"
> "You dont have to buy it. It wont
>   cost you anything to look."
> He unpacked the big black box. She saw the strands of his auburn hair glinting in the afterglow. [This phrase echoes her perception of Tom.] His back bulged against his white shirt as he stooped. He pulled out a square brown graphophone. She bent forward, looking. Lawd, but its pretty! She saw the face of a clock under the horn of the graphophone. The gilt on the corners sparkled. The color in the wood glowed softly. It reminded her of the light she sometimes saw in the baby's eyes. Slowly she slid a finger over a beveled edge; she wanted to take the box into her arms and kiss it.
> "It's eight o'clock," he said.
> "Yeah?"
> "It only costs fifty dollars. And you dont have to pay for it all at once. Just five dollars down and five dollars a month."
> She smiled. The white man was just like a little boy. Jus lika chile.[17]

Wright makes the opposition part of the sentence structure, as he constantly alternates between Sarah and the salesman, or Sarah and the graphophone. The confrontation reaches its height of incongruity when her view of the record player as a beautiful, seemingly animated, and quasi-sacred object is interrupted by the salesman's absurd-sounding statement, "It's eight o'clock"—which seems to echo the beginning of *Alice in Wonderland* when the White Rabbit with pink eyes says, "Oh dear! Oh dear! I shall be too late," and surprises Alice by actually taking a watch out of its waistcoat pocket, looking at it, and hurrying on. The salesman's talk about the clock-graphophone, its price, and the possible payment plan is equally incongruous and makes him a little like Franklin. From Sarah's point of view, the salesman is equally funny and childish.

As the excerpt suggests, Wright very consciously establishes the contrast. In "Long Black Song," Wright most especially makes use of a very elaborate set of repetitions and variations that give the story its forcefulness and cohesion. Told as an interior monologue, with occasional first-person sentences in dialect by Sarah, the story develops through associations of words and images in Sarah's mind.

Wright saw the story as an attempt at starting from Ernest Hemingway, yet he also wanted to "dig deeper into the character [of Sarah] and try to get something that [would] live." He said in 1938 that to

> make an implied social comment about her, I tried to conceive of a simple peasant woman, whose outlook upon life was influenced by natural things, and to contrast her with a white salesman selling phonographs and records.
>
> I tried to make out of that story a social comment implied in the very nature of the story itself. You might call it an indictment of the conditions of the South, letting the consciousness of the woman speak for the Negro people.[18]

Wright thus attempted to make Sarah's (like Bigger Thomas's) consciousness speak for the Negro people *in general*, and he here proceeded with this generalizing tendency by fitting the leitmotifs and repetitions into a polarized set of opposites.

The verbal system that emerges is very dense. Many repetitions intensify the effect and illustrate Sarah's state of mind, her associative thinking in images and direct sensations, and not in abstractions, in feelings rather than in measurable temporal categories. In that respect, "Long Black Song" is more reminiscent of Jean Toomer's "Blood-Burning Moon" (as James Giles noted); of Wright's favorite literary work, Gertrude Stein's "Melanctha" (as Edward Margolies observed); or of William Faulkner's Benjy section in *The Sound and the Fury* than of Hemingway.[19]

The shifts in Sarah's associations are sometimes marked by the "Bang! Bang! Bang!" Wright always liked to render sounds in writing[20] (This, literally, is what the word "graphophone" means.) He uses Ruth's banging against the old clock as a rhythmically recurring leitmotif. As did the *"Brrrrrrriiiiiiiiiiiiiiiiiiiiiinng!"* in *Native Son*, the "Bang! Bang! Bang!" in "Long Black Song" is not only the sound of the clock but also the apparent symbol of the arrival of modernity and the foreshadowing of a violent apocalypse. Repeated eleven times (one time less than the hours of the clock), the "bangbangbang" gives a pulse to the story and suggests the power of the clock, its associations with sex, and (enhanced by the song played on the phonograph) the apocalyptic approach of the end of time.[21]

Other words and phrases that are repeated throughout the story, sometimes with special intensity in one section, help to create word patterns and image clusters that dramatize and make concrete the clash between Sarah's natural world and the world of time and money:

She, black	white man
bare feet, toes	shoes
"We git erlong widout time"	"Its eight o'clock"
rooster crowing	clock
home	far away, death
a vast peace	war, kill
God/Lawd	science
Sarah's lullaby: the suns going down	the graphophone's "ringing coils of music"

Obviously critical of the intrusion of the machine, Wright yet refrains from making the rural world appear idyllic and uses the contrast to sketch the grim alternative the protagonists face of either dying or escaping traumatized.

"The Gilded Six-Bits"

"Long Black Song" shares its outline—or, at least, the beginning of the plot and some of its contrastiveness—with Zora Neale Hurston's short story "The Gilded Six-Bits," which was first published in *Story* magazine in August 1933. Wright and Hurston were antithetical spirits in many ways. However, as authors born in the rural South who made their careers in the urban North, both were attracted to the plotline of an adultery story to fictionalize modernization.[22]

Missie May is taking a bath, looks at the clock, and realizes that her husband, Joe Banks, is about to arrive from his job at the factory. When he comes, he, as always, throws silver dollars at the door, which she picks up and piles up next to her plate. This time, he brings $9 from work that way, but his pockets are also stuffed with sweets for his wife. While they are eating the ham hocks dinner that the wife has prepared, Joe says that he wants to take Missie May to a new ice cream parlor operated by a stranger, Mister Otis D. Slemmons from Chicago, whom Joe worships as a black Rockefeller or Ford and who has the distinction of owning a $5 gold piece for a stickpin and a $10 gold coin on his watch chain, in addition to a mouthful of gold teeth.

Joe is excited after their visit to Slemmonses' parlor, whereas Missie May thinks that the gold would look better on Joe. They have been married for about a year, and Joe is eager to have a child. Yet one night when Joe comes home early from his shift at the plant, he finds Slemmons in bed with his wife, beats him, chases him away, and is left with the golden watch charm in his hands, which he now uses as a symbolic reminder of Missie May's unfaithfulness. Only after months of acting sullenly like a "stranger" and keeping the gold coin between them does Joe relent, and they make love again, but Missie May finds the gold piece in their bed the next morning and wonders whether he meant it as "payment" for her lovemaking. She then discovers, however, that it is merely a gilded half-dollar and not a $10 gold piece, as Slemmons had pretended it was in front of villagers' eyes. Soon Missie May is pregnant. Before too long, a baby boy is born who, according to Joe's mother, looks exactly like the husband. Now Joe feels reconciled, goes to Orlando, and buys the whole gilded four-bits worth of candy kisses for his wife.[23] When he returns to the house, he throws $15 in wages on the floor, and the couple's life continues as it was before the Slemmons episode.

The similarities of Wright's and Hurston's stories are obvious.[24] Both stories contrast natural time with clocked time, focus on the intrusion of the capitalist ethos as a sexual seduction, give the seducer a Chicago dimension, portray the female character as the more traditional one who yet yields to the temptation from the snake of the salesman of leisure (whether he is in the graphophone or ice cream line), and show that the glitter of modern capitalism is not made of gold but is merely gilded.

Perhaps indebted to the tradition of winding up the clock on a certain occasion in *Tristram Shandy*, both "Long Black Song" and "The Gilded Six-Bits" surround the clock imagery with erotic contexts (as did Hurston's ditty on that Johnson gal), combining the appeal of modern time with that of sex. In both stories, too, the intrusion is imagined not simply as a loss of innocence, but as adultery and unfaithfulness to good husbands. In both cases, the heroines' breasts are the locus of the transformation. Sarah's breasts, in her "natural" state offered to her baby, are touched sexually by the salesman, and Hurston first describes the still faithful Missie May in the bathtub with a phrasing that already evokes and contrasts with the ice cream parlor: "Her stiff young breasts thrust forward aggressively like broad-based cones with the tips lacquered in black" (60). At the end, Joe buys so many candy kisses because the baby boy can "suck a sugartit" (70).[25] In both stories, too, the contrast between "feet" and "shoes" plays a part: Silas brings shoes from town for his barefoot wife, and Joe expresses his wish for a child with the reiterated phrase "making little feet for shoes" (65, 69).

Yet Wright and Hurston conclude their stories in a virtually antithetical fashion. For Hurston, natural time (and the period of pregnancy and childbirth, which, significantly, is not given in precise, measured time and thus throws some doubt on the cuckolded husband's paternity) works as a great healer.[26] For Wright, the story steers toward a violent catastrophe. Hurston's seducer is black, which gives the story an intraracial focus (that is characteristic of much of Hurston's oeuvre), whereas Wright's modern tempter is white, which intensifies the dramatic interracial collision. "If it were anybody but a white man," Sarah ponders when she considers pleading with Silas, "it would be different." Sarah knows that she cannot simply go to Silas and ask forgiveness; Missie May acts penitently for long enough to heal Joe's wounded pride, although, of course, with the help of childbirth (which in "Long Black Song" took place a short time *before* the story began). Hurston here and elsewhere writes humorously; Wright writes typically with a seriousness that admits only the occasional wry laugh at the absurdity of man's fate.

Hurston's story stresses the resilience of the folk couple, their "adaptability" to the conflict situation of adultery,[27] and their ability to resolve a crisis peacefully—so peacefully, in fact, that to the ignorant white clerk from whom Joe buys the candy at the end, the black couple seem to be typically happy darkies, minstrels who know nothing of conflicts. "The sun, the hero of every day, the impersonal old man that beams as brightly on death as on birth, came up every morning and raced across the deep blue dome and dipped into the sea of fire every evening" (64), Hurston writes—but she chooses birth as the resolution of her tale.[28] In "Long Black Song," however, the clash between the spirit of the city and that of the country certainly brings death, even though Sarah and Ruth escape from the scene of the battle. Hurston's pastoral concept is that of the idyllic place (as Robert Bone has argued); Wright, however, speaks more for the picaresque logic of running away or dying. Wright's story is linear; Hurston's, circular. Wright is decidedly "male"; Hurston, "female" and often regarded as protofeminist.[29]

Wright and Hurston

The differences between these stories that start out so similarly point to a larger opposition between two writers who were at odds with each other while each claimed to be telling the truly representative tale that would incorporate blacks into the American story. Thus, in "What White Publishers Won't Print" (1950), Hurston emphasized not only the analogies of blacks and Jews in the American imagination—according to her, publishing houses shied away from printing love stories about either group unless such works involved racial tension—but also the significance of *all* minorities for the country: "But for the national welfare, it is urgent to realize that the minorities do think, and think about something other than the race problem. That they are very human and internally, according to natural endowment, are just like everybody else."[30] Wright similarly struck an incorporating note in a blurb he prepared for the publicity of *Black Boy*:

> [To] those whites who recall how, in the early days of this land, their forefathers struggled for freedom, BLACK BOY cannot be a strange story. Neither can it be a strange story to the Jews, the

Poles, the Irish, and the Italians who came hopefully to this land from the Old World.[31]

Yet despite their shared attempt to parallel the black story with that of other ethnic groups in America, Hurston and Wright differed dramatically in style and attitude toward their materials. Wright stressed the psychological and social dimensions of racial oppression and interracial conflict, whereas Hurston described the style of folkways and foodways and tried to capture specific characteristics of black language that she recorded in black communities. It is symptomatic that one of Wright's stories, "Almos' a Man," was fittingly illustrated in serious WPA style by Thomas Hart Benton, whereas Hurston had *Mules and Men* illustrated by the slicker Miguel Covarrubias, who had earned his fame as a *Vanity Fair* artist.[32] Wright represents World War I with an allusion to the plotline that Frantz Fanon was later to consider the prototypical Third World story: the black veteran who has fought for a country that denies him his right to live when he returns. Hurston instead incorporates the phrase "bookooing," which black soldiers had picked up in France (from the word *beaucoup*).[33]

Although he occasionally has been mislabeled as a naturalist, Wright was seriously dedicated to modernism. The third part of his Joycean novel *Lawd Today*, set on a single day, bears a motto from T. S. Eliot's *The Waste Land*, and the text incorporates Stein's "a rose is a rose is a rose."[34] Wright also alludes to Eliot when he calls Chicago an "unreal city."[35] In one version of his manifesto "Blueprint for Negro Writing," Wright invokes James Joyce's famous phrasing when he encourages black writers to "forge in the smithy of our souls the uncreated conscience of our race," an adaptation of Joyce that was later echoed by Ralph Ellison.[36] Similarly, the ending of "Bright and Morning Star," as Kinnamon has argued,[37] is a response to the conclusion of Joyce's "The Dead." Wright held up Stein's "Melanctha" as the best modern prose piece in the collection *I Wish I Had Written That* (1946), wrote a blurb for and reviewed Stein's *Brewsie and Willie* (1946), and described in *American Hunger* how, under the influence of *Three Lives*, he composed "disconnected sentences for the sheer love of words" for example: "The child's clumsy fingers fumbled in sleep, feeling vainly for the wish of its dream."[38] Wright was fascinated by D. H. Lawrence, experimented with Faulknerian stream-of-consciousness sentences in *Native Son*, and explained, as we saw, that "Long Black Song" was an attempt to extend Hemingway's technique. For Wright, the question was "What would life on Chicago's South Side look like when seen through the eyes of a Freud, a Joyce, a Proust, a Pavlov, a Kierkegaard?"[39]

Hurston's irrepressible optimism contrasts sharply with Wright's modern temper, and her literary influences are fairytales, folklore, and mythology (she especially liked the Norse gods), while among her favorite authors were Rudyard Kipling, Robert Louis Stevenson, Hans Christian Andersen, and such lesser contemporaries as Robert Wunsch (to whom her first novel is dedicated) and Fannie Hurst (for whom Hurston worked as a secretary for a while).[40]

According to Wright's manifesto "Blueprint for Negro Writing," writers had to radicalize folkloric materials and put things into perspective: "Negro writers must create in their readers' minds a relationship between a Negro woman hoeing cotton in the South and the men who loll in swivel chairs in Wall Street and take the fruits of her toil."[41] By contrast, Hurston explained why she was *not* a protest writer:

> You cannot arouse any enthusiasm in me to join in a protest for the boss to provide me with a better hoe to chop his cotton with. Why must I chop cotton at all? Why fix a class of cotton-choppers? I will join in no protests for the boss to put a little more stuffing in my bunk. I don't even want the bunk. I want the boss's bed.[42]

One can imagine from the terms of the polarization that Wright and Hurston did not like each other's fiction. They said so freely in public. In October 1937, Wright reviewed Hurston's *Their Eyes Were Watching God* for the radical *New Masses* under the title "Between Laughter and Tears":

> Miss Hurston can write; but her prose is cloaked in that facile sensuality that has dogged Negro expression since the days of Phillis Wheatley. Her dialogue manages to catch the psychological movements of the Negro folk mind in their pure simplicity, but that's as far as it goes.
>
> Miss Hurston *voluntarily* continues in her novel the tradition which was forced upon the Negro in the theater, that is, the minstrel technique that makes the "white folks" laugh. Her characters . . . swing like a pendulum eternally in that safe and narrow orbit in which America likes to see the Negro live: between

laughter and tears. . . . In the main, her novel is not addressed to the Negro, but to a white audience whose chauvinistic tastes she knows how to satisfy. She exploits that phase of Negro life which is "quaint," the phase which evokes a piteous smile on the lips of the "superior" race.[43]

These comments are largely applicable to "The Gilded Six-Bits," in which Wright might have shared the clerk's opinion of Joe and Missie May as minstrels—Hurston's minstrels, however.

Although Wright's attack on Hurston has been widely noted and often viewed in contemporary criticism as a male writer's put down of a disadvantaged female colleague, Hurston responded in kind when it was her turn to review Wright's *Uncle Tom's Children* only a few months after Wright's review of *Their Eyes Were Watching God* appeared:

This is a book about hatreds. Mr. Wright serves notice by his title that he speaks of people in revolt, and his stories are so grim that the Dismal Swamp of race hatred must be where they live. Not one act of understanding and sympathy comes to pass in the entire work. . . . Since the author himself is a Negro, his dialect is a puzzling thing. One wonders how he arrived at it. Certainly he does not write by ear unless he is tonedeaf.

She specifically writes that in "Long Black Song,"

the hero gets the white man most Negro men rail against—the white man who possesses a Negro woman. He gets several of them while he is about the business of choosing to die in a hurricane of bullets and fire because his woman has had a white man. There is lavish killing here, perhaps to satisfy all male black readers.[44]

And, as if thinking of Silas or Wright, she quipped on another occasion that a Museum of Unnatural History might contain the stereotyped doll of "the most amoral character before a share-cropper's shack mumbling about injustice. Doing this makes him out to be a Negro 'intellectual.' It is as simple as all that."[45]

It probably deserves mention that Wright was by no means the more established writer when the exchange took place. Wright was younger than thirty and had not yet published a single book when his attack on Hurston appeared in the low-circulating *New Masses*; Hurston was Wright's senior by seventeen years, the author of two novels and two non-fiction collections, and a former Rosenwald fellow, who was completing her second Guggenheim fellowship year when she attacked Wright's first published book in the widely read *Saturday Review*. Hers was the "only unfavorable review" of *Uncle Tom's Children* by a black critic.[46]

Anthropological and Sociological Tendencies

The opposition between Wright and Hurston was serious and deep, informed by their personal dispositions and political differences. Yet Wright's and Hurston's oeuvres, as well as their differences, can be fruitfully approached from the divergent orientation of the disciplines of anthropology and sociology.[47] Both were, indeed, formally or informally students of these disciplines. Hurston was the privately educated alumna of the Robert H. Hungerford Normal and Industrial School in Eatonville, the Morgan Academy, Howard University, Barnard College, and Columbia University Graduate School. She received her doctoral training from a central figure of twentieth-century anthropology, Franz Boas; did fieldwork for Melville Herskovits; and wrote for Ruth Benedict. Wright, who was largely self-taught, came across sociology in an informal way. He finished only the eighth grade at the public Smith Robertson School and beyond that had only one more term of formal schooling at the Lanier High School, in Jackson, Mississippi. But Wright's aunt was under the supervision of the Chicago social worker Mrs. Louis Wirth, and thus Wright encountered the thinking of the Chicago School of sociology at its height (Robert E. Park, Robert Redfield, Louis Wirth), an encounter that was intensified through his friendship with the Chicago sociologist Horace Cayton.

Both Wright and Hurston specifically recognized their stories in these disciplines. Wright "sensed that Negro life was a sprawling land of unconscious suffering, and there were but few Negroes who knew the meaning of their lives, who could tell their story."[48] How did he become one of those storytellers? Citing Hamlet's admonition to Horatio, Wright admits to his own "dumb yearning to write, to tell my story." Yet he adds:

But I did not know what my story was, and it was not until I stumbled upon science that I discovered some of the meanings of the

environment that battered and taunted me. I encountered the work
of men who were studying the Negro community, amassing facts
about urban Negro life, and I found that sincere art and honest science were not far apart, that each could enrich the other. The huge
mountains of fact piled up by the Department of Sociology at the
University of Chicago gave me my first concrete vision of the forces that molded the urban Negro's body and soul. . . . It was from
the findings of men like . . . Robert E. Park, Robert Redfield, and
Louis Wirth that I drew the meanings for my documentary book,
12,000,000 Black Voices; for my novel, *Native Son*; it was from their
scientific facts that I absorbed some of that quota of inspiration necessary for me to write *Uncle Tom's Children* and *Black Boy*.[49]

Hurston is equally specific in characterizing her academic indebtedness: "I needed my Barnard education to help me see my people as
they really are."[50] And elaborating on anthropology as a lens for her
perception, Hurston writes that the folklore she was familiar with since
childhood was too close to her, fitting her "like a tight chemise," so she
"had to have the spy-glass of Anthropology to look through at that."[51]

Both Wright and Hurston paraphrase their mentors in their works.
Wright thus summarizes Redfield's description of the advent of machine
production in a way that also illuminates "Long Black Song":

Holy days became holidays; clocks replaced the sun as a symbolic measurement of time. As the authority of the family waned,
the meaning of reality, emotion, experience, action, and God
assumed the guise of teasing questions.[52]

Hurston echoes Boas's environmentalism and universalism when she uses
what one might call anthropological vernacular and writes in her autobiography, "It seemed to me that the human beings I met reacted pretty
much the same to the same stimuli. Different idioms, yes. Circumstances
and conditions having power to influence, yes. Inherent difference, no."[53]
The problem of adaptation was therefore equally crucial to Hurston and
Boas.

These relationships between scholars and writers were not one-way
streets. Chicago sociologists saluted and endorsed Wright. Thus, the
aged Park (who originally wanted to become a novelist and had worked

as a journalist and Booker T. Washington's ghostwriter) asked to meet Wright and got up, with difficulty, to shake the hands of the thirty-four-year-old writer in respect.[54] Cayton described how Wright asked him for "sociological concepts" while writing *12 Million Black Voices*. "I explained to him the idea of urban versus rural, of culture versus civilization, or a sacred versus a secular society," Cayton remembered. "I talked about the differences between societies in which folkways determine the way of life and those which are governed by contracts rather than promises."[55] Cayton also reviewed Wright's works and gave *Native Son*, *12 Million Black Voices*, and *Black Boy* his fullest sociological endorsement:

> For every adjective which Wright used we have a label, for every move that Bigger took, we have a map; for every personality type he encountered we have a life history. . . . [I]n general a large research project which was carried on in Chicago's Black Belt for a period of four years substantiated the entire thesis of "Native Son."
>
> [In *12 Million Black Voices*] he has translated into literary form the polar types of social organization: the anthropological concepts of Robert Redfield—culture and civilization—and the sociological concepts of Louis Wirth—sacred and secular societies.
>
> Richard Wright has had but one story to tell. That story is how it feels to be a Negro in the United States. . . . In *Black Boy* he has retold it. . . . Although he relies mainly on the psychoanalytic frame of reference in selecting incidents of his life, he has brought to play on this material all the insight he has derived from sociology, anthropology, and literature. Indeed, all these instruments were necessary to achieve an objectivity which would allow him to tear himself out of the context of his every day environment and describe the life of Negro people through his own personality.[56]

Hurston similarly was supported by the anthropologists. In her autobiography she reports that Boas—whom she called "Papa Franz"—once remarked in a fatherly fashion:

> "Of course, Zora is my daughter. Certainly!' . . . Just one of my missteps, that's all." The sabre cut on his cheek, which it is said he got in a duel at Heidelberg, lifted in a smile.[57]

Boas's student Ruth Benedict published Hurston's first scholarly pieces in the *Journal of American Folklore*, for which she was then the editor,
and Boas himself, solicited by Hurston (who had also requested that Benedict "sort of edit" the manuscript),[58] wrote the preface to *Mules and Men*:

> It is the great merit of Miss Hurston's work that she entered into
> the homely life of the southern Negro as one of them and was
> fully accepted as such by the companions of her childhood. Thus
> she has been able to penetrate through that affected demeanor by
> which the Negro excludes the White observer effectively from
> participating in his true inner life.[59]

Sterling Brown strongly disputed this statement, which was echoed by
Hurston in the book itself. Brown, who could also be critical of Wright
and thought "Long Black Song" weak in characterization and structure,
and who reviewed Hurston's *Their Eyes Were Watching God* favorably,
commented on Hurston's *Mules and Men* that it failed to represent the
total picture because it omitted the dimension of bitterness and anger.
"Unfortunately," Brown writes, Hurston's book "does not uncover so
much that white collectors have been unable to get. The tales ring genuine, but there seem to be omissions. The picture is too pastoral, with only
a bit of grumbling about hard work, or a few slave anecdotes that turn
the tables on old master." What seems missing to Brown is "bitterness."[60]
  The differences between anthropology and sociology, the disciplines
Hurston and Wright were attracted to, were widely debated in the period. What seemed clear was that anthropologists were more concerned
with "culture," "folk," "tradition," and "adaptation," whereas sociologists
looked into "civilization," "an urbanized population," "modernization,"
and "conflict." As Philip Gleason has argued, the Boasian anthropologists
in the period leaned toward an "internalist approach to the study of human
groups—they focused primarily on the group considered in itself, its norms,
institutions, and the patterns that gave it coherence." The Parkian sociologists, by contrast, "highlighted the processes of interaction *between* groups"
that were "being thrown into contact with each other, were reacting to
each other, and mutually influencing each other in all sorts of ways." Thus,
"folk culture" often suggested the internalist perspective, whereas "urban
civilization" summoned the interactionist approach.[61] In this sense, Hurston
was a rural internalist, while Wright was an urban interactionist.

Of course, the two disciplines were not always easy to distinguish. There was some city in the village, and some village in the city, as became apparent when Redfield (an anthropologist but a student of Park's and, incidentally, also Park's son-in-law) investigated his Tepoztlán, a "traditional" village, yet located near Mexico City, and he noted that "several phonographs are . . . making city songs popular."[62] One of Redfield's chapters is tellingly titled "The Folk in a City World." Anthropological and sociological approaches could not always be separated.

In the March 1940 issue of the *American Journal of Sociology*, two related articles, by Robert Redfield and Louis Wirth, set out in a complementary fashion to clarify the relationship of anthropology and sociology by deemphasizing the dichotomy between them. Redfield's "The Folk Society and Culture" starts out with the story of two blind men who are investigating an elephant: one studies the legs, while the other measures ears, trunk, tail, and body. Explaining his parable, Redfield argues that anthropology and sociology have dealt with different aspects of a whole: "The whole is society."[63] Instead, he would like to see their enterprises not as parallel but as complementary, as one focuses on the "primitive" and the other on the industrial. Reviewing his own work, Redfield concludes that Tepoztlán was a village that shared some features of a modern city with others of a primitive tribe and hence was a good place for the study not of any pure folk (which he specifies as tribal and peasant society), but of the development from primitive to urbanized man. He suggests that culture in the anthropological sense implies an integral whole, traditionally organized from birth to death—a demand met in fewer and fewer places around the globe. Wirth's "Urban Society and Civilization" looks at "culture" and "civilization" as two poles of human existence and states quite clearly: "What we call civilization as distinguished from culture has been cradled in the city."[64]

Paralleling Redfield's discussion, both "Long Black Song" and "The Gilded Six-Bits" show the presence of modernity in the rural worlds of Mississippi and Florida. In "Long Black Song," Silas is already perfectly assimilated to "the practical version of the American way."[65] He has driven a car, is a good merchant of his crops, brings town gifts to a wife who is eager for more leisure culture, and is, on the whole, the perfect Franklinian spirit. Sarah and Silas already own a clock that, at the beginning of the story, serves as the baby's toy. There is also, in "Long Black Song," a type of repetition that was not emphasized in the contrastive premodern–modern reading: there are many repeated words and images that develop *connections* between the worlds so sharply polarized—for example, between Silas and the salesman, the baby and the salesman, Silas and the white mob, Tom and the salesman, the baby and the graphophone, the baby and the black–white battle, and so on—links, in short, between the worlds juxtaposed in the story:

cricket	crickets
teat (baby, Tom)	breasts (salesman)
gourd (baby)	gourd (salesman)
baby's eyes	clock and graphophone box
tinkle (Silas's wagon)	tinkle (salesman's belt)
afterglow (Tom)	afterglow (salesman)
white bright days and deep desire of dark black nights (Tom)	white bright days and deep desire of dark black nights (salesman)
$250	$40, $50 (salesman)
shoes (Silas)	shoes (salesman)
bastard (Silas speaking)	bastard (white mob speaking)
overalls (Tom)	overalls (Silas)
toy (baby)	like toy dolls (black and white)

In "The Gilded Six-Bits," the factory (ironically, a fertilizer plant) where Joe works on the night shift appears in the first paragraph, and the symbol of money plays an important part in the natural, prelapsarian state of the couple's sexual relations.[66] There is also a clock in the house, and Missie May's first line is, "Humph! Ah'm way behind time t'day," another variation on the White Rabbit's exclamation from *Alice in Wonderland*. It is furthermore noteworthy that Joe (who, incidentally, laughs at Slemmons in his bedroom like a "chessy cat" [66]) becomes a "strange man" (like Otis Slemmons), and by the end of the story, when he tells the clerk that he has been around "spots and places" (70), he applies to himself the phrase that he had earlier used as Slemmons's trademark.[67]

It therefore seems plausible to assume that both Wright and Hurston were aware that they were exaggerating the drama of modernization. After all, for Hurston it was problematic to settle on Eatonville as the locus of folk culture. Redfield had argued that secluded rural southern blacks and, to a lesser extent, Appalachians had the only true folk cultures in America. Yet Hurston's Eatonville hardly was such a secluded community, for it was modern, named after the Captain Josiah C. Eaton of the Civil War, on whose land it was founded, and incorporated on August 18, 1887, barely three-and-a-half years before the author was born. It had Sears and Roebuck streetlights, and as Hurston stressed in her rationale for *Mules and Men*, it contained a cross section of Negroes from all over the South as well as from the North and the West, hardly the classic place for studying unscathed traditional folk. Hurston herself was born on January 15, 1891, in Notasulga, Alabama, and was a migrant to Eatonville, although she seems never to have mentioned that fact. Perhaps Hurston's persistent claim that Eatonville was her birthplace was an attempt to bypass these difficulties through autobiographical invention. For Wright, the traditional rural setting was already disrupted by war and aspects of modernization (such as segregation) and characterized by modern violence—a violence Wright was given to exaggerate when he used autobiographical material.

Both writers inscribed themselves into their stories as not only the embodiments of folk from the rural areas where they had grown up but also the modern commercial seducers, the phonograph- and ice-cream-vending figures who are as distanced from folk as the writers were from their own southern childhood environments when they made their careers in northern cities. One need only compare "Long Black Song" with Wright's memories of working as a salesman of insurance policies in Chicago and of meeting a simple young woman who extends sexual favors in return for not paying her ten-cent premium, or "The Gilded Six-Bits" with the image of Hurston's arrival in Eatonville with a diploma and a Chevrolet to recognize the autobiographical dimensions of the modernizers and seducers—even though they are portrayed as white by a black author and male by a female writer.[68]

Versions of Folklore and Modern Time

If anthropology and sociology are merely two ways to look at an elephant, the idea of *the* "true black story" between "folklore" and "modern time" may well be Hurston's and Wright's elephant. It was what they saw in folklore and modern time that marked their difference. For example, there is an interesting story in Hurston's *Mules and Men* in which a man takes a turtle on a string as if it were a pocket watch on a chain; when asked what time it is, he pulls out the turtle and says, "It's quarter past leben and kickin' like hell for twelve." [69] In Wright's *12 Million Black Voices* there is another passage about time that again illuminates the difference between the two writers:

> If a white man stopped a black man on a southern road and asked: "Say, there, boy! It's one o'clock, isn't it?" the black man would answer: "Yessuh."
>
> If the white man asked: "Say, it's not one o'clock, is it, boy?" the black man would answer: "Nowsuh."[70]

In another example, Hurston cites the following song in *Mules and Men*; it is a song, she told Herbert Halpert in 1939, that is entitled "Ever Been Down" and that she heard in Palm Beach in 1933:

> Ah'd ruther be in Tampa with the Whip-poor-will,
> Ruther be in Tampa with the Whip-poor-will
> Than to be 'round here—
> Honey with a hundred dollar bill.[71]

In his novel *Lawd Today* (which was completed in 1937 but published posthumously in 1963), Wright uses a verse that is sufficiently similar to reveal its origin in the same folkloric family, yet it is different enough to serve as an illustration here: *"Lawd, I'd ruther be a lamppost in Chicago than the president of Miss'sippi."* Wright liked the verse enough to vary it in *12 Million Black Voices* to read, "We'd rather be a lamppost in Chicago than the president of Dixie!"[72]

Hurston published polished, singable, and rhythmic verses that are addressed to someone called "Honey" and have a predominantly personal meaning (one might say "folklore *pour* folklore"). In contrast, Wright rendered two rough-hewn versions that start as a prayer but in their development from "Lawd, I'd ruther" to "We'd rather" increasingly stress collective secular social consciousness ("folklore in perspective"). Hurston's speaker faces a choice that seems slightly absurd but not really that bad (why is Tampa with a whip-poor-will better than staying put with money and the addressee?) and seems to advocate reassuringly (if somewhat quizzically) going to the (apparently nearby) city, "where the water taste like wine,"[73] as opposed to staying in the country. Wright's voice expresses a wry sense of bitter humor with a social cutting edge: remaining in Mississippi or Dixie must be worse than death if being a Chicago lamppost (another metallic object, evocative of a violent death by hanging—or, at least, a not exactly humorous reification) is preferable to being a leader in the South. Both tendencies—the "internalist" personal-humorous and the "interactionist" political-serious—were probably present in black folklore of the period. Lawrence Levine, for example, cites the following version:

> Lord, I rather be in Mobile in a hollow log
> Than to be here treated like a dog.[74]

This is a version that rhymes and continues the prayer format yet also has a clear social perspective. The selective and divergent emphasis that Wright and Hurston made in their folk materials is telling.

Finally, while early in their careers Hurston and Wright were interested in how the clock as a symbol of modern time affected African American characters, both also intensified the representation of time as they matured as writers, a process that a study of textual variants in their works reveals.

For example, Hurston renders her "folk-tale" of how blacks got their color at least three times (in 1935, 1937, and 1942), with variants that are worth attention.[75] Most important, she intensified the conflict between God's demand for punctuality and the blacks' failure to comply with it. In the 1935 version, God set a day for giving out color and waited three-and-a-half hours for the blacks-to-be.[76] In 1942, however, God said:

> Tomorrow morning, at seven o'clock *sharp*, I aim to give out color. Everybody be here on time. I got plenty of creating to do tomorrow, and I want to give out this color and get it over wid. *Everybody* be 'round de throne at seven o'clock tomorrow morning.[77]

Now God waits for only one-and-a-half hours before sending Gabriel out to find the missing folk. While the outline of the tale remains the same, God's insistence on punctuality is strengthened while his patience for latecomers diminishes. The concept of God's clocked time in confrontation

with a "natural" people shows the pressure of modernization even on such
at times statically conceived entities as "traditional" folklore.

A glance at Wright's manuscripts shows that he intensified the presence
of clocks while also persistently removing elements of resilient folk life
from his narrative enterprise. Particular critical concern has centered on
one of his parenthetical remarks in *Black Boy*, probably the first widely read
American autobiography by a person not of Anglo-Saxon background,
that draws a partly very unsympathetic character. (In reviewing *Black Boy*,
W. E. B. Du Bois calls the hero "self-centered," "foul-mouthed," and
a "loathsome brat.") Significantly, upon the occasion of an impending
relocation, the grandmother tells the young protagonist to say good-bye
to his friends, but he refuses and then broods about "the strange absence
of real kindness in Negroes, how unstable was our tenderness, how lacking in genuine passion we were, how void of great hope, how timid our
joy, how bare our traditions, how hollow our memories, how lacking
we were in those intangible sentiments that bind man to man, and how
shallow was even our despair."[78] Du Bois sarcastically commented on this
paragraph, "Born on a plantation, living in Elaine, Ark., and the slums
of Memphis, he knows the whole Negro race!" Ralph Ellison took more
than one occasion to reflect, with varying results, on Wright's strategy in
his devastating parenthetical observations. Yet it was the kind of statement
at which Wright arrived by radicalizing his own experience into a general
psychogram of "the Negro mind" that would, he hoped, strengthen the
call for action and social change, especially for desegregation. As Alice
Deck has shown, Wright worked hard at this parenthetical remark, and
at an early stage, the phrase "absence of real kindness in Negroes" still
read "*abundance*"—before Wright crossed out "abundance" and ultimately
replaced it with the word "absence." The coldhearted individual aberrant
boy who does not want to say good-bye to his friends before relocating
had been transformed into an allegory of "the Negro," multiplied by
twelve million, so to speak.[79]

It is a process of rewriting that resulted in the famous beginning of
Native Son, too. In conclusion, I cite the opening of the novel, according
to the typescript preserved at the New York Public Library's Schomburg
Center for Research in Black Culture:

One moment he was sound asleep and then the very next a loud
knock at the door made him jerk fully awake; he leaned upon

his elbows in bed, staring unblinkingly into darkness, listening with that muscular tensity of a man trying to decide if harm is threatening or not. There was a short silence in which he wondered if he had heard anything; he thought that perhaps he had been dreaming. But the knock came again, sharp and hard, and he relaxed, thinking, Somebody's knocking. . . . Suddenly he felt the cold air of the room and slid back beneath the cover.

"Ma!" he called softly.

Directly after he had spoken the knocking stopped and a muffled voice called.

"Sister Thomas!"

He closed his eyes and gritted his teeth.

"Oh, Sister Thomas! You sleep?" asked a muffled voice.

He lifted his head an inch from the pillow.

"Ma!" he called. "Somebody's at the door!"

A grunt came from the darkness.

"Hunh?"

"Ma!"[80]

This earlier version of the beginning of *Native Son* still described black family life as poor but *human* life, in which characters do not brutally kill rats but interact with one another and the neighbors. In other words, they still have those "intangible sentiments that bind man to man." They are also the subjects of sentences. The final and famous opening of *Native Son*, with the "*Brrrrrriiiiiiiiiiiiiiiiiiiinng!*" was, then, not the first thing that had occurred to Wright's supposedly naturalistic mind but the result of a carefully worked-out process—perhaps inspired by the social scientists from whom Wright learned "his story"—of providing the reader with "perspective," which Wright defined as "the frame in which the picture is hung" and "that part of a novel that is remembered long after the story is forgotten."[81] The startling ringing of the alarm clock that distinguishes the published version from the early manuscript certainly was such a part.

Figure 8.1. Winold Reiss, *Zora Neale Hurston.* Pastel on Whatman board, ca. 1925. (Courtesy of Renate Reiss.)

CHAPTER 8

Of Mules and Mares in a Land of Difference; or, Quadrupeds All?

June 1951: Using a fable of mules running after white mares, Zora Neale Hurston polemicizes against communism and racial integration in American Legion Magazine.

PERHAPS A CULTURE can best be understood by critics who lay bare what may be covered up and who question what is taken for granted, even by their own initial hypotheses. The term "cultural criticism" implies a truly critical position from which the surrounding culture is being surveyed, analyzed, compared with others, and, most important, criticized. When we set ourselves the goal to recover and reappraise critical traditions in the study of American culture, we are compelled to ask which historical processes have separated us from these traditions. What makes such traditions now appear to be older schools of thought, and what is it that seems problematic about them to many intellectuals of the present? Why are such traditions not simply available but in need of recovery? A better understanding of the intervening historical processes would seem a useful first step toward pursuing the questions of how we can recover what is valuable in cultural criticism of the past and

SOURCE: Werner Sollors, "Of Mules and Mares in a Land of Difference; or, Quadrupeds All?" *American Quarterly* 42, no. 2 (1990): 167–190. Reprinted with permission by Johns Hopkins University Press. Copyright © 1990 American Studies Association.

how we can stimulate the current state of American studies by calling attention to, drawing on, and criticizing earlier theorizing.

Whether the 1960s really mark the division between the now and the then in cultural criticism is perhaps less easily ascertained than that a shift has been experienced. As the reflections by critics such as Leo Marx and the late Henry Nash Smith suggest, their older vocabulary included such phrases as "myth and symbol" and "increasing complexities of modern industrializing societies" instead of the now preferred terms "ideology" and "capitalism." Such semantic changes seem to be representative of many others in the United States, as well as in Europe. When David Schneider reissued his 1968 study *American Kinship* in 1980, he added a new chapter in which he wondered whether ethnicity would not challenge his generalizations about America. Others have been critical of the bias toward high culture and of the exceptionalist practice in past American studies, which rarely compared the United States with other countries while stressing its uniqueness on the basis of a few cultural items of which only a small class of Americans may have been aware.[1] A thorough conceptualization of the intellectual changes brought about since the 1960s would be helpful today.

One such change is the marked increase in challenges to universalism that have affected not only the discourse about nationalism, ethnicity, and gender but also the intellectual procedure of generalizing about American culture in an international context. An important reason for this change lies, of course, in the overt and hidden exclusivism of the old generalizations. When, for example, Barrett Wendell, who introduced the teaching of American literature to Harvard University at the beginning of the twentieth century, used the word "American," he thought of it as signifying one branch of the Anglo-Saxon family. Contemplating the fearful possibility that among Harvard's students "either an Ethiopian or a Hebrew" might win the Jacob Wendell Scholarship (thus forcing him to dine with him), he was relieved that the students had "all been Americans, and, with hardly an exception, gentlemen." Even a scholar of the eminence of Gunnar Myrdal drew a parallel between Negroes and women in an appendix to *An American Dilemma* (1944) that seems virtually blind to the existence of black women.[2] The phrase "women and minorities" that Philip Gleason called attention to continues that tradition. Nancy Cott's discovery of an entry in *Current Biography* on Charles and Mary Beard that speaks about only *him* is another case in point. And the question repeatedly directed at Jesse Jackson whether he is black or American suggests that in political rhetoric, the generalization "American" still does not automatically include the category "black."

In scholarship, however, the recovery of cultural activity outside the (often falsely generalized) mainstream has been impressive, and the definition of "the American" has been broadened. It is now common knowledge, for example, that the year 1620 may be less meaningful to black history than the year 1619, and 1920 may be a more important caesura for American women's history than World War I. That does not mean that one cannot construct the outline of a history that encompasses such differences, yet the compatibility of the subcultures with the culture has received relatively little attention, and the shared features of American culture have tended to disappear from view. Little work seems to be under way that investigates the new meanings of America that are emerging after much particularistic scholarship, and calls for a new synthesis (such as those made by Thomas Bender and T. J. Jackson Lears) seem to provoke much criticism, even of a hostile nature. And while the deconstructive argument has been made against such abstract generalizations as "America" and "culture," it is not always applied with equal rigor against such similarly problematic generalizations as "women's literature," "ethnic history," and "the Jewish experience."

I would like to sketch a twofold undertaking, starting with a report on now rarely considered arguments against the *Brown v. Board of Education of Topeka* decision of 1954 that were made not by white southerners but, somewhat surprisingly, by two interesting culture critics, one black and one Jewish. After regarding some questions that these essays raise, I touch on the changes that have taken American culture criticism from universalism to difference in the recent past.

My first example is by Zora Neale Hurston, the Alabama-born and Howard-, Barnard-, and Columbia-educated black anthropologist and author of such novels as *Their Eyes Were Watching God* (1937), whose reputation has recently undergone a revival that has made many of her works available in reprint and for classroom use. *Many* but not all—among Hurston's uncollected works is the essay "Court Order Can't Make Races Mix." The essay is occasionally referred to yet hard to locate, because it was published only once, in the *Orlando Sentinel* in 1955. In an essay from 1971, Darwin T. Turner mentions that Hurston "protested against the 1954 Supreme Court declaration that 'separate' schools are not equal.

The decision, she wrote, insulted Negroes by implying the inadequacy of their schools." Parts of Hurston's essay were cited in Robert Hemenway's careful biography, the book that helped to set off the Hurston revival.[3] Mary Helen Washington argues that in the essay, Hurston took her "most highly controversial stand." Washington at first sounds like Turner but then goes on to make the essay part of a *positive*, proto-militant stance that lets Hurston explicitly appear as a precursor of the 1960s rather than as a conservative. Hurston's attitude, Washington writes, "was consistent with her cultural philosophy that blacks had adorned a rather pallid American culture with colorful, dramatic, and dynamic contributions. In every art form, she saw truly original expression rooted in black culture." Washington concludes:

> Little wonder, then, that she, as well as many other southern blacks, feared that they would be the losers in the integration plan. It is both ironic and sad to realize that Hurston would not have been denounced for any of these views in the sixties or seventies. She might even have been considered militant.[4]

Sandra M. Gilbert and Susan Gubar write that Hurston was sometimes criticized by black writers, such as Richard Wright and Alain Locke, for "the conservative cast" of her essays: "Yet the basis for Hurston's rejection of Northern liberalism was clarified by a letter she wrote to the editor of a Florida newspaper . . . for Hurston argued that integration denied the value of already-existing black institutions."[5] Finally, Elaine Showalter states that Hurston's "determination to write from inside black culture and to withstand fashionable issues of racial tension or oppression . . . antagonized her male contemporaries" such as Richard Wright, Sterling A. Brown, and Ralph Ellison.[6]

With such descriptions, our interest in recovering the text of this writer's clarification of her most highly controversial stand is awakened. As if it were not only a rarity to find an essay by a prominent black writer of the 1950s *against* integration (Du Bois's controversial statement on segregation stems from the 1930s), we are promised, in addition, the presence of pre-1960s ethnic pride, and even a hint of pre-1980s feminism (as the piece seemed to annoy only *male* writers).

Hurston's "Court Order Can't Make Races Mix," an open letter to the *Orlando Sentinel* published on August 11, 1955, is, indeed, a very interesting document.[7] The short (twelve-paragraph) letter to the editor is written flippantly in a way Hurston herself calls "thinking out loud," and the center of it is taken up with an amplification of what Hurston, the author of *Mules and Men* (1935)—calls "the doctrine of the white mare." She explains:

> Those familiar with the habits of mules are aware that any mule, if not restrained, will automatically follow a white mare. Dishonest mule-traders made money out of this knowledge in the old days. Lead a white mare along a country road and slyly open the gate and the mules in the lot would run out and follow this mare. This [Supreme Court] ruling being conceived and brought forth in a sly political medium with eyes on [the election of] '56, and brought forth in the same spirit and for the same purpose. It is clear that they have taken the old notion to heart and acted upon it. It is a cunning opening of the barnyard gate with the white mare ambling past. We are expected to hasten pell-mell after her.

The story was illustrated, apparently by the *Orlando Sentinel*, with a small cartoon depicting a white mare with a question mark over her head and a sign reading "desegregation" while on the other side of the fence a black mule is thinking, "I just want my own pasture improved." Hurston goes back to the story later in the essay and confesses that, personally, she is "not persuaded and elevated by the white mare technique." She concludes the essay with the statement, "That old white mare business can go racking on down the road for all I care."[8]

Hurston is obviously critical of the very story she is telling, yet her rejection of integration also seems clearly suggested in the parable. As the critics promised, Hurston *does* invoke racial pride. She regards the court ruling "as insulting rather than honoring [her] race" and says that at issue is the "self-respect" of her people. She asks a very good question: "How much satisfaction can I get from a court order for somebody to associate with me who does not wish me near them?" Therefore, she claims the Indian's pride that knows no whine—hence, the Indian has never been spoken of as a minority: "It is inconceivable of an Indian to seek forcible association with anyone." These are interesting statements for a recuperation of cultural criticism, statements that help in speculations about the reasons black writers, as Mario Materassi has argued, have remained relatively uninspired by *Brown v. Board of Education*.[9] Thinking specifically about education, Hurston ventures even further. She writes:

> If there are not adequate Negro schools in Florida, and there is some residual, some inherent [here Hurston echoes the court's opinion that segregated schools are "inherently unequal"] and unchangeable quality in white schools, impossible to duplicate anywhere else, then I am the first to insist that Negro children of Florida be allowed to share this boon. But if there are adequate Negro schools and prepared instructors and instructions, then there is nothing different except the presence of white people.

By the logic of this questioning, she praises the work of a black educator in Florida and suggests enforcing compulsory education and hiring more truant officers and social workers as better strategies than school integration. Her argument is at odds with that of such black social scientists as Kenneth Clark, who were cited by the court for documenting the negative effects of segregated schools on schoolchildren.[10]

Some of the historical and political contexts in which Hurston arrives at her critique of school desegregation also come troublingly close to those invoked by southern white conservatives. The worst periods in the quick history she drafts are "the days of the never-to-be-sufficiently-deplored Reconstruction" (when the belief that Negroes want nothing more than to associate with whites was also current) and the New Deal (when only the "stubborn South and the Midwest kept this nation from being dragged farther to the left than it was"). She seems to consider seriously that the desegregation decision was only a trial balloon and precedent designed to keep southerners busy while more serious attacks on the political system could be launched: "What if it is contemplated to do away with the two-party system and arrive at Govt. by decree?" What she senses behind such deceptive maneuvering is the American left. Hurston, in 1955, specifically warned the readers about attempting integration at a time that

> the nation is exerting itself to shake the evils of Communist penetration. It is to be recalled that Moscow, being made aware of this folk belief, made it the main plank in their campaign to win the American Negro from the 1920s on. It was the come-on stuff. Join the party and get yourself a white wife or husband.

This allusion to a communist conspiracy probably found some resonance in the McCarthyist period to which Hurston here alludes.[11]

There is a dimension to Hurston's conservatism that deserves mention. When Hurston, in a southern newspaper (and, as we saw, in *American Legion Magazine*) of the 1950s, described school desegregation as a revival of a supposed Communist Party plan for interracial marriages, she may inadvertently have lent support to the familiar white racist equation of integration with miscegenation, and her argument, even with her sharp and proud criticism of the white mare technique, may have mobilized the most virulent and paranoid white fears about integrated education.[12] Hurston's essay may present some problems for post-segregationist ethnic and feminist endorsement. Even though she invokes ethnic pride, her political conservatism is pronounced and hardly would seem 1960ish if it had been voiced by another writer.[13] Yet may not one decade's conservatism turn out to contain the next decade's radicalism—and, by the way, vice versa? May not one generation's political correctness appear to successors merely as a set of "fashionable issues" (as Showalter puts it)?

My second example has some features in common with the first yet takes them in a different direction. In 1957, Hannah Arendt, the political thinker and author of the classic study *The Origins of Totalitarianism* (1951), was invited by George Lichtheim, one of the editors of *Commentary* (then a liberal magazine) to write an article on the implications of the struggle for integration. Her now largely forgotten essay "Reflections on Little Rock" was inspired, as she explicitly stated in a follow-up piece, by a newspaper picture showing a "Negro girl on her way home from a newly integrated school; she was persecuted by a mob of white children, protected by a white friend of her father, and her face bore eloquent witness to the obvious fact that she was not precisely happy."[14] Arendt proceeded to imagine the situation from the point of view of a black mother and a white mother to arrive at a political analysis of the importance of legally sanctioned segregation for the South. (A similar procedure was undertaken thirty years later by Anthony Lewis in *Common Ground*, his book on the busing crisis in Boston.) Arendt offered a rare "liberal-conservative or conservative-liberal" analysis (as Sidney Hook put it) that also predicted some problems that did arise: she specifically feared in the late 1950s that mob ideology and mob organization around race questions might "one day even prove more explosive in the big Northern urban centers than in the more tradition-bound South" (47). Like Hurston, Arendt had doubts about the wisdom of forcible school integration. Arendt's answer to her own question about what she would do if she were a Negro mother closely resembles Hurston's stance:

> Under no circumstances would I expose my child to conditions which made it appear as though I wanted to push its way into a group where it was not wanted. . . . I would feel that the Supreme Court ruling, unwillingly but unavoidably, has put my child into a more humiliating position than it had been in before. (179)

Arendt's analysis was provocative in questioning more generally whether children's education was the best arena in which to initiate the type of social integration of which adults still seemed to be afraid. Arendt distinguished between a public and a private realm (in which parents' rights were an important factor; unlike Margaret Mead, Arendt was not amused by a culture in which parents were becoming obsolete). In a move that seems to invert Hurston's, Arendt made a passing reference that the right to intermarriage was one of the most fundamental rights still violated by state laws in twenty-nine of the forty-nine states and yet a right rarely if ever demanded by civil rights activists:

> Indeed, with respect to unconstitutional legislation, the Civil Rights bill did not go far enough, for it left untouched the most outrageous law of southern states—the law which makes mixed marriage a criminal offense. The right to marry whoever one wishes is an elementary human right compared to which "the right to attend an integrated school, the right to sit where one pleases on a bus, the right to go into any hotel or recreation area or place of amusement, regardless of one's skin color or race" are minor indeed. Even political rights, like the right to vote, and nearly all other rights enumerated in the Constitution, are secondary to the inalienable human rights to "life, liberty and the pursuit of happiness" proclaimed in the Declaration of Independence; and to this category the right to home and marriage unquestionably belongs. It would have been much more important if this violation had been brought to the attention of the Supreme Court; yet had the Court ruled the anti-miscegena-

tion laws unconstitutional, it would hardly have felt compelled to encourage, let alone enforce, mixed marriages. (49–50)[15]

To evade white southerners' emotional associations of social and sexual integration (that were often made in anti-integrationist texts), authors of pro-integration rhetoric of the 1950s generally avoided or played down references to intermarriage. Arendt turns the tables and puts miscegenation into the foreground of a political line of argument that clearly favors desegregation while drawing a sharp distinction between canceling the legal framework on which segregation rested and *enforcing* integrationist social practices (such as school integration). It is not surprising that her argument, made shortly after the Supreme Court avoided the intermarriage issue in *Naim v. Naim* (1955), and a decade before the court struck down laws prohibiting interracial marriages in *Loving v. Virginia* (1967), had an electrifying effect. As David Spitz perceived it:

> If we are to bring Southern white citizens to accept what they regard as a more far-reaching personal association growing out of desegregation in the public schools, it will be, in part, because they accept the argument that intimate sexual relations between the races are no necessary consequence of this. There is, consequently, no surer way to prevent acceptance of the principle of equal educational opportunity for the Negro in the South than to push the issue of miscegenation into the forefront at this time. (64)

To some readers it seemed as if Arendt was suggesting to forget about the bulwarks, and to storm the citadel first. Arendt explicitly did not "advocate" intermarriage but argued that it was not promising to start with the enforcement of children's school integration while segregation was still entrenched in a huge web of important legal relationships for adults— among which the ban on intermarriages had an absurd prominence.

Because of disagreements among the editors (Norman Podhoretz and Elliott Cohen favored while Martin and Clement Greenberg and David Sher opposed printing the essay), *Commentary* delayed its publication for a long time. When *Commentary* let Arendt know that the piece, set in galleys (and circulating among New York intellectuals), would still not appear in the February 1958 issue, she withdrew it. Meanwhile, Sidney

Hook's reply to Arendt for *Commentary*, which had also made it to the galley stage, was published in a revised and only indirectly polemical form, even though Arendt's article had not seen print yet, in a special issue of *New Leader*; one could order it in bulk as a pamphlet, together with Mao's "Let a Hundred Flowers Bloom."[16] On September 7, 1958, Irving Howe requested Arendt's essay for the more radical *Dissent*. When the article finally appeared in that publication in the winter of 1959, it was prefaced with a strong disclaimer by the editors of *Dissent* (among the other members of the editorial board were Lewis Coser, Norman Mailer, Meyer Schapiro, and Michael Walzer) that invited readers' responses and stated quite bluntly:

> We publish [Arendt's article] not because we agree with it—quite the contrary!—but because we believe in freedom of expression even for views that seem to us entirely mistaken. Because of Miss Arendt's intellectual stature, the importance of her topic, and the fact that an earlier opportunity to print her views had been withdrawn, we feel it is a service to allow her opinion, and the rebuttals to it, now to be aired freely. (45)

Arendt's piece was thus sandwiched in *Dissent* between this editorial statement and two "rebuttals." (This makes an *American Quarterly* disclaimer, published as a headnote to an article by Viola Sachs, seem mild, indeed.) The rebuttals that followed were "Pie in the Sky," a highly emotional polemic by Melvin Tumin, and David Spitz's "Politics and the Realm of Being." Tumin sharply accused Arendt of ignorance, at best, and anti-Negro feeling, at worst; Spitz defended antimiscegenation legislation—without any *Dissent* disclaimers—arguing that since Arendt thought the right to intermarriage was a private matter in which the state had no right to interfere via segregationist legislation, "the logic of her position would require her to argue . . . that incest" was also a "purely private" matter (57). This parallel, which Spitz surprisingly amplified with some scriptural exegesis, may sound absurd, yet connections between incest and miscegenation are a staple in racial fiction, as well as legislation.[17]

   Arendt was reminded by her critics that what the oppressed seek is "not the right to be accepted as brother-in-law but as brother" (63), and she was called an "ardent champion" of intermarriage (67). In the next issue of *Dissent*, Sidney Hook (who also gave his version of the reason Arendt's essay had not appeared in *Commentary*, implying that she had withdrawn the piece after seeing his reply) expressed deep shock at Arendt's proposal and felt that she gave "priority to agitation for equality in the bedroom rather than equality in education" (203), a phrasing that Arendt, in a further response, repeated in disbelief (204). Critics such as Spitz and Hook specifically asserted that Arendt had misrepresented black interests in this matter; they claimed that the issue of intermarriage was meaningless to blacks. Arendt replied (45–46) that she had her doubts about that (especially when thinking about the educated strata) and that "oppressed minorities were never the best judges on the order of priorities in such matters" (a phrasing for which both Tumin and Spitz took Arendt to task as "snobbish" or "cavalier"; Ralph Ellison, too, commented on Arendt's "Olympian authority," although he seemed more concerned about her remarks about the failure of the parents).[18]

Arendt's explicit intention to "break the dangerous routine in which the discussion of these issues is being held from both sides" helped to generate a debate. The discussion surrounding her intervention is worth recovering because it illuminates the powerful associations of integration and miscegenation made even by liberal intellectuals. It may well be that the history of sharp debates and controversial occasions, of cultural transmissions and oppositions might prove even more profitable for our time than the biographically oriented recovery of Great Culture Critics.

Finally, it is interesting to note a certain ambiguity in Arendt's essay as far as ethnic identification is concerned. On the one hand, as a universalist intellectual she clearly felt free to speak for the whole body politic (including blacks and whites); without citing any Afro-American voices, she did not hesitate to suggest another course of action than the one officially proposed by black organizations (such as the National Association for the Advancement of Colored People) in the 1950s; and she had no difficulties making her argument simply on the strength of empathy with a Negro schoolgirl and her mother. On the other hand, Arendt must have experienced the ethnic ambience of this debate strongly enough to feel obliged to define her own position vis-à-vis race prejudice in the American South in ethnic terms:

> Like most people of European origin I have difficulty in understanding, let alone sharing, the common prejudices of Americans

in this area. Since what I wrote may shock good people and be misused by bad ones, I should like to make it clear that as a Jew I take my sympathy for the cause of the Negroes as for all oppressed or underprivileged peoples for granted and should appreciate it if the reader did likewise. (46)

While empathy with and speaking for other groups was still possible, universalism had also reached a crisis point: there were cultural boundaries that made even the understanding of certain prejudices difficult. Arendt's concession to what she seems to have perceived as an American cultural requirement to back up one's argument by one's descent was turned against her by more than one of her opponents, most of whom also were Jewish. They argued that because she was an "outsider" and "an aristocrat, not a democrat, at heart" (63), her piece illustrated "how little Europeans understand our race problems" (205). (The pronoun in the first person plural concerns us more.)

Hurston, too, could speak both from an inside perspective (in the vernacular) and in a universalist fashion, succeeding precisely to present a specifically black culture as universal. Both Arendt and Hurston received some of the strongest reactions from their peer groups: black writers and Jewish intellectuals, respectively.[19] Hurston, in her mix of ethnic pride and political conservatism, and Arendt, in her ambivalence about backing up a universalist assertion with a particularist genealogy, seem to take a middle position on the road from universalism to increasing ethnic identification. It is this development that I would like to consider for the remaining time.

Scholarly work nowadays is self-consciously introduced with statements that no attempt is being made to tell a single, unified story about America. As Emory Elliott puts it:

No longer is it possible, or desirable, to formulate an image of continuity when diversity of literary materials and a wide variety of critical voices are, in fact, the distinctive features of national literature. . . . [T]he history of the literature of the United States is not one story but many different stories.[20]

The fault lines of the different stories are those of ethnicity and gender; hence, such statements do not seem shaped by the postmodern recognition that *all* generalizations and cultural constructions are suspect (including not only those concerning nationality but also those about ethnic groups, sex, or historical period). It is as if Michel Foucault's example of the ungeneralizable "Chinese" classification of animals (at the beginning of *Les mots et les choses*) were applied only to the American mainstream. Within what used to be the subcategories of the broader term "American literature and culture," however, "continuity" and a unified story may be presented without the same hesitation. Thus, Gilbert and Gubar write:

> No single anthology has represented the exuberant variety yet strong continuity of the literature that English-speaking women have produced between the fourteenth century and the present. . . . Although this history cannot be adequately defined by the categories and chronology customarily used to organize "mainstream" literature, its contours document [Virginia] Woolf's thesis that women's "books continue each other."[21]

One may not generalize about the continuity of American literature, but one is permitted to do so in the equally problematic case of literature by women.

The cohesiveness of women's literature written in English, however, also experiences further interferences, and less from historical than from ethnic factors. The modernized text of the fourteenth-century Christian visionary Margery Kempe seems to present no problem of direct cultural access: the introduction to her excerpts brings her closer to the concerns of today's students by stressing that she "decided, after almost twenty years of marriage and fourteen children, that she was meant to be married not to her husband but to Christ."[22] Yet when it comes to introducing Maxine Hong Kingston, a contemporary of the editors who was born in America and educated in California, they suggest cultural distance and difference:

> No doubt because this artist has so brilliantly illuminated the intricate processes by which "femininity" is constructed in a culture different from our own, the novelist Kay Boyle has written with delight that *The Woman Warrior* is "a woman's book that has the vitality to take one far, . . . from the domestic grievances of American suburbia, . . . into the wit, and the love, and grief, of another place entirely."[23]

Thomas Ferraro has called attention to and questioned the strategy by which a Chinese American author is assigned to "a culture different from our own" and "another place entirely."[24] One result is that, at least by negation, a unified culture can be reinstated, even made normative, and claimed with the possessive pronoun "our." That culture seems characterized by suburbia, domestic grievances—and fourteenth-century Christian mystics who presumably were white. Unified presentations even of American culture seem possible after all today in such short-hand and often clichéd negative characterizations. Yet the belief that one should not overtly generalize about American culture and the concomitant distancing strategies that move certain American cultural texts symbolically to "another place entirely" are widespread.

Once upon a time, however, American culture was imagined as one place. When the term "American" was broadened and made more inclusive in the 1930s and 1940s, this was generally accomplished not by opposing universalism but by appealing to it. The introductions to anthologies of the period provide us with examples. In *Readings from Negro Authors* (1931), Otelia Cromwell, Eva B. Dykes, and Lorenzo Dow Turner (who was Zora Neale Hurston's literature professor at Howard) suggest that school reading programs in American literature could take advantage of "the worth-while productions of Negro authors":

> Negro literature demands no unique method of approach, no special interpretation of the rules of craftsmanship, because the standards of literary form are based upon universal principles. A short story written by a Negro is good, bad, or indifferent in so far as it is a good, a bad, or an indifferent short story.[25]

These are sentiments one rarely finds in printed documents of today. They are echoed in the famous anthology *The Negro Caravan* (1941), edited by Sterling A. Brown, Arthur P. Davis, and Ulysses Lee. While the editors make a special claim for Negro authors as the "ultimate portrayers of their own,"[26] and carefully assess what distinguishes their writings from those of their white counterparts (i.e., a common rejection of popular stereotypes and a common "racial" cause—except, perhaps, for Hurston, who is represented generously), they conclude that "writings by Negroes do not seem . . . to fall into a unique cultural pattern." They elaborate this point:

Negro writers have adopted the literary traditions that seemed useful for their purposes. . . . Phillis Wheatley wrote the same high moralizing verse in the same poetic pattern as her contemporary poets in New England. While Frederick Douglass brought more personal knowledge and bitterness into his antislavery agitation than William Lloyd Garrison and Theodore Parker, he is much closer to them in spirit and form than to Phillis Wheatley, his predecessor, and Booker T. Washington, his successor. . . . Without too great imitativeness, many contemporary Negro writers are closer to O. Henry, Carl Sandburg, Edgar Lee Masters, Edna St. Vincent Millay, Waldo Frank, Ernest Hemingway, and John Steinbeck than to each other. The bonds of literary tradition seem to be stronger than race. (6–7)

Brown, Davis, and Lee believe that the "Negro writes in the forms evolved in English and American literature" (7). They

consider Negro writers to be American writers, and literature by American Negroes to be a segment of American literature. They believe that it would be just as misleading to classify Clifford Odets' play about Jewish life as "Jewish literature" or James T. Farrell's novels of the Chicago Irish as "Irish literature" or some of William Saroyan's tales as "Armenian literature." (7)

The reason for their firmness in this matter is the fear that with such headings the literature will be treated separately, "by certain critics, white and Negro, in an alcove apart," and the "next step is a double standard of judgment, which is dangerous for the future of Negro writers" (7). They append a long comparative chronology for the "American Scene" and the "Negro World."

I think it is fair to consider these statements representative of the intellectual ferment that led to the incorporation of minorities into the American story and that strengthened the broader redefinition of the term "American."[27] The particular stories that were being told served to illuminate the human story; hence, international and interethnic understanding were stressed. What the works by many of the older culture critics and writers have in common is precisely their shared assumption that social generalizations are possible and that universal assertions are not only desirable but also the central task of any culture critic, whether the work is concerned with large cultures or small subcultures. (It was not as if "American" stood for universal and "subculture" for the particular.) Thus, Franz Boas's explicit goal in graduate instruction was "to develop a juster appreciation of foreign nations and to bring out those elements in our own civilization which are common to all mankind."[28]

The intervening years seem to have changed things considerably. What the editors of the anthologies most desired—the reading of Afro-American texts in American classrooms—has, to some extent, come about. Yet what they most dreaded has also happened. Various forms of multiple standards have become the rule in current critical practice, as has the division of American literature (in the *Columbia Literary History*, for example) into subcategories according to the authors' ethnicity or gender (often matched by their critics' characteristics). The bonds of race and sex now seem to be considered stronger than those of literary and cultural traditions, and some culture critics have set it as their goal to strengthen these bonds by attempting to show exactly what the editors of *The Negro Caravan* did not believe existed: "gemeinschafty" subcultures (this is Michael Lacey's nice adjective) understood as independent essence, not also as parts of larger wholes and dialogues. Whether in discussions about aesthetics or about reading lists, universalism is regarded as naïve, passé, or a thin camouflage of power relations. As Andrew Delbanco has noted, criticism of American culture now often has a different character from criticism of black culture.[29]

How did this extreme shift come about? How did the universalist tradition that had such integrative force rupture? Whenever the turning point was, the change had become highly visible in 1969, when *The Negro Caravan* was reprinted and Julius Lester wrote a new introduction in which he reported that the

> desire of black writers of the past to be accepted as American writers and not as black writers was a reaction against seeing their work treated by white publishers as "exotic," as something never to be considered as worthy of the same serious consideration given to white writers, particularly when those white writers were writing about blacks.

Yet he was hardly optimistic about the change:

The black writer of the 1960s does not have this particular problem, but the present emphasis on blackness and the corresponding denial of Americanness is as false as [the] denial of blackness. The black American writer must realize that his blackness has been acted upon and has reacted to forces that are peculiarly American. Thus, his black experience is different from that of the Jamaican, Brazilian, or Guinean. Indeed, there is something very American about the present romanticization of blackness. The present attitude is not one which will most easily free the black American writer spiritually to do that which only he can do—illuminate the consciousness of Man through the specifics of his own particular black experience.[30]

Lester's cosmopolitanism (in language that may seem gender-specific to later readers) is neither nostalgic nor progressive. Would not his balancing of various attributes (black, American, New World, writer, human being, and so on) be useful for cultural inquiry today? Since all generalizations are problematic, could not "particularist" studies (of nations or ethnic groups) stress comparisons and connections? And could not generalizing investigations (e.g., of modernization) resort to various particularisms to test the validity of the generalizations? Thus, studies of "the American character" would have to be both internationally comparative and able to accommodate, for example, W. E. B. Du Bois's famous remark about the American Negro's twoness; whereas particularizing studies about "the black experience" might call attention to Du Bois's uses of Exodus and Paul's letter to the Corinthians (for "veil"), Goethe's *Faust* (for "two souls"), Hegel (for "consciousness"), and Emerson (for "double-consciousness") to make a special predicament more widely intelligible—in a rhetorical fashion that other ethnic groups used, as well, as the widespread use of the "veil" metaphor illustrates.[31] One investigation American studies might undertake now is a testing of the hypothesis ventured by Albert Murray that the "mainstream is not white but mulatto,"[32] a metaphor that, because it presupposes the existence of black-white interaction in a Creole culture, may run against the kind of sentiments that also opposed "miscegenation."

Such a program is hardly what animates American studies today. Instead, what Lester refers to as "romanticization" has become the dominant tendency—applied to an ever increasing array of targets. This development seems all the more ironic since the 1960s and 1970s also witnessed the generation of extremely suggestive theories of ethnicity—by Fredrik Barth, Abner Cohen, Georges Devereux, and Herbert Gans—that have had relatively little influence on American studies.[33]

In conclusion, I offer two instances that illustrate the forces under which universalism collapsed. The first instance comes from a new validation of the category of experience (as opposed to tradition) that gained acceptance in the course of the neo-Romantic Beat Generation. What was characteristic of this loose grouping of writers, which included Jack Kerouac and Allen Ginsberg, who had a prodigal son relationship to Lionel Trilling, was a praise of spontaneity and originality. In the late 1950s, the black modernist writer LeRoi Jones (who would become Amiri Baraka in 1968) was an adherent of Kerouac's "Essentials of Spontaneous Prose" and especially liked Kerouac's position according to which only the author can fully understand and enjoy a work of art. Kerouac had drawn on Wilhelm Reich (with the suggestion that writers have to "come"), and in a contribution to *Evergreen Review* in 1959, Jones expanded this parallel between the joys of the creative and the procreative act:

> The pure ecstatic power of the creative climax can never be the reader's; even though he has traced and followed frantically the writer's steps, to that final "race to the wire of time." The *actual* experience of this "race" is experienced *only* by the writer.[34]

The key concept of "experience" is located in the "ecstatic power" of the author's "creative climax"—and it is essentially inaccessible to readers. (Even the joys of voyeurism seem excluded, and the modernist's spontaneous overflow of powerful feelings seems to take place in public solitude.)

In the mid-1960s, Jones began to apply this exclusive concept of "experience" no longer only to artists but also to blacks as a whole. In a panel titled "Jazz and Revolutionary Nationalism" held in 1965 and transcribed in *Jazz* magazine in November 1966, he asserted that in America a white listener could never understand the music of Archie Shepp, Ornette Coleman, or Albert Ayler. Jones tellingly described the difference between white listener and black musician as "the difference between a man watching someone have an orgasm and someone having an orgasm."[35] The sexual metaphor, once used to separate any artist's experience from that of any audience, reappears to separate the black experience (now shared by black performers and black audience) from that of white audiences. The universal aspects of the differentiation between artists and audiences were substituted by an ethnic scenario that separates blacks and whites in art, love, life, and even in death. (The deaths of the white civil rights workers Michael Schwerner and Andrew Goodman for a brief time could appear to Jones as essentially different from that of their fellow freedom fighter James Chaney.)

The writer's attack on universalism from the point of view of an eth-no-artistic community was paralleled by a critic's counterpart. Richard Gilman's famous review of Eldridge Cleaver's *Soul on Ice* (1968) reported a supposedly new tradition—even a "genre"—of black writing that start-ed with *The Autobiography of Malcolm X*:

> That universality is not among the incentives and preoccupations of this writing is something that makes for its particular, if some-times provisional strength. . . . [*The Autobiography*'s] way of look-ing at the world, its formulation of experience is not the potential possession—even by imaginative appropriation—of us all; hard, local, intransigent, alien, it remains in some sense unassimilable for those of us who aren't black.[36]

All the key words of the 1980s are present: unassimilable otherness, another place entirely—yet it is a rhetoric that also constitutes a strong "we" out of "those of us who aren't black" and who, by the way, silent-ly claim the autobiographical tradition as somehow "white." (Harriet Beecher Stowe was still very aware that Saint Augustine was an African.) Malcolm and Cleaver may have been shaped by the "white" Western tradition, but they are not contributing to it, Gilman argues. He arrives at a chilling definition of difference, in conscious contradistinction to Shakespeare's universalism (in the play that can no longer be taught in the public schools of New York City):

> The Negro doesn't feel the way whites do, nor does he think like whites—at the point, that is, when feelings and thought have moved beyond pure physical sensation or problems in mathemat-ics. "Prick me and I bleed," Shylock rightly said, but the differ-ence begins when the attitude to the blood is in question: Negro

suffering is not of the same kind as ours. Under the great flawless arc of the Greco-Roman and Judeo-Christian traditions we have implicitly believed that all men experience essentially the same things, that birth, love, pain, self, death are universals; they are in fact what we mean by universal values in literature and consciousness. But the Negro has found it almost impossible in America to experience the universal as such. [37] (25)

From such insights Gilman draws the conclusion that he will give up the habit of the judge-critic when he reads this new genre of black literature:

I don't wish to continue in this strange and very contemporary form of injustice, that of sanctioning Negro thought from the standpoint of white criteria. I will go on judging and elucidating novels and plays and poetry by Negroes according to what general powers I possess, but the kind of *Negro writing* I have been talking about, the act of creation of the self in the face of that self's historic denial by our society, seems to me to be at this point beyond my right to intrude on. (30)

Gilman's relativist withdrawal deserves to be compared with Boas's ability to sustain—as Richard Handler has shown—his belief in science, "despite the fact that the scientific study of other cultures made possible a newly critical awareness of the biases inherent in even the scientist's perspective."[38] In Gilman's response to critics of the original article, he called for a "moratorium on the public act of judgment."[39] It was his way to deal with the threat he sensed in this literature "to our historical belief in the universality of ideas and values" (27). Gilman concludes:

To look at each other now in this country, black and white, across a gulf of separate speeches, gestures, intentions, hopes, is more *reasonable* than to go on insisting that Negroes or any other group [*sic*] have got to be enrolled under the ancient Western humanist flags, so that progress can be guaranteed and chaos averted. (27–28)

Gilman's call for a discontinuation of the act of interethnic judgment in certain matters has been widely debated and criticized. As Randall

Kennedy noted, Gilman reviews and judges anyway.[40] Gilman calls the
Malcolm-Cleaver style of repudiation "clumsy, painful and confused"
and hovers on a passage by Cleaver he finds beautiful and impressive; his
argument thus has a rhetorical quality.

Yet no matter what arguments can be made against them, the challenges to universalism represented here very selectively by one writer's
and one critic's stance took hold like Turner's frontier thesis once did,
and the academic climate in the United States has changed. "Negroes or
any other group" (as Gilman puts it) can now be placed outside universal
categories (which, thereby, are depleted of any meaning), and it is in this
world of difference that cultural criticism is operating. The United States
has been described (inspired by Hegel and Tocqueville) as a nation whose
citizens prefer migration to revolution. What we may be witnessing is
the intellectual migration from "American culture" to various alternative
cultures and subcultures—which, however, may not be "other places
entirely" but may turn out to look very much like the old shells that were
left behind. Exceptionalist studies of the American character have gone
out of fashion, yet their format may well be resurrected in areas such as
ethnic studies. In surveying recent American scholarship, H. C. Porter
finds the Indian described now as peaceable, merciful, uncomplicated,
egalitarian, and kind to animals. "Indeed," Porter concludes whimsical-
ly, "the Indian seems to have most of the virtues of small-town Middle
America, as portrayed in the Andy Hardy films."[41] Some pieties simply
may have migrated from "Americans" to "ethnics."

We may feel happier in this new world of difference. But, on one
hand, what if our students had to discover anew that if they accept the
challenge against generalizations, then mules and mares are hardly very
safe terms in Foucault's Chinese animal classification? And on the other
hand, if students continue to make generalizations, may they not also
speak of mules, mares, and even stallions as quadrupeds?

Figure 9.1. Carl Van Vechten, *W. E. B. Du Bois*, 1946. (Photo by Carl Van Vechten. Used with permission of the Van Vechten Trust, Beinecke Library, Yale University.)

CHAPTER 9

The Autobiography of
W. E. B. Du Bois

September 25, 1959: The FBI observes as a "security matter" that W. E. B. Du Bois has received $25,000 as part of the International Lenin Peace Prize Award.

WHAT AN INTERESTING, long life W. E. B. Du Bois lived, spanning nearly a century. Born in the year 1868, when Wagner's opera *Die Meistersinger von Nürnberg* was first performed, Du Bois was an exact contemporary of Maxim Gorky, was a year older than Mahatma Gandhi, and was two years older than Lenin and Rosa Luxemburg—and he outlived them all. In the year in which Du Bois died, 1963, Samuel Beckett's *Play* was shown, an American astronaut orbited Earth (five years after the launching of the Soviet Sputnik hastened the space race), the Polaroid camera was invented, computers were being perfected, and Elvis Presley was already a few years past his first wave of popularity. Du Bois lived from the first decade after Charles Darwin published *The Origin of Species* to the space age, with his middle years during World War I and the Russian Revolution. "I have lived a good and full life," he writes near the end of *The Autobiography of W. E. B. Du Bois: A Soliloquy*

SOURCE: Werner Sollors, "Introduction," in *The Autobiography of W. E. B. Du Bois: A Soliloquy on Viewing My Life from the Last Decade of Its First Century,* by W. E. B. Du Bois (New York: Oxford University Press, 2007), xxiii–xxx. Copyright © 2007 by Werner Sollors.

on Viewing My Life from the Last Decade of Its First Century (first published posthumously in 1968). In his youth, he continues, "we talked of flying as impossible and joked at man's attempts. Yet I read of the first successful flights; and myself in 1921 flew from Paris to London. I have flown tens of thousands of miles since, over land and sea." He finds that "the most startling miracle" of his time was Sputnik, a "triumph of Reason."[1]

Impressive, too, were the changes in race relations that took place during Du Bois's lifetime. An African American from a free colored family, Du Bois was born just a few years after the end of slavery and a generation before the peak of imperialist colonialism in Africa; he died six years after Ghana's independence and just a day before the March on Washington that brought the American Civil Rights Movement to a high degree of visibility. In *The Autobiography*, Du Bois twice mentions the "unexpected and extraordinary success" that Arthur Spingarn's and Thurgood Marshall's legal work achieved "in a series of court decisions which culminated in the decision of the Supreme Court in 1954, outlawing race segregation in the schools and other public facilities" (333). This was "unexpected" because Du Bois "assumed that legal discrimination along the color line would last much longer than it may" (392). Yet he also remembers that in his high school years, boys did not pair about with girls, whereas by the 1950s high schools had become "social centers and even matrimonial agencies, particularly in the South." In this changed "concept of the high school" Du Bois also sensed a source of "the fanatical resistance to desegregation as at Little Rock" (94).

During Du Bois's lifetime the world changed very dramatically, and he found many occasions to reflect on his life in its historical setting, including two earlier autobiographical works, *Darkwater* (1920) and *Dusk of Dawn* (1940). His posthumously published *Autobiography* specifically does not claim "final and complete authority," for autobiographies "are always incomplete, and often unreliable." What he offers to the reader instead is "the Soliloquy of an old man on what he dreams his life has been as he sees it slowly drifting away; and what he would like others to believe" (13). In thinking, or dreaming, about what his life has been, Du Bois develops four major narrative strands that are intertwined and at times also augmented with materials incorporated from his earlier books, going back all the way to *The Souls of Black Folk* (1903), as well as from other sources and documents.

Personal Life

First, and perhaps most interesting, there are completely new personal revelations in *The Autobiography*, written with the candor of an old man. Du Bois not only reviews his childhood years in Great Barrington, Massachusetts, and reflects more fully than ever on the figure of his grandfather and on his own years at Fisk, Harvard, Berlin, and the University of Pennsylvania, but he also offers startling comments about his sexual initiation and his general views of sexuality. Some of these recollections Du Bois also recorded on tape at the time that he was writing *The Autobiography*.

"My Birth and My Family" starts as if to illustrate the dreamlike quality with which he recalls his childhood, but then couples the dream with an all-important historical fact. "I was born by a golden river and in the shadow of two great hills," he begins lyrically, but continues, "five years after the Emancipation Proclamation, which began the freeing of American Negro slaves" (61). He also explains later that his Housatonic River "was 'golden' because of the waste which the paper and woolen mills poured into it" (83). He mentions being afraid of the Irish children who called him by racial slurs and attacked him, and he remembers becoming conscious of "the pressure of the 'veil of color'; in little matters at first and then in larger" (83), but he makes no mention of the episode of having his calling card refused by a girl, a newcomer, the episode that led to the most famous "double consciousness" passage in *The Souls of Black Folk*.[2] The story of his grandfather Alexander Du Bois becomes particularly vivid, and the reader learns more details about Du Bois's own childhood; his controversial commencement speech at Harvard; his professors; his bold letter to Rutherford B. Hayes, after which he received the fellowship to study in Berlin; and his relationship there with his landlord's daughter Dora Marbach ("We confessed our love for each other" [161]).

The chapter entitled "My Character" is especially revealing and permits a fuller understanding of Du Bois, somewhat beyond the cliché of his being an extraordinarily restrained "Victorian." Yes, there is confirmation that he may be an old-fashioned gentleman who retained "an interest in what men are rather than what they do," who could only twice in his life induce himself to gamble, was uninterested in whiskey drinking in saloons, and "could never get wildly enthusiastic even over baseball" (283).

Yet without shyness he explicitly blames his New England schooling for his "inexcusable ignorance of sex" at the time that he "went South to Fisk at 17" (279). "I actually did not know the physical difference between men and women," he writes, and this ignorance not only made him the subject of ridicule by his peers but also turned "one of the most beautiful of earth's experiences into a thing of temptation and horror." As a result, he "fought and feared what should have been a climax of true living" (280).

One hardly believes one's eyes reading what the supposedly staid Du Bois writes about being "literally raped by the unhappy wife who was [his] landlord" in rural eastern Tennessee, about "a brief trial with prostitution" in Paris, about cohabitation with a Berlin shopgirl, and finally about being "literally frightened into marriage" (280). He comments about his marriage of fifty-three years to Nina Gomer that her "life-long training as a virgin, made it almost impossible for her ever to regard sexual intercourse as not fundamentally indecent" (281). Even though he always had more friends among women than among men, he clearly wished to have had an earlier education about sex, a less troubled attitude toward marital sexual intercourse, and a greater tolerance toward homosexuals—of whose existence he had "no conception" before an incident that he relates (282). These are sides of Du Bois's character that he rarely revealed elsewhere.

Work Life

Du Bois's lofty goals, but also his travails, obstacles, and petty fights about the details of his organizational work for the Civil Rights Movement and especially for the National Association for the Advancement of Colored People (NAACP), as well as his academic and editorial work for various universities and for *The Crisis*, *Phylon*, and his *Encyclopedia Africana* project, become clearer in the second strand of his narrative, even though he says little about his own major works, from *The Suppression of the African Slave Trade* (1896) to *Black Reconstruction* (1935); his novels; or his fascinating five-month trip to Nazi Germany in 1936. These sections present such information as an account of Du Bois's appeal to the United Nations

Commission on Human Rights in 1946–1947 and offer candid views of his contemporaries while also illustrating his lifelong commitment to searching for appropriate academic and political tools for the fight against race hatred and inequality.

The reader learns that NAACP Secretary Walter White, with whom Du Bois had to work when editing *The Crisis*, "was absolutely self-centered and egotistical to the point that he was almost unconscious of it. He seemed really to believe that his personal interests and the interest of his race and organization were identical" (293). According to Du Bois, Oswald Villard, a member of the NAACP's board of directors, was married to a racist wife from Georgia, so that Du Bois "could never set foot in his house as a guest, nor could any other of his colored associates" (256). *The Autobiography* is a rich source for understanding the institutional and personal contexts in which Du Bois worked in Philadelphia and Atlanta, at the beginnings of the Niagara Movement, in the NAACP, and in his Pan-Africanist engagements. As Du Bois's biographer David Levering Lewis has stressed, Du Bois's answer to the race problem remained that "knowledge based on scientific investigation" (197) could cure it—and Du Bois's faith in science is articulated throughout *The Autobiography*.[3]

Communism

Irving Howe liked the sections on Du Bois's childhood and youth, as well as those about his academic and civil rights career, deeming these parts "a classic of American narrative: composed in a lovely if old-fashioned formal prose, rich in portraiture of late nineteenth-century New England, and packed with information and opinion about the early years of Negro protest." Howe expressed disappointment, however, in the account of the "less than glorious" years of Du Bois as a communist, and he found that those parts in *The Autobiography* "read as if they came from the very heart of a mimeograph machine."[4]

Indeed, Du Bois has a dramatically different voice in the third narrative strand, those sections that express his view of the world since he began to admire, and in 1961 joined, the Communist Party. Here Du Bois speaks at times with party-line certainty and makes large global pronouncements, some of which sounded painful to non-Stalinist read-

ers and reviewers when the book was first published and sound almost
unbelievable now, decades after the end of Soviet communism, as strange
as propagandistic socialist realist paintings for which there is now a new
vogue. Fittingly, Du Bois mentions that "Lawrence Bradshaw, sculptor
of the great head of Karl Marx, did my head" (409).

Not only does Du Bois condemn the Marshall Plan; praise East
Germany for "developing the faith of Karl Liebknecht and Rosa Luxemburg and becoming a socialist state, after the pattern of the Soviet
Union" (23); and suggest that in Soviet-dominated Poland, Hungary,
and Czechoslovakia the communist governments had the support of the
"overwhelming mass of their inhabitants" (28). He also refuses to "judge
Russia in the matter of war and murder" (290) and even praises the Red
Army for refusing to take part in the Warsaw uprising against the Nazis
("a premature attack") and for stopping the Hungarian "anti-commu-
nist revolt [that] led to the effort to overthrow communism" in 1956
(28). Du Bois clearly saw the Soviet Union as the strongest opponent
to color prejudice and the strongest guarantor of world peace, and he
believed that communist China—not Taiwan or Hong Kong—was on
the road to the future.

Howe deemed Du Bois's communist commitment "soiled both
morally and intellectually."[5] Richard Kostelanetz found such passages
"faintly embarrassing" in an autobiography that originally appeared
in a publishing house—International Publishers—that advertised such
other works as Karl Marx and Friedrich Engels's *German Ideology* and
a book entitled *Unbroken Record: Soviet Treaty Compliance.*[6] Hugh Davis
Graham saw in these chapters "a mindless apology to Stalinism" that
was "unworthy" of Du Bois.[7] Truman Nelson went further, asserting
that these narrative parts with which the book begins so prominently
must have been inserted into the text by its editor, Herbert Aptheker.
Nelson claimed to have received a carbon copy of the typescript of
The Autobiography from Du Bois's widow, Shirley Graham Du Bois, in
1965; according to Nelson, the typescript begins with what is chapter
6 in the version that was published in 1968; and the first five chapters
and the italicized interlude on "communism" are, in fact, more or less
exclusively devoted to Du Bois's communist worldview.[8] It would be
interesting to compare the Nelson manuscript with the published version of the book.

Yet the communist voice is not limited to the first five chapters, to the first sixty pages, but is audible throughout the narrative. Reviewing his well-known dispute with Booker T. Washington ("not an easy person to know" [243]), Du Bois writes, "Neither I nor Booker Washington understood the nature of capitalistic exploitation of labor, and the necessity of a direct attack on the principle of exploitation as the beginning of labor uplift" (236). In somewhat anachronistic retrospect, he finds his ambitious pre–World War I Atlanta University program for the interdisciplinary study of African Americans "weak on the economic side," because "it did not stress enough the philosophy of Marx and Engels and was of course far too soon for Lenin" (217). And in the chapter "The Depression," he offers self-critical assessments of having "blamed the Communists when I thought their agitation made the ignorant Scottsboro boys suffer for the sins of others, and failed to give those same Communists credit for making the Scottsboro case known to the civilized world" (306). As William E. Cain put it, *The Autobiography* "places exacting political pressure on its readers, who face a potent array of pro-Soviet claims."[9]

Views of an Old Man

The last note that Du Bois strikes—and it is apparent especially in the postlude—is that of a self-consciously old and mature-sounding man vis-à-vis America at the time of the culture of consumption of the 1950s and the growing youth culture of the 1960s. Gilbert Osofsky found in *The Autobiography* "not the least hint of crabbiness or senility," but Du Bois is quite sarcastic in his comments on post–World War II America.[10] "The highest ambition of an American boy today is to be a millionaire," he writes. "The highest ambition of an American girl is to be a movie star" (416). Most characteristic of his America was "the attempt to reduce life to buying and selling" (418). For Du Bois, America was in the hands of men such as John Foster Dulles, "fools who rule us and are today running wild in order to shoot a football into the sky where Sputnik rolls in peace around the earth" (415).

Nobody would have expected Du Bois to be an Elvis Presley fan, but it is still surprising that he comments at all on the Elvis cult, seeing it more or less as part of the decline of America: "When Elvis Presley goes through the motions of copulation on the public stage it takes the city police to hold back teen-age children from hysteria" (416). And facing the youth cult of the 1960s more generally, he comments tartly, "Youth is more courageous than age because it knows less. Age is wiser than youth because it knows more" (414).

Assessment

Is *The Autobiography* a hodgepodge, then? Is it "largely an anthology of previous self-portraits" and "a flawed and disappointing book in certain ways," as some have viewed it?[11] Certainly, far more critics have written about *The Souls of Black Folk* than have dared to face *The Autobiography*.[12] Yet perhaps *The Autobiography*, despite the four major voices in which it was written, is not as disjointed as it may seem at first, for what may hold these strands together is Du Bois's lifelong wish for some form of public *recognition*, individual and collective—the sort of recognition that Du Bois experienced vicariously through Goethe, for whom he had an abiding love and whom he quotes, mentions, or alludes to repeatedly in *The Autobiography*, even though "Goethe" does not appear in Aptheker's index to the book.

When he writes how he viewed his "program of life" at Fisk, Du Bois recites Goethe's famous last words, "mehr Licht!": "In essence I combined a social program for a depressed group with the natural demand of youth for Light, more light" (123). At Atlanta University, "amid a wide desert of caste and proscription, amid the heart-hunting slights and jars and vagaries of a deep race-dislike," he finds that "men may lie and listen and learn of a future fuller than the past, and hear the voice of Time," which turns out to be Goethe's voice from *Faust:*

Entbehren sollst du, sollst entbehren.

Thou shalt forego, shalt do without. (212)

This passage was part of Faust's complaint to Mephistopheles that this is the eternal song he hears that makes life so tiresome and unfulfilling. It reappears in a dramatic speech Du Bois incorporates here that his second wife, Shirley Graham Du Bois, delivered for him in Accra, Ghana, warning people around the world, and especially people of color and racial minority populations, that the West

> offers to let some of your smarter and less scrupulous leaders become fellow capitalists with the white exploiters, if in turn they induce the nation's masses to pay the awful cost. This has happened in the West Indies and in South America. This may yet happen in the Middle East and Eastern Asia. Strive against it, with every fibre of your bodies and souls. A body of local private capitalists, even if they are black can never free Africa; they will simply sell it into new slavery to old masters overseas. (403)

This, Du Bois adds, turning to Goethe, "is a call for sacrifice. Great Goethe sang, 'Entbehren sollst du, sollst entbehren'—'Thou shalt forego, shalt do without'" (404). What is so moving about Du Bois is that he articulated such exhortations to the Third World in terms of his Western, and particularly German, cultural repertoire, which also made him a perhaps unusual Pan-Africanist admirer of Wagner and Beethoven.

On his way back from Europe to Wilberforce in 1896, Du Bois wrote a letter to a friend, which he quotes in *The Autobiography*: "I must step, walk, stumble and climb now: for the *Lehrjahre* [learning years] were passed—I fancied—and the *Meisterjahre* [adult years] begun" (184). Alluding to Goethe's Wilhelm Meister again, Du Bois writes, "Of greatest importance was the opportunity which my *Wanderjahre* in Europe gave of looking at the world as a man and not simply from a narrow racial and provincial outlook" (159). Perhaps Du Bois hoped for a Wilhelm Meister–like ending to his own bildungsroman—an ending in which the searching, learning, and wandering apprentice-protagonist ultimately becomes "master" and part of the Society of the Tower that had secretly watched over him.[13]

Du Bois's experience was full of disappointments in this regard. Throughout his life exposed to acts of racial discrimination, he found his academic hopes repeatedly dashed. Proposing a broad program in the study of the Negro to Harvard, Columbia, and the University of Pennsylvania in 1899, he found that "they paid not the slightest attention to this challenge" (199). About his Atlanta conferences he writes that "as far as the American world of science and letters was concerned, we never 'belonged'; we remained unrecognized in learned societies and academic groups. We rated merely as Negroes studying Negroes, and after all, what had Negroes to do with America or science?" (228).

More than half a century after graduating from Harvard, Du Bois could not join a white college friend at the Harvard Club; he kept having to worry about being able to meet white people as an equal; and at eighty-two he received not public acknowledgment and admission to a benevolent Society of the Tower, but a criminal indictment as a "foreign agent," an outgrowth of Cold War McCarthyist political paranoia. The seemingly endless documents of Federal Bureau of Investigation and U.S. State Department surveillance of the old scholar-activist only show that Du Bois's wish for a publicly recognized status in America was cruelly mocked by government agencies that put him on a frequently updated "Security Index card"; monitored his travels, speeches, and correspondence; withheld his passport; made "pretext telephone calls" to his residence; interviewed his neighbors; and kept voluminous news clippings about their subject under file number 100-99729.

For the old Du Bois—he started writing *The Autobiography* when he turned ninety in 1958—it must have been the ultimate irony to find that having "lived to an age of life which is increasingly distasteful to this nation" (414) provided yet a new ground—old age—on which recognition could be withheld from America's "most conspicuously educated Negro." As much as he may have desired it, his life in America was not a Wilhelm Meister–like bildungsroman.

Having moved from innocence to experience and from ignorant naïveté to educated maturity, the aged Du Bois was still deprived of public recognition in his homeland. Thus, he soliloquizes at the end of his life, reveals private aspects of his character, reviews his career as a civil rights activist, and takes on an old man's voice of wisdom. However, he also proudly mentions some of the many honors and appreciations that he received abroad, especially in the communist countries and the Third World. He was awarded the Lenin Prize (which carried quite a fortune of $25,000, as the government surveillance documents keep pointing out) and honorary doctorates, of economics at Humboldt University in East Berlin, of the science of history at Charles University in Prague, and of historical science at Lomonosov University in Moscow. He met with figures of the greatest historical importance, such as Mao Tse-tung and Nikita Khrushchev. And finally, he received Kwame Nkrumah's invitation, which he accepted, to move to postcolonial, independent Ghana, where Du Bois worked on his *Encyclopedia* project until his death in 1963.

Figure 10.1. Roger Pic, *Funnyhouse of a Negro*. Production at Théâtre de France starring Toto Bissainthe, 1968. (From Geneviève Fabre, *Le théâtre noir aux Etats-Unis* [Paris: Editions du Centre National de la Recherche Scientifique, 1982].)

CHAPTER 10

Owls and Rats in
the American Funnyhouse

Adrienne Kennedy's Drama

January 14, 1964: Funnyhouse of a Negro *opens at the East End Theatre and wins the Obie award.*

O-PRODUCED BY EDWARD ALBEE at the East End Theatre in New York City on January 14, 1964, Adrienne Kennedy's *Funnyhouse of a Negro* won the prestigious Obie Award given out annually by the *Village Voice* for the best off–Broadway plays. Kennedy has lived up to the promise of that prize and continued to create an impressive body of one-act plays and other works. *The Owl Answers* was produced in 1965, and *A Beast Story*, a year later. This was followed by *A Rat's Mass* (first presented in 1966 at the New American Theater in Rome), *A Lesson in Dead Language* (1966), *Sun* (commissioned by the Royal Court Theatre, London, 1968), *An Evening with Dead Essex* (1974), *A Movie Star Has to Star in Black and White* (first performed at the New York Shakespeare Festival in 1976), *Lancashire Lad* (1980), *Black Children's Day* (1980), *Robert* (1983), and *A Diary of Lights* (1987). Kennedy also did adaptations of John Lennon's *In His Own Write* (*W*, 1967); of Euripides's *Electra and Orestes* (*E*, 1980), as well as of *Iph'egenea* (1983); and of Flaubert's *Madame Bova-*

SOURCE: Extract from Werner Sollors, "Owls and Rats in the American Funnyhouse: Adrienne Kennedy's Drama," *American Literature* 63, no. 3 (September 1991): 507–532. Copyright © 1991 by Duke University Press. Republished by permission of the publisher.

ry. Some of her plays were collected under the title *In One Act* (1988). Among her more recent plays are *The Film Club* (1992), *She Talks to Beethoven* (1991), and *The Ohio State Murders* (1998). After publishing *People Who Led to My Plays* (1987), unusually stylized and regarded by Ishmael Reed as a "new form of black autobiography," which sheds much light on the influences on her hermetic writings, she continued prose experimentation with *Deadly Triplets: A Theatre Mystery and Journal* (1990).[1]

Half a century after *Funnyhouse*, Kennedy's oeuvre still awaits recognition as a full-fledged modern American attempt at rewriting family tragedy. Her most important plays explore the tragic condition of daughter, mother, father, sibling, and lover in the web of American race and kin relations.

Funnyhouse of a Negro

In her first produced and published play, *Funnyhouse of a Negro*, Kennedy pursues her themes with a haunting intensity that gives the play a probing and ritualistic quality. The mysteriously divided and related characters repeat sentence sequences in such a way that a structural pattern emerges that seems more precisely definable than the enigmatically ambiguous action, the dreamlike funnyhouse set, or the intense imagery. Eight names appear in the dramatis personae (*F*, 252; *I*, 1), yet four of them are described as "one of herselves": the Duchess of Hapsburg, Queen Victoria, Patrice Lumumba, and Jesus are aspects of Sarah, who is defined as "Negro." The central character, who was partly inspired by a sixteen-year-old neighbor in her mother's hometown of Montezuma, Georgia, Sarah Clara (*P*, 35), is thus in the majority on-stage. The Mother, Landlady (the Funnylady), and Raymond (the Funnyman) together have only a small number of lines compared with those given to Sarah and "Herselves." The list of characters thus suggests that *Funnyhouse of a Negro* is a drama of a divided self.[2]

In the play Kennedy has taken the contemplation of "Sarah" to the breaking point at which the central character splits into several antagonistic aspects that collide dramatically. Such a dramatic strategy is especially suited to shed light on a social world in which human beings belong to more than one community. Kennedy focuses on the moment in which different modes of identifying are in sharp, deadly conflict. She portrays her central character not as unified or whole but as a collage of multifaceted and contradictory selves (who are not only black and white or male and female but also father's daughter and mother's daughter, ruler and martyr, stoic and revolutionary, dead and alive, carnal and spiritual, young and old, hairy and bald, glamorous and humble, and proper and lascivious). The antithesis between Victoria and Lumumba may thus be seen as that between empire and anticolonialism; Jesus and the Duchess of Hapsburg may relate to each other as love and lust; the Duchess and Victoria may represent the conflict between a scandalous and a proper woman; Lumumba and Jesus may embody militancy and forgiveness. Sarah, however, is all of these masks, and each of the selves is a person in the original sense of the word "persona," mask. Rosemary Curb emphasized that Sarah's selves "are not the historical persons whose names they carry and whose costumes they wear, but fragments of Sarah's mind, so real as to seem separate persons."[3]

Yet why did Kennedy specifically choose as Sarah's personae the Duchess of Hapsburg, Queen Victoria, Lumumba, and Jesus? In *People Who Led to My Plays*, the author elucidates some associations from which these figures emerged. "Jesus" seems to evoke for Kennedy, apart from the memories of a Christmas pageant (*P*, 11) and an Easter sermon (*P*, 21), the image of a child-loving savior on gilt-edged Sunday school cards (*P*, 11; *B*, 191) that later merged with her impression of Giotto's fresco of the marriage of Joseph and Mary (*P*, 34). This connection comes to the foreground in the vignette *"Jesus and my parents' marriage,"* when the news of the separation of Kennedy's parents makes her create a different savior figure: a "punishing Jesus; berserk, evil, sinister" (*P*, 123).

While the figure of Jesus is thus linked with the images of the marriages of Kennedy's parents' and of Mary, Patrice Lumumba, the first prime minister of the independent Congo who was assassinated in 1961 while Kennedy was staying in Ghana, is connected with her father, her African patrimony, and her quest for a black hero: "Just when I had discovered the place of my ancestors, just when I had discovered this African hero, he had been murdered. . . . Even though I had known of him so briefly, I felt I had been struck a blow. . . . I remembered my father's fine stirring speeches on the Negro cause . . . and Du Bois' articles in *The Crisis* which my father had quoted. . . . There was no doubt that Lumumba, this murdered hero, was merged in my mind with my father" (*P*, 119–120).

As Lumumba represents the quest for African origins, Kennedy's Queen Victoria stands for the culmination of a long-lasting interest in

English descent. When her mother said that "most of the white people of Montezuma's families came from England," Kennedy says, "I realized dimly that this meant some of our ancestors too had come from England, since, like most 'Negro' families in the town, we had white relations as well as 'Negro.' I became very interested in 'England'" (*P*, 22). This interest became active during a stay in London: "The statue we saw of Victoria in front of Buckingham Palace was the single most dramatic, startling statue I'd seen. Here was a woman who had dominated an age. In my play I would soon have the heroine, Sarah, talk to a replica of this statue. . . . The *statue* would reveal my character's secrets to herself" (*P*, 118).[4]

In the stage directions of *Funnyhouse of a Negro*, the plaster cast is described as "a sitting figure, one of astonishing repulsive whiteness, possessing the quality of nightmares and terror" (*F*, 271; slightly altered in *I*, 11). The queen, an image of white arrogance, also evokes a myth of royal origins that is extended to Africa when Kennedy sees the Liberian presidential palace and observes Ethiopian princesses in a hotel: "Royalty was not only Queen Victoria, or even Antigone. Perhaps I myself and my heroines were descended from royal African blood" (*P* galleys, 103).

Finally, the Duchess of Hapsburg was the beautiful sister of the Belgian King Leopold II, Carlotta Maria Amelia, better known as the wife of Maximilian, the well-intentioned but ill-fated Hapsburgian Emperor of Mexico. Carlotta turned insane when the Mexican enterprise failed and her husband was executed upon Benito Juarez's victory. Her part was played by Bette Davis in William Dieterle's film *Juarez* (1939), which was based on Franz Werfel's antiexpressionistic "dramatic history" *Juarez und Maximilian* (1927), as well as on Bertita Harding's *The Phantom Crown* (1934). *Juarez*, with a screenplay co-written by John Huston, develops a persistent bird imagery centering on the song "La Paloma," which Carlotta translates for her husband, culminating in the scene in which the volley by which Maximilian is executed stirs up a dove that seems to cross the ocean and reach Carlotta spiritually in her chamber in Europe (an image that evokes the Annunciation). In *Juarez*, Carlotta reminds Max that they are at the site "of the very halls of Montezuma," a remark that must have carried special meaning for Kennedy, whose father's and mother's family roots were in the Georgia town Montezuma. *Juarez* impressed Kennedy so deeply that she visited Chapultepec Castle in Mexico, the seat of the last Hapsburgs in America: "I bought many postcards of the palace and the Duchess of Hapsburg and saved them.

One day the Duchess of Hapsburg would become one of my characters' most sympathetic alter egos or selves. . . . European royalty in an alien landscape. Soon my Duchess of Hapsburg would exist in an alien persona, that of the character of the Negro writer" (*P*, 96–97).

The choice of Sarah's four diverse personae carries quite a particular associative baggage. Yet the aesthetic strategy of changing identities that Kennedy first admired in the horror film *The Wolf Man* (*P*, 16–17) subverts any attempt to interpret the selves as fixed symbols. It is difficult to say that "Queen Victoria" always stands for "X" and Lumumba for "Y" in the play. Kennedy does not choose to differentiate characters who consistently represent the diverse qualities of the Duchess of Hapsburg, Queen Victoria, Patrice Lumumba, or Jesus in Sarah. What unites the masks is a shared concern for lineage (holy, familistic, or aristocratic) against the contradictory images that they also represent. Whether they face a complicated heritage or a tragic destiny, whether they are powerful or insane, Kennedy's figures refer to a descendant's confrontation with a family legacy that is highly contradictory and embodies deep antagonisms.

While the divided selves seem separate in some of the stage directions, their unity becomes apparent in the monologues and dialogues of the play. From the very beginning, the selves speak repetitions and variations of identical lines, at times in unison. The effect is that of a rhythmical incantation and is evocative of Gertrude Stein's experiments with word repetitions. The sentences are spoken at times as if in dialogue, and at other times as if the selves had the same first person singular. The section in which all four selves speak at once (about the father) is representative:

> He never tires of the journey, he who is the darkest one, the darkest of them all. My mother looked like a white woman, hair as straight as any white woman's. I am yellow but he is black, the darkest one of us all. How I hoped he was dead, yet he never tired of the journey. It was because of him that my mother died because she let a black man put his hands on her. Why does he keep returning? He keeps returning forever, keeps returning and returning and he is my father. He is a black Negro. They told me my father was God but my father is black. He is my father. I am tied to a black Negro. He returned when I lived in the south back in the twenties, when I was a child, he returned. Before I

was born at the turn of the century, he haunted my conception, diseased my birth . . . killed my mother. He killed the light. My mother was the lightest one. I am bound to him unless, of course, he should die.

But he is dead.

And he keeps returning. Then he is not dead.

Then he is not dead.

Yes, he is dead, but dead he comes knocking at my door. (*F*, 270; *I*, 20–21)

In an ironic allusion to the queen's famous question in *Snow White* (see *P*, 20–21, 24)—"Who's the fairest of them all?"—this "returning father" passage illustrates the tormented self-examination of a character who has internalized a negative black image associated with the father and idealized a contrastive white mother symbol. She cannot recognize herself as "Negro" and blames her father for "returning" in her as blackness.

The stage directions suggest that the four selves' speeches are "mixed and repeated by one another," and that this section is "repeated several times." At this point the sentences about the "returning father" are already familiar: they have previously been spoken, or varied on, in the opening "dialogue" between Victoria and the Duchess (*F*, 254; *I*, 3–4), the description by the Funnylady (*F*, 259; *I*, 9), the "conversation" between Funnyman and the Duchess (*F*, 260–262; *I*, 9–11), and the Duchess's and Jesus's incantation in unison (*F*, 267; *I*, 17). Kennedy consciously applied the principle of poetic repetition, which she learned from Edgar Allan Poe (*P*, 117–118).

The chorus-like form also echoes Greek tragedy, with which Kennedy feels a special affinity (*P*, 88, 108), as did Countée Cullen when he wrote a new version of Euripides's *Medea* in 1934 and Wole Soyinka, who published his *Bacchae* in 1973. *Funnyhouse of a Negro*, by the author who also adapted *Electra and Orestes*, may be considered a modern revisiting of Greek family tragedy. The masks with their "great dark eyes that seem gouged out of the head" (*F*, 253; *I*, 3) evoke Oedipus, and the dominant issues are the "recognition of myself" (*F*, 257; *I*, 6)—or, paradoxically, the "recognition against myself" (*F*, 263; *I*, 13)—the "identity" of Sarah and herselves, and the answer to the question "Who am I?" that many sentences in the play address. The tragic conflict between race and kin relations in America has previously been dramatized by such writers as

Paul Green (whose *White Dresses* may be echoed in Kennedy's costumes) and Langston Hughes (whose *Mulatto* might be regarded as a son's drama in the same way that *Funnyhouse* is a daughter's play). Kennedy has transformed the conflict from a social confrontation between characters into a traumatic psychological drama within a self, and her modern structuring of family tragedy does not lead to one unambiguous plot.[5]

The action, rendered unsummarizable by different versions that are left in suspension, reaches a climax when Sarah is seen having hanged herself at the end. But did she kill her father when Lumumba died? Did he kill himself? Is he dead at all? Or will he always return, although dead? These questions cannot be answered on the basis of the play's text, which lets the Negro/daughter and Lumumba/father become partly identical while allowing another wide range of speculations about an equally identical mother. For example, when the dark faceless man appears (*F*, 262; *I*, 11), the audience expects him to be the father who has been said to be knocking, but he identifies himself as Lumumba and then speaks the daughter's lines. Familial relations are sustained in name but obscured in fact.

Unstable characters and ambiguous action are supported by a "dream setting" (*P*, 108) that is constantly transforming itself. The play takes place in several spaces, which are both real and unreal. Sarah says, "These are the places I exist in. I know no places. That is I cannot believe in places. To believe in places is to know hope and to know the emotion of hope is to know beauty. It links us across a horizon and connects us to the world. I find there are no places, only my funnyhouse" (*F*, 257; *I*, 7). The various sets form a house of mirrors, the funnyhouse of the title, that, according to Kennedy, was inspired by a Cleveland "amusement park attraction whose gates are flanked by two enormous grimacing figures—a metaphor for America 'where real places don't exist, only bizarre houses'" and where one can feel the "white world . . . ridiculing the Negro."[6] Kennedy may also have thought of the famous ending of Orson Welles's film *The Lady from Shanghai* (1947).

The play can yet be said to have a clear structure, and this derives from the pattern of repetition and variation and from the systematic use of imagery, especially that of hair loss and of birds. The one-act play is thus divided into twelve sections of dialogue, monologue, or chorus that are, singly or in pairs, interrupted by pantomimes or changed settings.[7] There are two major rhetorical counterpoints to the "returning father" passage: the "Roman ruins" and the "African savior" sequences.

The chant of the four selves is contrasted, in the musical fashion of an antiphony, by Sarah's two monologues, the longest passages of the play (*F*, 255–258, 264–266; *I*, 5–7, 14–15). They are spoken from the point of view of a creative consciousness that gives a rationale for the personae and for the aesthetic refusal to submit to "logical relationships" or the ordered force of "themes" or "statements" (*F*, 258; missing in *I*).

However, a part of the first monologue, the "Roman ruins" passage (see *P*, 123), is also the basis for another ritual of repetition that transcends the character Sarah's boundaries: "It is my dream to live in rooms with European antiques and my Queen Victoria, photographs of Roman ruins, walls of books, a piano, oriental carpets, and to eat my meals on a white glass table. I will visit my friends' apartments which will contain books, photographs of Roman ruins, pianos, and oriental carpets. My friends will be white. I need them as an embankment to keep me from reflecting too much upon the fact that I am a Negro. For, like all educated Negroes—out of life and death essential—I find it necessary to maintain a stark fortress against recognition of myself" (*F*, 256–257; *I*, 6). This passage, which connects the theme of a split heritage with the character's refusal to accept part of it—or to recognize herself in that part—is repeated, with variations, by Lumumba (*F*, 263; *I*, 13) and, at the very end of the play, by the Funnyman (*F*, 272; *I*, 23).

The third rhetorical unit, the "African savior-white dove" passage, comes from Sarah's second monologue and uses particularly magical language: "My father—his mother wanted him to be Christ. From the beginning in the lamp of their dark room she said—I want you to be Jesus, to walk in Genesis [perhaps alluding to Lake Gennesaret (Matthew 14:22–34)] and save the race. You must return to Africa; find revelation in the midst of golden savannas, nim [i.e., "neem" or margosa] and white frankopenny trees, white stallions roaming under a blue sky, you must walk with a white dove and heal the race, heal the misery, take us off the cross. . . . His father told him the race was no damn good. He hated his father and adored [adores in *F*, 264] his mother. His mother didn't want him to marry my mother and sent a dead chicken to the wedding" (*F*, 264; *I*, 14). This is spoken not by Jesus (a yellow-skinned hunchback dwarf in the play) but by the Negro Sarah, repeated by her a page later, and finally varied on by the Funnylady (*F*, 267–268; *I*, 17–19). It is also echoed in Kennedy's own description of Africa: "white beaches that were filled with wild white horses running from the trees" (*P*, 121).

The contrapuntal structure of these three major sequences that are repeated and varied on in the play provides a rhythm (comparable to the pulsating drum beat in Eugene O'Neill's *Emperor Jones*) that deepens the themes of conflictual heritage, failed self-recognition, mission, sacrifice, decline, murder, and suicide, without resolving these issues. The three rhetorical units parallel Sarah's self-division as they variously articulate the difficult balance between a black patrimony and a white legacy that wants to deny, usurp, or kill blackness—as well as the hope for a black messiah who will set the record straight. In this respect, Kennedy is reminiscent of authors such as Charles W. Chesnutt and Jean Toomer, who created racially mixed characters as allegories of a country that refuses to acknowledge the black dimensions in its own makeup.

The powerful imagery of the play supports its structure and strengthens its intensity. Among the strongest images in the play is the eerie loss of hair. Kennedy writes about Picasso's portrait *Madame H. P.* (1952), "Often when I was depressed, my hair fell out, as my mother's hair fell out when I was born because of the ether she had to take during a difficult labor. At the Museum of Modern Art I had found a postcard of Picasso's *Madame Hélène*. Her hair seemed a living thing, an image I would soon use in my play *Funnyhouse of a Negro*" (*P*, 117; see *P*, 36). In *Funnyhouse*, the hairloss image is articulated by Sarah (*F*, 257, 264; *I*, 6, 14), the Duchess (*F*, 261; *I*, 10), and Lumumba (still identified only as "He" [*F*, 262] or "man" [*I*, 11]); described by the Funnylady (*F*, 259; *I*, 8); and connected by the Mother with the paranoid theme of rape by blackness (*F*, 255; *I*, 4). As hair comes to an independent, horrifying life of its own, the living beings from whose head it comes are closer to death. The association of her birth with the Mother's hair loss may strengthen Sarah's tragic death wish, her desire "not to be" (*F*, 256; *I*, 5). The theme of hair—whether "straight as any white woman's" (*F*, 254; *I*, 3) or "unmistakably Negro kinky hair" (*F*, 257; *I*, 6)—often used in literature as a racial identifier, is first transformed into the existential fear of hair loss, but that fear, too, remains explicitly connected to "race" when the Landlady says, "Her mother's hair fell out, the race's hair fell out because he left Africa, he said" (*F*, 267; *I*, 18). Once the Duchess's (possible) death is enacted on the stage, the hair-loss rhetoric subsides.

The bird imagery of the white dove, the dead chicken, the ravens, and the owl also balances both racial and existential aspects. The "search for the white dove" (*F*, 265; "doves" in *I*, 14–15) may allude to the animal that was sent from Noah's ark (Genesis 8:8); the Christian image of the Holy Ghost and of baptism (Matthew 3:16; Mark 1:10); the Holy Spirit of the Annunciation (Luke 1:35); the dove that was present during Mary's wedding on the Giotto fresco Kennedy cherished (*P*, 88); or the biblical wish, "Oh that I had wings like a dove! for then I would fly away, and be at rest" (Psalms 55:6). This passage comes from one of Kennedy's favorite books of the Bible (*P*, 89, 102) and is close in spirit to the line "Sometimes I feel like a feather in the air" that is repeated in the spiritual "Motherless Child" (which Kennedy heard her mother sing on Sunday mornings [*P*, 97]). In the African American tradition, the motif of flying (e.g., in "The Flying African" that Toni Morrison drew on in her novel *Song of Solomon* [1977], which also parallels the father's suicide attempt in Kennedy's play *A Movie Star Has to Star in Black and White* [*M*, 60; *I*, 89]) is often an expression of a yearning for an escape to freedom, a return to Africa, or for spiritual transcendence in death (which was, of course, also the use Dieterle's *Juarez* made of the dove image). The dead chicken, sent by the father's mother to the wedding, is an evil omen; it is also a metaphorical expression of the child's wish that the parents had never married, an extension of the wish not to be or not to have been born. The "great black ravens" that are flying about (*F*, 253; *I*, 2) evoke the white-black color contrast that permeates the play; they (in conjunction with the motif of a mysterious knocking at the door) may also have been inspired by Poe, who let his black raven contrast with the white bust of Athena, whose bird is the owl.[8] Sarah's mother "spoke of herself trapped in blackness" and "preferred the company of night owls" (*F*, 265; *I*, 15). This is an image that Kennedy would develop further in *The Owl Answers*. Kennedy's bird imagery, which may also go back to her excitement about African bird masks (*P*, 121) or her love for Chekhov's *The Seagull* (*P*, 101), manages to remain evocative and does not settle on one meaning.

The director Gerald Freedman made the comment that "Kennedy is a poet of the theater. She does not deal in story, character and event as a playwright. She deals in image, metaphor, essence and layers of consciousness."[9] Kennedy also stated that she uses people such as Lumumba, Queen Victoria, and Jesus as "metaphors really" (*G*, 46). She stressed metaphor, citing a passage from Aristotle: "The greatest thing by far is to be a master of metaphor. It is the one thing that cannot be [learned from others] and it is also a sign of genius since a good metaphor implies an intuitive perception of the similarity in dissimilars" (*P*, 105).[10] Kennedy has this grasp, and her plays are studies in the intuitive perception and carefully crafted expression of the similarity of dissimilars, both in the world of objects and in the inner lives of characters. In a striking way, she manages to sustain both identity and difference in all aspects of dramatic construction.

The Owl Answers

In *The Owl Answers* (1965), the presentation of changing sets and characters continues and intensifies the strategies undertaken in *Funnyhouse of a Negro*. In the new play, the connections between the various selves of Clara Passmore are "metaphoric": "SHE WHO IS CLARA PASSMORE WHO IS THE VIRGIN MARY WHO IS THE BASTARD WHO IS THE OWL" (*O*, 170; *I*, 25). The character Clara was inspired again by her neighbor Sarah Clara (*P*, 35), by Kennedy's mother, and by her mother's half-sister, Aunt Martha, who also introduced Kennedy to Shakespeare (*P*, 102, 122; *O*, 175; *I*, 31). In Clara, whose telling last name may describe a desire to "pass" for white, illegitimacy, racially mixed identity, conflicts between father and mother, and cultural tensions between England and America converge. The set is a collage of Old World and New World places, all of which strangely coexist: "*The scene is a New York subway car is the Tower of London is a Harlem hotel room is St. Peter's*" (*O*, 171; *I*, 26). Three major characters have similarly alternating identities: Mother–Reverend's Wife–Anne Boleyn, Goddam Father–Richest White Man in the Town–Dead White Father–Reverend Passmore, and White Bird–Reverend Passmore's Canary–God's Dove.[11] There is a Negro Man, and the figures of Shakespeare, Chaucer, and William the Conqueror form the Greek chorus of an English literary tradition whose "*lines throughout the play are not spoken specifically by one person but by all or part of them*" (*O*, 172; *I*, 27) and challenge Clara's claim to English ancestry. The first word of the play, which this English chorus addresses to Clara, is "Bastard" (*O*, 172; *I*, 27).

Once again, family relations are complex (and reminiscent of Hughes's meditation on the destruction of family by race in *Mulatto*). Clara's identities as white man's "blood" daughter or bastard, black cook's daughter, and black reverend's foster daughter rotate—not to mention Virgin Mary and owl. *The Owl Answers* also uses the word "ancestor" when one would expect "descendant." For example, Shakespeare and Company say, "If you are his ancestor why are you a Negro?" (*O*, 172; *I*, 28), and the Dead Father echoes, "If you are my ancestor why are you a Negro, Bastard?" (*O*, 175; *I*, 31). Ancestry and descent thus merge symbolically, and repetition, again, is an important structural element of the drama. In a later passage, however, She refers to England as the place of "our ancestors" (*O*, 184; *I*, 42; see also *P*, 22), following the common usage. Yet this ancestry denies Clara a place, whether as descendant or as ancestor. In terms of literal kinship, She does not bear the name of her White Father (Mattheson) that would establish an ancestral entitlement. It is as if half her parentage did not count in the strange racial genealogy that Clara confronts. She (like Hughes's Bert, who also may not use his father's name, Norwood) has to enter her own father's house through the back door (*O*, 179; *I*, 36). Now that the father has "died today or was it yesterday" (an allusion, perhaps, to the beginning of Albert Camus's novel *The Stranger*), She is not even permitted to attend his funeral (*O*, 176–177; *I*, 33). St. Paul's universalist promise of a Christianity without ethnic boundaries (Galatians 3:26–28) seems forgotten in St. Paul's Chapel, where the father's funeral takes place but where Clara is not permitted to go. England, the home of the Brontës (*O*, 176, 183; *I*, 33, 41), does not welcome the avid *Jane Eyre* reader (*P*, 14, 36–37, 43, 45, 47, 62–63, 86, 110–111) and makes her feel alien and solitary in the familiar settings of Dickens and George Eliot, of Anne Boleyn and Mary Queen of Scots. Clara repeatedly speaks the loaded sentence "I was the only Negro there" (*O*, 179, 181, 185; *I*, 36, 39, 42).

Refused acceptance in the father's world that is so clearly a part of her, Clara denies her own relationship to the father and tries to create new, alternative father (and God) figures for herself on the New York subway: "I am Clara Passmore. I am not His ancestor. I ride, look for men to take to a Harlem hotel room, to love, dress them as my father, beg to take me" (*O*, 180; *I*, 37–38). The taunting White Bird and the Mother keep interrupting the scene in which she takes the Negro man to the hotel room. Finally, the Mother stabs herself with a butcher knife (that could come from Eugene O'Neill's *All God's Chillun Got Wings*), saying, "I know the way to St. Paul's Chapel, Clara" (*O*, 186; *I*, 44), and is transported by White Bird to the top of St. Peter's dome. Clara, however, does not follow her to find her dead father through her own death. After the Dead Father is briefly seen, too, Clara fends off and tries to attack with the knife the Negro man whom she ostensibly sought out on the subway. Now she *"suddenly looks like an owl"* and speaks the last words, "Ow . . . oww," whereupon "DEAD FATHER *rises and slowly blows out candles on bed*" (*O*, 187; "FATHER" in *I*, 45). Her transformation into an owl is complete.

This metamorphosis has been prefigured from the first character description to many owl references throughout the play, among them the following passage by Clara that echoes the title:

> They are dragging his body across the green his white hair hanging down. . . . I must get into the chapel to see him. I must. He is my blood father. God, let me in to his burial. . . . I call God and the Owl answers. (*Softer.*) It haunts my Tower calling, its feathers are blowing against the cell wall, speckled in the garden on the fig tree, it comes, feathered, great hollow-eyed with yellow skin and yellow eyes, the flying bastard. From my Tower I keep calling and the only answer is the Owl, God. (*Pause. Stands.*) I am only yearning for our kingdom, God. (*O*, 185; *I*, 43)

No image in Kennedy's oeuvre has received more extensive treatment than that of this owl.[12] An additional way to look at the owls as night birds emerges from Kennedy's African vignette *"The owls and myself"*:

> The owls in the trees outside the Achimota Guest House were close, and at night, because we slept under gigantic mosquito nets, I felt enclosed in their sound. In the mornings I would try to find the owls in the trees but could never see them. Yet, at night in the shuttered room, under the huge white canopied nets, the owls sounded as if they were in the very center of the room. I was pregnant again. And there were difficulties. I had to stay in bed for a week, as I bled. I listened to the owl sounds, afraid. (*P*, 121–122; cf. *P*, 102)

The image of the bird is associated here with pregnancy (as was the dove of the Annunciation), but unlike the bird that solemnized Mary's marriage in Kennedy's favorite Giotto fresco (*P*, 34, 88; *O*, 184; *I*, 42), the owl is secretive. It is audible only at night; invisible in the day. Clara's transformation into an owl may thus reenact the father's family relationship that existed only at night. It is also possible, however, that the owls, as part of Kennedy's elaborate system of bird images, represent a somber alternative to Maeterlinck's blue bird of happiness (*P*, 3, 72) or go back to the finger rhyme *Little Piggies* from Kennedy's childhood: "Little Piggies were my toes who went to market, who stayed home, who cried ow-ow-ow [*not* the customary "we-we-we"] all the way home" (*P* galleys, 23). Kennedy's next plays, *A Beast Story* (1966) and *A Rat's Mass* (1966), continue the investigation of animal imagery as a part of magical transformations and as counterstatements to one of the staples of modern racism.[13]

Later Plays

A Lesson in Dead Language (1966) presents a chorus of Pupils who intone, "I bleed. I bleed. Ever since I became a woman, I bleed. Like Caesar will I bleed away and die? Since I became a woman blood comes out of me. I am a pinnacle tumbled down" (*L*, 39; *I*, 52). The allusion is to Shakespeare's *Julius Caesar*—or to Joseph Mankiewicz's film adaptation of 1953 "with Louis Calhern, Brando and James Mason" that Kennedy remembers seeing; the character of Calpurnia, Caesar's wife, was played by Greer Garson; Kennedy adds, "I bought the recording of the movie and played it for my father" (*P*, 78). The setting of Kennedy's play is a Latin class that turns into an absurd ritual of instruction and repetition, vaguely reminiscent of Eugène Ionesco's play *The Lesson*. Caesar's death and the end of childhood (or the beginning of woman's sexual maturity and her initiation into adult culture) are metaphorically related through the shared omen of the blood that accompanies both events. Hence, Calpurnia's dream, a warning to Caesar of the Ides of March, is recited by the Pupils who have started to menstruate. The play also derives from Kennedy's sheer fascination with Caesar: "Three years of Latin made me more interested in him than in any other figure except Jesus. Caesar, his campaigns, his armies, his assassination, the betrayal by Brutus on the steps of the Capitol. How I loved him" (*P*, 63).[14]

In *A Movie Star Has to Star in Black and White* (1976), Kennedy returned to projected aspects of a central self, taking on directly the myth of Hollywood: "All the colors are shades of black and white" (*M*, 53; *I*, 80); there is film music; and the actors are made up to look exactly like Bette Davis, Paul Henreid, Jean Peters, Marlon Brando, Montgomery Clift, and Shelley Winters. "Supporting roles are played by the mother, the father, the husband" (*M*, 55; *I*, 81). And in what seems to be an ironic inversion of the earlier technique, "A bit role is played by Clara" (*M*, 55; *I*, 81). The play thus promises to be the realization of Kennedy's dream: "If I were an actress I would want to play roles like Bette Davis" (*P*, 78). Indeed, the play opens with the Columbia Pictures lady announcing, "Summer, New York, 1955. Summer, Ohio, 1963. The scenes are *Now, Voyager, Viva Zapata!* and *A Place in the Sun*" (*M*, 55; *I*, 81). The three scenes into which the play is divided (an unusual procedure for Kennedy, whose other major plays are all undivided one-act plays) are each set in a film, as well as in a "real" place (hospital lobby, brother's room, and Clara's old room). In each scene, the characters who have the names of movie stars and are made up to look just like them are positioned in key moments of the respective film.

Yet the lines they speak do not come from the movies, as the first address by "Bette Davis" to "Paul Henreid" makes clear: "When I have a baby I wonder will I turn into a river of blood and die? My mother almost died when I was born. I've always felt sad that I couldn't have been an angel of mercy to my father and mother and saved them from their torment. I used to hope when I was a little girl that one day I would rise above them, an angel with glowing wings and cover them with peace. But I failed" (*M*, 56; *I*, 83). These words echo Sarah's feeling toward her mother in *Funnyhouse of a Negro* and birth traumas and blood imagery from Kennedy's other plays. Bette Davis also says, in a fashion familiar from Kennedy, "My father used to say John Hope Franklin, Du Bois and Benjamin Mays were fine men" (*M*, 57; *I*, 84; see also *P*, 12, 15). Indeed, *A Movie Star* is so strong in its retrospective quality that it includes a passage about the writing of *A Lesson in Dead Language*: "The main image is a girl in a white organdy dress covered with menstrual blood" (*M*, 63; *I*, 94). It even incorporates the character Clara (the "bit role"), who on five occasions in the play reads from "her play" *The Owl Answers*, including the section that contains the title of the play in the sentence "I call God and the Owl answers" (*M*, 60; *I*, 89).

Whereas other adaptations of popular culture have led to the creation of characters who speak the lines of movie actors (e.g., in Woody Allen's *Play It Again, Sam*), Kennedy lets the movie stars speak only her lines. No other character emerges that is fully exempt from this projection, except perhaps the male stars. The stage directions indicate that Montgomery Clift, Paul Henreid, and Marlon Brando are mute: "*If they did speak they would speak lines from their actual movies*" (*M*, 65; *I*, 98). Kennedy does not create a character like Bette Davis but turns Bette Davis into Kennedy's character. The autobiographical dimension in her work is so forceful that it may explain this unusual strategy of projection.

The family foreground is a condensed representation of misery: the brother has an almost lethal accident, and there are flashbacks to a suicide attempt by the father, the separation of father and mother, mental depression, and the mother's detailed account of racial segregation (*M*, 57; *I*, 84) that complements a shorter passage in Kennedy's memoir (*P*, 33–34). Autobiographical elements abound in the play: Georgia and Cleveland (where Kennedy's socialization took place) are mentioned; the father wears a Morehouse sweater (Kennedy's father, C. W. Hawkins, was educated as a social worker at Morehouse College); the husband is sent to Korea (as was Kennedy's husband, Joseph); and "Bette Davis" mentions going to such movies as *A Place in the Sun*.

The films are not randomly chosen. In *Now, Voyager*, the background to the first scene, the patient Charlotte Vale (Bette Davis) undertakes an ocean voyage on the recommendation of her psychiatrist, Dr. Jaquith (Claude Rains), to escape her domineering mother and restrictive Boston society. Charlotte meets the unhappily married Jeremiah Durrance (Paul Henreid) on board and strikes up a relationship, which begins her emancipation and her cure. At a crucial moment, Charlotte confronts her mother (played by the British actress Gladys Cooper). Invoking her psychiatric counselor, she exclaims, "Dr. Jaquith says that tyranny is sometimes an expression of the maternal instinct. If that's a mother's love, I want no part of it. I didn't want to be born. You didn't want me to be born, either." When she hears this, the mother has a heart attack and dies. This scene in Irving Rapper's movie, which takes its title from a line in Walt Whitman's poem "Now Finalé to the Shore," was referred to by Jeanne Thomas Allen as a "declaration of independence to the imperious Boston matriarch."[15] Later, Charlotte develops a supportive relationship with Tina, the daughter of Jeremiah Durrance, her (by then renounced) lover. Jerry's daughter also was never wanted by her mother. This aspect of *Now, Voyager* reinforces the "never was born" motif, the death wish in Kennedy's works, with its sources in tragedy and spirituals. It is no coincidence that Kennedy also associated *Now, Voyager* with her own first trip to Europe and her beginnings as a published writer.

The films *A Place in the Sun* (George Stevens, 1951) and *Viva Zapata!* (Elia Kazan, 1952) form the backdrop to the second half of Kennedy's play. The scene in *A Place in the Sun* (based on Theodore Dreiser's novel *An American Tragedy* [1925]) to which Kennedy's play alludes is the death by drowning of the pregnant working-class girl Alice Tripp (played by Shelley Winters) while her lover George Eastman (Montgomery Clift)— who really wishes that Alice were dead—is ready to pursue his love affair with the upper-class woman Angela Vickers (Elizabeth Taylor). Interestingly, the film anticipates and juxtaposes the death scene with the ominous sound of a loon and continues the bird metaphor with the image of a bird in a cage that the prison guards on death row look at after George has been sentenced to die.[16] The key sequences from *Viva Zapata!* are the wedding night and the moment when Emiliano Zapata (Marlon Brando) teaches Josefa (Jean Peters) how to read, thus paralleling the figure of Kennedy's Clara, the reader and emergent writer who is reliving her development as a dramatist. Ruby Cohn has stressed that Kennedy's film scenes also contrast sharply with the family foreground: falling in love (*Now, Voyager*) with family quarrel and divorce; wedding (*Viva Zapata!*) with the parental argument in the hospital where the brother is lying without consciousness; and the pregnant Alice's death (*A Place in the Sun*) with the pregnant Clara's divorce.[17]

With *A Movie Star Has to Star in Black and White*, Kennedy's dramatic work has come full circle, and there is a certain logic to her turning toward autobiographical prose after it. Her plays are the condensed expression of a theatrical mind that has integrated the diverse autobiographical elements of family history; the tragic paradox of American race relations in the twentieth century; and the impulses of popular culture, as well as of high modernism and European and African art, into an effective aesthetic form.

Figure 11.1. Alix Jeffry, *Dutchman*. LeRoi Jones on the set, with the director Edward Parone, Al Freeman Jr. as Clay, Jennifer West as Lula, and other members of the cast. (Alix Jeffry photograph [MS Thr 416]. Copyright © Houghton Library, Harvard University.)

CHAPTER II

LeRoi Jones/Amiri Baraka,
Dutchman

March 24, 1964: An absurd drama of lyrical introspection opens at the Cherry Lane Theater and has an explosive effect.

WITH THE SUCCESSFUL PRODUCTION of *Dutchman* in 1964, LeRoi Jones/Amiri Baraka became the nationally and internationally known "fierce and blazing talent" (*New York Herald Tribune*) who shocked fascinated audiences with his "murderous rage" (*New York Times*).[1] Frequently reprinted and performed, filmed in England under the direction of Anthony Harvey, and adapted in France for Jean-Luc Godard's movie *Masculin Féminin* (1966), *Dutchman* is Baraka's most familiar, as well as his most intensely analyzed and highly praised, play. A social drama of lyrical introspection, it is also a play from the theater of the absurd that effectively integrates social myths with private themes, literary surrealism, and political ethnocentrism.

Dutchman stages the encounter of a twenty-year-old, middle-class Negro and a thirty-year-old, white bohemian woman as an absurdist ritual on the New York subway. The woman, Lula, flirts with the young man, Clay; her aggressive hipness makes Lula the dominant partner in

SOURCE: Werner Sollors, "Dutchman," in *Amiri Baraka/LeRoi Jones: The Quest for a "Populist Modernism,"* by Werner Sollors (New York: Columbia University Press, 1978), 117–133, 284–288. Copyright © 1981 by Werner Sollors.

their interchange. In the presence of other subway passengers, her attacks become harsher and more and more provocative, and when the black man responds with a rhetorical tirade, he is stabbed to death by the aggressive white woman who, at the end of the play, prepares for her next victim, another young black man.

The realistic elements of *Dutchman* are outweighed by absurd drama techniques, which make the play provocative and unsettling.[2] The introductory stage directions suggest that the protagonists are not fully individualized characters in the sense of realistic drama but reified types whose encounter takes place in a dreamlike, Kafkaesque setting that is both specific and vague:

> *Opening scene is a man sitting in a subway seat, holding a magazine but looking vacantly just above its wilting pages. . . . The train slows after a time, pulling to a brief stop at one of the stations. The man looks idly up, until he sees a woman's face staring at him through the window; when it realizes that the man has noticed the face, it begins very premeditatedly to smile. The man smiles too, for a moment, without a trace of self-consciousness. Almost an instinctive though undesirable response.*[3]

The stage directions refer to "a man" (not to his name, Clay) and reify the woman, Lula, by making her *face* the subject of her action: not "the woman" smiles, but her face; "it" does it "premeditatedly," whereupon "the man" makes an "instinctive" response. As in many plays of the absurd, the characters are objects of an external situation and of internal instincts, puppets rather than persons, body parts rather than full personalities. There is a difference between "the woman's face," which brings about the initial action, and "the man," who only responds, but both figures are involved in a ritualistic situation. Initially, the woman's face takes *visual* possession of the man by staring at him. It is also a shift in visual perspective that underlines the victimization of characters by their environment. In the first scene "the man" "*is sitting alone. That is, only his seat is visible, though the rest of the car is outfitted as a complete subway car. But only his seat is shown*" (4). In the beginning of the second scene, the setting is "*the same as before, though now there are other seats visible in the car. And throughout the scene other people get on the subway*" (22).

This slight change in perspective makes other seats and, very soon, other passengers visible to the audience and the protagonists. Seeing and being seen by, others become a necessary part of Clay's and Lula's drama. When Lula is closest to Clay, at the "groovy" end of the first scene, she says significantly, "And we'll pretend the people cannot see you, that is, the citizens. And that you are free of your own history. And I am free of my history. We'll pretend that we are both anonymous beauties smashing along through the city's entrails" (21). Yet Baraka asserts, and reminds us by including the presence of "others" in scene 2, that this liberation from one's own history is only make-believe and superficial, at best. When Lula first becomes aware of the presence of other "riders of the coach, white and black" (3), the stage directions describe her as suffering a "*mild depression, but she still makes her description* [of a night with Clay to be spent in her 'tenement'] *triumphant and increasingly direct*" (24). Clay's reaction to the presence of others is more naïve: "*Notices another person entering, looks quickly, almost involuntarily up and down the car, seeing other people in the car.* Hey, I didn't even notice when they got on" (25).

Clay and Lula desire "invisibility" as an escape from history into a transracial sexual encounter in a Bohemian "groove." The hostility between them is at its lowest point in the play when the other passengers appear. The presence of these "citizens" increases Lula's aggressiveness and helps to reveal that her idyllic description was an illusion, that the situation between Clay and her does not leave them this "liberated" alternative. Lula acts as if obsessed, and Clay responds, in a gesture reminiscent of the opening scene, "almost involuntarily." As more and more people board the train and move closer to the two main figures, the private dialogue between Clay and Lula assumes, increasingly, the character of public address expressed in more and more aggressively obscene language. Only when the others laugh with Lula at Clay does Clay raise his voice and address the passengers directly, and only after Lula has reached an agreement with the "citizens"—"All right! *The others respond*" (37)— does she stab Clay (whose body is, fittingly, disposed of collectively by the group of train riders).

The mere presence of the black and white riders of the coach illustrates that the world turns what might have been a harmless flirtation or a loving relationship into plain aggressiveness and murder.[4] No psychological character transformation is caused by the physical presence of the "citizens," for *Dutchman* does not show the infringement of others on Clay's and Lula's consciousness as a realistic process that gradually changes their attitudes. Instead, it posits this infringement of social and

historical forces on the "instinctive" responses of "characters"—fatalis-
tically and in the absurdist tradition—as having started long before Lula
and Clay ever met.[5] If *Dutchman* is a play about the "Fall of Man," then
the expulsion from Eden is complete before the beginning of the play.[6]
The ending of the play finally and irrefutably demonstrates that Lula's
desire for Clay was for him as not an object of love but as an object of
racism. In a forceful adaptation of a common absurd drama technique,
Baraka leads his play to a circular ending:

> LULA *busies herself straightening her things. Getting everything in order.*
> *She takes out a notebook and makes a quick scribbling note. Drops it in*
> *her bag. The train apparently stops and all the others get off, leaving her*
> *alone in the coach. Very soon a young Negro of about twenty comes into*
> *the coach, with a couple of books under his arm. He sits a few seats in*
> *back of* LULA. (37)

The full circle, which makes the play end the way it began and therefore
allows for an eternal repetition of the same plot, is achieved in slightly
different ways in the two authoritative *Dutchman* editions.[7] Both versions
make clear that Lula will repeat her murderous acts after the formal
end of the play; however, the Morrow edition introduces the theme of
black brotherhood, represented by the old conductor with an Uncle Tom
mask.[8] The Parone version limits itself to an unambiguous emphasis on
the circular structure by ending the play just as Lula is biting into an
apple, an exact repetition of the beginning of scene 1.

The absurdist circular ending of *Dutchman* is part of a conscious literary strategy that demonstrates that Lula is caught in a situation of compulsive repetition. At times, she is even aware of her affliction: "But it's
always gentle when it starts" (13); "A gray hair for each year and type I've
come through" (13); "How could things go on like that forever? Huh?
. . . Except I do go on as I do. Apples and long walks with deathless
intelligent lovers" (28).

The ending underlines the elements of the play that make it the por-
trayal of a hopeless situation in which the Clays and the Lulas, as social
masks rather than as individuals, are trapped. It is not, the ending suggests, a unique occurrence but a rule that *Dutchman* presents.

In this respect, *Dutchman* is more "European absurdist" than, for
example, Jack Gelber's *The Connection*, which employs a circular struc-

ture to convey the hopelessness of the drug addict scene, or Edward Albee's *Zoo Story*, which shows a deadly confrontation between two men who represent the different worlds of New York's East Side and Upper West Side. Eugène Ionesco's *The Lesson*, although more mathematical and humorously detached than *Dutchman*, uses reified role players (professor and student) to demonstrate the rule that education is a continuous form of rape and murder. After the student has been stabbed by the professor and her body disposed of, the doorbell rings, and the professor prepares for his next victim. The interrelationship of power and sexuality and the obsession with language as a form of possible communication that turns into a tool of domination further link *The Lesson* with *Dutchman*.

Baraka's play also shows certain affinities to pre-absurdist European theater, Thus, *Dutchman* parallels August Strindberg's *Miss Julie* in theme and plot structure. In both plays, there is a confrontation between a man and a woman separated by social barriers—class structure or color line—and the protagonists' mutual attraction is possibly a result of that very barrier. Strindberg's Jean and Baraka's Clay imitate the men of the dominant class/race, whereas the women in both plays are attracted by the very otherness (of class or color) in the men they tempt. Julie drinks beer and dances to the fiddle at Midsummer Eve; Lula tries to lure Clay to do a black dance and uses hip language. Moreover, in both *Miss Julie* and *Dutchman*, the women are the aggressors. Both plays have a brief intermission (rare in one-act plays) that suggests physical closeness or sexual union yet also marks the beginning of the inevitable end of the relationship. While this parallel does not extend to the tone of the plays, it illustrates the statement of *Dutchman* as a social drama: the protagonists cannot transcend their backgrounds; there is no hope for an individual rapprochement; the social chasm cannot be bridged. To adhere exclusively to such an interpretation, however, is to ignore passages of the dialogue and to overlook the connections that link *Dutchman* to Baraka's earlier works.

Drama of the Self

Like Jones's early drama "The Eighth Ditch," *Dutchman* is a drama of the self.[9] While it is generally accepted that Clay is a projection of and spokesman for Baraka, Lula, too, expresses many of Baraka's ideas in his own language. Clay and Lula are not merely depersonalized, absurd, two-faced social symbols; they are also endowed with elements of their creator's self. They represent different temporal aspects of an artistic consciousness that has split into opposing forces. Lula first becomes visible to Clay as he looks "blankly toward the window" of the train; this suggests the genesis of the woman out of Clay's mirror image. Seen this way, the beginning of *Dutchman* is an elaboration of Baraka's narcissistic mirror-window images in the early poetry.[10] Again, the dark window is a "grey glass" and reveals, at first, only an image of a "white Negro."

In the first scene of *Dutchman*, Clay represents those familiar black bourgeois hang-ups that Baraka previously satirized in poetry and prose. Clay is the "buttoned down" Negro par excellence, the incorporation of Baraka's rejected black middle-class background in New Jersey. Clay is a "type" from the "dead" world of unconditional assimilationism, of "lukewarm sugarless tea" (8) and tall skinny black boys with phony English accents (10), of "hopeless colored names," like Jones's own baptismal name Everett, "creeping out of New Jersey" (15), of "three-button suits" (18), social-worker mothers and would-be Christians (31).

In her taunting of this "Black Baudelaire" (19–20), Lula attacks Clay's middle-class mask from the point of view of bohemianism and thus represents a later stage of Baraka's development. Ten years older than Clay, she is perceptive to the point of omniscience: she knows everything about Clay's life, his place of origin, his destination on the train, and his friends' names. She is even aware of Clay's most intimate incestuous memories, or fantasies, and she knows all about black manhood, which Clay so energetically represses. In Baraka s own words, Lula says "essentially true things" to Clay.[11] More than that, Lula is perhaps everything Clay does not permit himself to become. Lula mocks Clay's three-button suit (18) and entices him, more and more aggressively, to "Rub bellies. Rub bellies" (30). Lula's suggestions for a sexual, racial, political, and aesthetic self-liberation are largely those of Jones/Baraka's poetry:

> LULA: Come on, Clay. Let's rub bellies on the train. . . . Clay! You middle-class black bastard. Forget your social-working mother for a few seconds and let's knock stomachs. Clay, you liver-lipped white man. You would-be Christian. You ain't no nigger, you're just a dirty white man. Get up, Clay. Dance with me, Clay.
>
> CLAY: Lula! Sit down, now. Be cool.

LULA (*Mocking him, in wild dance*): Be cool. Be cool. That's all you
know . . . shaking that wildroot cream-oil on your knotty
head, jackets buttoning up to your chin, so full of white man's
words. Christ. God. Get up and scream at these people. (31)

The scream Lula wants Clay to express so that he can "break out" of his
shell of false consciousness is, of course, the scream of the "thing" inside
in Jones's poem "An Agony. As Now," the scream of "Black Dada Nihilismus." At this point, Parone's edition of the play is even more explicit
in making that connection; here, Lula continues her invective with an
allusion to the title of the play:

LULA: Get up and scream at these people. A dada man. Like
scream meaningless shit in these hopeless faces. . . . Clay, you
got to break out. Don't sit there dying the way they want you
to die. Get up.[12]

Baraka's familiar aesthetic strategy of escaping from a middle-class "death"
by becoming a "dada man" is expressed, in *Dutchman*, by a white female
persona; the opposing black male part of the divided self is at first reluctant
to adopt this program of artistic rebellion. Confronted with Lula's harsher
insults, with her Uncle Tom invective, and with her playing the dozens
about his mother, Clay finally does "get up." He grabs Lula and slaps her
"as hard as he can, across the mouth" (33).

This gesture brings the interaction between black bourgeoisie and
bohemia to an abrupt end. Virtually without any development, the protagonists change their functions to themselves, to each other, to the other
train riders, and as artistic self-projections. The other sides of their Janus
faces suddenly emerge. If until this point Lula was the protagonist of the
play, Clay now becomes the hero. As he drops the bourgeois masquerade,
he assumes the role of Baraka's more contemporary mouthpieces. In his
three-page address, the most famous section of *Dutchman*, he voices his
aggression and pent-up violence and posits a black mystique, an inner
identity of repressed murderous instincts held back forcefully by masks
and sublimated only by artistic expression:

The belly rub? You wanted to do the belly rub? . . . Belly rub is
not Queens. Belly rub is dark places, with big hats and overcoats

held up with one arm. Belly rub hates you. Old bald-headed four-eyed ofays popping their fingers . . . and don't know yet what they're doing. They say, "I love Bessie Smith." And don't even understand that Bessie Smith is saying, "Kiss my ass, kiss my black unruly ass." Before love, suffering, desire, anything you can explain, she's saying, and very plainly, "Kiss my black ass." And if you don't know that, it's you that's doing the kissing. Charlie Parker? Charlie Parker. All the hip white boys scream for Bird. And Bird saying, "Up your ass, feeble-minded ofay! Up your ass." And they sit there talking about the tortured genius of Charlie Parker. Bird would've played not a note of music if he just walked up to East Sixty-seventh Street and killed the first ten white people he saw. Not a note! And I'm the great would-be poet. Some kind of bastard literature . . . all it needs is a simple knife thrust. Just let me bleed you, you loud whore, and one poem vanished. A whole people of neurotics, struggling to keep from being sane. And the only thing that would cure the neurosis would be your murder. Simple as that. I mean if I murdered you, the other white people would begin to understand me. You understand? (34–35)[13]

Clay's address is often cited as the pumping black heart of the New Black Aesthetic and of the Black Arts Movement of the 1960s and hailed as an act of political liberation or deplored as a dangerous advocacy of violence. While it is true that, at this point in *Dutchman*, Clay becomes a black nationalist spokesman who rejects his middle-class background to affirm a restoration of sanity for the wretched of the earth, he articulates, at the same time, what Lula asked of him. He fulfills Lula's and Baraka's conception of Dadaism as established in Jones's poem "Black Dada Nihilismus" and paraphrased by Lula's demand for "a dada man." However, Baraka advances Clay one step further by subjecting him to the surrealist exaggeration of Dadaism. In the central scene of *Dutchman*, Clay, who once thought of himself as a black Baudelaire, has become a black Breton. His address is not merely a racial address in the tradition of Frantz Fanon; it also shows strong affinities to André Breton's "Second Manifesto of Surrealism" (1930), which claims a surrealist tenet of "total revolt, complete insubordination, of sabotage according to rule" and "expects nothing save from violence":

The simplest Surrealist act consists of dashing down into the street, pistol in hand, and firing blindly, as fast as you can pull the trigger, into the crowd. Anyone who, at least once in his life, has not dreamed of thus putting an end to the petty system of debasement and cretinization in effect has a well-defined place in that crowd, with his belly at barrel level.[14]

The way Clay adapts Breton's simple act of anti-art is, of course, ethnic: it transforms an example of European surrealism into what seems to be American racial realism. Perhaps it is interesting that Godard's movie version of this scene in *Dutchman* restored Breton's pistol shot in lieu of Lula's knife thrust.[15]

Yet Baraka-Clay's concept of black surrealism leaves the arbitrariness of the "simplest Surrealist act" only partly intact, directed as it is against the first ten *white* men. Clay sees art as a neurotic perversion of violence and violence as the only act that will restore the black man's sanity. Clay may thus be seen "surrealizing" black nationalism and "ethnicizing" surrealism. This fusion of aesthetic and racial avant-gardism makes Clay's speech a forceful example of Baraka's strategy of populist modernism and a key passage for the avant-gardist Black Arts Movement of the 1960s.

Significantly, Clay advocates racial violence in the course of formulating an answer to an *artistic* dilemma, and the aesthetic quality of his argument seems to outweigh his concern for the political implications of black creativity. If murdering whites is "the simplest Surrealist act" for black Bretons, Clays, dada men, then Clay shies away from surrealism, except as a shocking aesthetic theory, and concludes his statement with characteristic lyricisms. No matter what he says, he seems more concerned with being understood than with taking his surrealist solution as literally as does Lula. Clay hopes to escape into the shelter of artistic sublimations that was Baraka's abode: "Safe with my words, and no deaths, and clean, hard thoughts, urging me to new conquests" (35).[16] At the end of his speech, Clay the artist reaches for his books; Lula, silently and businesslike, gets out her knife.

Lula, too, has been transformed, from the omniscient bohemian into an incorporation of everything that is murderous in white Western society, and the black dance she tried to entice Clay to do is now, as George Knox pointed out, a white *danse macabre*.[17] An agent of repression, Lula must crucify Christ, must silence Clay to bring the *Dutchman* ritual to an end. Before Clay's speech, Lula represented aesthetic protest as a challenge to Clay's middle-class mask; now Clay symbolizes the surrealist-realist threat of black nationalism to Lula as white America. Like the secretary in Camus's *State of Siege*, Lula is a bookkeeper of murder, who keeps a record in her notebook of the contracts she has fulfilled. However, she can quickly retransform herself into the aggressively flirtatious hipster when she senses new prey. The dramatic strategy of self-division has led Baraka, in *Dutchman*, to the creation of two opposing forces who furthermore are divided in themselves. The play's "corporate Godhead" (24) consists of a double Clay and a double Lula.

The mirror image of the white-oriented poet changes as the train moves on. The self-total's identity is increasingly polarized along racial lines, and the black part of the self is being killed by its white mirror image. As the black writer stares through a glass darkly, he sees a white woman with sunglasses who becomes a witch with a knife. She is a deadly metallic enclosure, Baraka's familiar "shell." This agonistic confrontation yields a scream and a formulation of a defiant aesthetic as the legacy of the sacrificed inner self.

Title and Myth

Dutchman is powerful as a drama because it functions as a social construct, as an absurdist play, as a drama of the self, and as a "modern myth" (3).[18] The mythical dimensions extend from the frequently observed Edenic connotations to American popular culture and to the African and Afro-American archetype of a white witch; from the names of the protagonists to setting and meaning of title. Clay, who is also identified with Christ, Uncle Tom, and Richard Wright's Bigger Thomas, denotes an Adamic quality as well as moldability; he is, at the same time, the "original man" out of whose mirror image Lula is created and the sacrificial lamb whose blood must be spilled to seal a new covenant. Lula is the apple-eating Eve but is also associated with Juliet, Tal*lula*h Bankhead, and "Lena the Hyena," the ugliest woman in a L'il Abner contest (with the connotation of the animal that preys on carcasses). Her name, Lula, summons up a line of associations that range from Frank Wedekind's Lulu to the biblical seductress Lilith and even to a lullaby. Her function as a compulsive manhunter and mankiller, a femme fatale on a *"Dutchman"* mission, also evokes the association with furies, witches, and vampires.[19]

As the white woman imagined and feared by a black man, Lula also is reminiscent of the West African goddess Erzulie, depicted as a white woman who "strolls slowly along, swings her hips, throws seductive glances at the men."[20] Among her lovers is, interestingly, Damballah, the serpent god of the "Crow Jane" poems and "Black Dada Nihilismus." But more fear-inspiring than the white goddess in Africa is the white witch in black America, about whom James Weldon Johnson warned his brothers. Johnson's portrait recalls Baraka's Lula: despite her youthful appearance, "Unnumbered centuries are hers," and she pursues her eternal manhunt behind a luring mask. "And back behind those smiling lips, / And down within those laughing eyes, / The shadow of the panther lurks, / The spirit of the vampire lies."[21]

The immortality of Lula the vampire and the infinite repetition of the action suggested by the circular ending give some weight to a reading of the title of the play as a version of the myth of the Flying Dutchman. Baraka's first stage directions strengthen that connection: *"In the flying underbelly of the city. Steaming hot, and summer on top, outside. Underground. The subway heaped in modern myth"* (3). This description of the setting places *Dutchman* both in the real and concrete location of the New York subway and in a nightmarishly mythical netherland of the unconscious, and the surrealistic "excursion into the midst of forbidden territory" is undertaken in a vague eternal present. How does the Flying Dutchman myth fit into this absurdist time and place? Critics have linked this myth to Lula, Clay, and subway; compared the libretto of Richard Wagner's opera to the text of Baraka's play; and searched for other direct and oblique connections. Hugh Nelson interprets the subway as the *Flying Dutchman* ship (as the French translator implicitly did when he called the play *Métro fantôme*, alluding to *Vaisseau fantôme*, the French version of *The Flying Dutchman*) and casts Lula as captain and the other passengers as crew. In his view, however, Clay lacks any association with the *Dutchman* myth and is therefore more "natural" in his reactions.[22]

In a more historical reading, Sherley Anne Williams suggested that while Lula "is likened to a ghost ship" in *Dutchman*, the title of the play is equally significant against the background of the slave trade, "for it was a Dutchman, a Dutch man-of-war, which brought the first black slaves to North America. America symbolically comes full circle through Lula's—the *Dutchman's*—murderous action. . . . What the Dutchman has given, the Dutchman also takes away."[23] These two dimensions of the play's title are not as unrelated as they may seem.[24] The connection between the Flying Dutchman legend and the slave trade is actually older than the motif of redemption through love, which was added to the myth by Heinrich Heine and Richard Wagner. In 1811, Dr. John Leyden, the Scottish poet and collector of folklore, imputed the *Flying Dutchman* curse to "the first ship which commenced the slave trade," in what may be the first printed occurrence of the phrase "Flying Dutchman" in the English language. Leyden's verses about the "spectre-ship, denominated the *Flying Dutchman*," are included in his *Scenes of Infancy: Descriptive of Teviotdale*:

> Stout was the ship, from Benin's palmy shore
> That first the freight of bartered captives bore:
> Bedimmed with blood, and sun, with shrinking beams,
> Beheld her bounding o'er the ocean streams;
> But, ere the moon her silver horn had reared,
> Amid the crew the speckled plague appeared.
> Faint and despairing, on their watery bier,
> To every friendly shore the sailors steer;
> Repelled from port to port, they sue in vain,
> And track, with slow unsteady sail, the main.
> The spectre ship, in livid glimpsing light,
> Glares baleful on the shuddering watch at night,
> Unblest of God and man! Til time shall end,
> Its view strange horror to the storm shall lend.[25]

Baraka's view of the slave trade as original sin, and of the legacy of slavery as a curse on America, makes plausible the relationship of *Dutchman* to the *Flying Dutchman*. The analogy between Baraka's play and the Flying Dutchman myth is most specific in the hopeless *situation* of the play, rather than in the characters.[26] The allusions to *The Flying Dutchman* thus strengthen the absurdist character of the play.

   Dutchman is a complex attempt to merge narcissistic mirror art and growing ethnocentric consciousness in a communicative gesture that is truly the kind of "high energy construct" that Charles Olson advocated. The play is Lula's and aesthetic protest's last stand. Lula is only the physical victor at the end of the play; spiritually, she has been exorcised. *Dutchman* indicates the direction Baraka's art would take: toward Clay's speech; into the contradictions of surrealism, artistic sublimation, and "real" action; into the slave-ship dimension of the play's title; and away from whiteness, femininity, and absurdism.

Figure 12.1. President Barack Obama and First Lady Michelle Obama dance at the 2009 Inauguration Ball. (Staff Sergeant Katherine McDowell, *Inauguration Day*, 2009. Navy Media Content Services, DVIDS: Defense Video and Imagery Distribution System, Web, April 15, 2015.)

CHAPTER 12

Obligations to Negroes Who Would Be Kin if They Were Not Negro

At the present moment there is no one dominant note in Negro literary expression. As the Negro merges into the main stream of American life, there might result actually a disappearance of Negro literature as such. If that happens, it will mean that those conditions of life that formerly defined what was "Negro" have ceased to exist, and it implies that Negroes are Negroes because they are treated as Negroes. . . .

If the expression of the American Negro should take a sharp turn toward strictly racial themes, then you will know by that token that we are suffering our old and ancient agonies at the hands of our white American neighbors. If, however, our expression broadens, assumes the common themes and burdens of literary expression which are the heritage of all men, then by that token you will know that a humane attitude prevails in America towards us. And a gain in humaneness in America is a gain in humaneness for us all. When that day comes, there will exist one more proof of the oneness of man, of the basic unity of human life on this earth.

—Richard Wright, "The Literature of the Negro
in the United States" (1957)

*May 14, 1965: At the American Academy of Arts and Sciences Confer-
ence on the Negro American, the sociologist Everett C. Hughes imagines "a
handsomely purple-black Negro woman in a décolleté white gown at the ball
celebrating her husband's inauguration as President of the United States."*

RICHARD WRIGHT, who died in Paris in 1960, was not quoted or mentioned in the special issues of *Daedalus* on "The Negro American" that were edited by Talcott Parsons and Kenneth B. Clark in 1965 and 1966. However, many contributors to the issues shared Wright's

SOURCE: Werner Sollors, "Obligations to Negroes Who Would Be Kin if They Were Not Negro," *Daedalus* (special issue on "Race in the Age of Obama," ed. Gerald Early) 140, no. 1 (Winter 2011): 142–153.

interest in confronting the conditions that have defined the lives of American Negroes and have caused them to suffer agonies at the hands of their white neighbors.[1] Wright's forward-looking comment, his imagining of a different and perhaps better future, anticipated a possible exhaustion of the African American narrative,[2] and the contributors to *Daedalus* likewise made cautious predictions for the future. Returning to those prophecies from several decades ago makes for a fascinating enterprise.

The most intriguing prophet from the *Daedalus* issues was Everett C. Hughes, whose essay "Anomalies and Projections" focused on the disturbance that racial distinctions have created in the American kinship system.[3] At the time Hughes was writing, people from other races could not be or become white people's kinfolk, and the proverbial Negro who married a white man's sister would not only sever the kin relationship between brother and sister but also bring shame on the white man that would justify violence, even to the point of killing the Negro. As Hughes explained, "There is a great moral fault—in the geological sense, and let us not quibble about the other sense—in American society when it comes to obligations to Negroes who would be kin if they were not Negro." Hence, *race* could "mean the difference between friend and enemy, one's own to be trusted or outsider to be feared, between life and death."[4] No wonder the white eye was trained to detect racial difference, although its ability to do so could vary in certain circumstances.

Hughes wrote his essay in 1965, but his examples still surprise the reader today:

> If the Negro does not wear one of the many uniforms of deference or of poverty or play some role in which we expect *Negroes* to appear, *the Negro*-ness might not be noticed. On the other hand, there might be situations in which it would be doubly noticed. Imagine a handsomely purple-black Negro woman in a décolleté white gown at the ball celebrating her husband's inauguration as President of the United States.[5]

Hughes thought about Negroes "in prestigeful positions" to contemplate such questions as, "Does the office outshine race or does race dim the luster of the office?" He imagined the broader possibility that in the future there might be "the full extension of the American bilateral kinship system to include mixed couples and their in-laws on both sides." Although

Hughes was writing two years before *Loving v. Virginia*, he ventured to claim, "Perhaps there will come to be cases where mixed couples and their children will be able to lead normal lives, with real uncles and aunts and cousins on both sides."[6]

THE PARALLEL BETWEEN Hughes's hypothetical scenario and Barack Obama's presidential campaign, election, inauguration, and family history is difficult to ignore. In his famous "race" speech, delivered in Philadelphia on March 18, 2008, candidate Obama reiterated his place within a multigenerational family network:

> I am the son of a black man from Kenya and a white woman from Kansas. I was raised with the help of a white grandfather who survived a Depression to serve in Patton's Army during World War II and a white grandmother who worked on a bomber assembly line at Fort Leavenworth while he was overseas. I've gone to some of the best schools in America and lived in one of the world's poorest nations.

Positioning himself as an ideal mediator between races, continents, and classes precisely because of his interracial family background, he added his marriage to the story: "I am married to a black American who carries within her the blood of slaves and slave owners—an inheritance we pass on to our two precious daughters." Obama employed his complex family story not only to suggest harmonious American fusion ("It is a story that has seared into my genetic makeup the idea that this nation is more than the sum of its parts—that out of many, we are truly one") but also to stress that having both black and white relatives gives him a more sober perspective on what is secretly felt on both sides of the color line. He pledged that his presidency would help overcome this racial "stalemate," and he offered unusually candid critical comments to both blacks and whites in an effort to reach for this goal and heal old racial wounds.[7]

After the inauguration, the *New York Times* (with the help of the genealogist Megan Smolenyak) researched Michelle Obama's ancestry, following up on Obama's hint that his wife carries "the blood of slaves and slave owners." Illustrated with an interactive family tree,[8] the *New York Times* story mentions a "union, consummated some two years before the

Civil War," representing "the origins of a family line that would extend from rural Georgia, to Birmingham, Ala., to Chicago and, finally, to the White House. Melvinia Shields, the enslaved and illiterate young girl ['perhaps as young as 15,' we are told elsewhere in the story], and the unknown white man who impregnated her are the great-great-great-grandparents of Michelle Obama, the first lady." The article concludes that this genealogy "for the first time fully connects the first African American first lady to the history of slavery, tracing their five-generation journey from bondage to a front-row seat to the presidency."[9] Hughes's observations about American society and its "obligations to Negroes who would be kin if they were not Negro" would seem to apply very directly to the white and the nonwhite branches of the first lady's family.

Of course, it was the inauguration ball that offered the uncannily literal fulfillment of Hughes's prophecy. Michelle Obama's white dress received much media attention on its own: the *New York Times* fashion critic Cathy Horn even called it "a bit revealing."[10]

Although it lacks an inaugural ball scene, the best-selling writer Irving Wallace's novel *The Man* (1964), which imagines the first black president, perhaps inspired Hughes. (When Obama was inaugurated, Wallace's son David Wallechinsky reminded the public of his father's novel, the first American novel about a black president; however, the book seems to have been largely forgotten.)[11] In *The Man*, President Douglass Dilman is not elected but ascends to his office as pro tempore leader of the Senate after the president and vice-president die in an accident abroad. Wallace calls attention to the significance of Dilman's first name with an epigraph by Frederick Douglass.[12] Dilman's late-night swearing-in ceremony inspires newspaper headlines that range from sensationalism to segregationism and racial pride:

NATION GASPS! A NEGRO IS PRESIDENT OF THE USA! . . .

NEGRO SENATOR MADE CHIEF EXECUTIVE BY FLUKE; JUDICIARY COMMITTEE MEETS TO DEBATE CONSTITUTIONALITY; CITIZENS PRO-TEST "UNFAIR" RULE OF MAJORITY BY MINORITY; REPRESENTATIVE MILLER PREDICTS "DISSENSION, DISUNITY, VIOLENCE" . . .

HALLELUJAH! EQUAL RIGHTS AT LAST! COLORED PRESIDENT OF SENATE BECOMES PRESIDENT OF US ALL! WORLD APPLAUDS TRUE DEMOCRACY!

Wallace's narrator mediates these varied reactions. He comments, "Several things were evident at once. To no one would he be simply a public servant who, by the law of succession, had become President of the United States. To both sides, and the middle, too, he would be the 'Negro' who had become President."[13]

Wallace's narrator reminds us of the question Hughes raises in his *Daedalus* essay, as well as how it might apply to the present—that is, does President Obama's office outshine race, or is the country divided between people who think it does and others still preoccupied with his ancestry? Contemporary responses to this question vary from high optimism to deep skepticism. In "Our Man Obama: The Post-Imperial Presidency," the Vietnamese American essayist Andrew Lam views Obama's election as a boost for a multicultural America because it symbolically strengthened the culturally subservient role Friday plays to Robinson Crusoe. The victory opened "the door wider to that growing public space in which Americans with mixed background and complicated biographies—Latino Muslims, black Buddhists, gay Korean Jews, mixed race children—can celebrate and embrace their multiple narratives with audacity."[14] Lam tempers his enthusiasm when he adds that, with the election, America has not moved into a utopia; that bigotry, racism, and struggles over resources and for power will remain with us. Yet he concludes on the hopeful note that Friday's/Obama's "talent is the ability to overcome the paralysis induced by multiple conflicting narratives and selves by finding and inventing new connections between them."[15] Ishmael Reed, who commented critically on the public responses "to the election of the first Celtic-African-American president," saw a sharp contrast between a celebratory façade and the media's continued practice of ignoring black voices: "On the day after the election the *New York Times* announced in its headline that Obama's election had broken a barrier, yet on the editorial page all of the poets who were invited to chime in were white. Some barriers remain."[16]

WHAT RELEVANCE does Richard Wright's "The Literature of the Negro in the United States" have for contemporary African American literature?[17] What themes emerge in literary works by young authors who achieved first recognition in the twenty-first century, who have Facebook sites and are Internet-savvy? Do their works conform to one or the other of Wright's choices? Do poetry, drama, and fiction in "the age of Obama" engage with some semblance of Everett Hughes's notion of extended kinship?

Young contemporary African American writers address race in many different ways in their works. Amina Gautier, a fiction writer in her early thirties, uses the thwarted fantasy of a happy extended family gathering for Thanksgiving to explore themes that transcend race. In her melancholy short story "Been Meaning to Say" (2008),[18] she follows the recently widowed grandfather Leslie Singleton, his surname a signal of his loneliness. His younger white neighbor, Joey Leibert, is about to sell his house, which is semi-attached to Leslie's but that Leslie has never seen from the inside. Although Leslie tells Joey that his daughter, Carole; his son-in-law, Martin; and his eight-year-old grandson, Amir, are all coming for Thanksgiving, his false hope becomes excruciatingly evident. Carole, an assistant professor whom the reader encounters only through cell-phone calls, seems distant from her father. Leslie, showing the first signs of senility, desperately misses his late wife, Iphigenia, and does not seem to want to pronounce his grandson's Arabic name; Leslie thinks of it as "mumbo jumbo." When a black family arrives on Thanksgiving to look at the Leiberts' house, Leslie feels strongly that they should not buy a house for their children. "They will grow up and they will leave it. They will leave you," he feels like saying to them.[19] The turkey is in the oven, underdone, but Leslie spends the holiday alone seated in front of the television with his remote control.

"Been Meaning to Say" is a short story of manners in which race plays no dominant or plot-constitutive role. Perhaps it does explain why Singleton has never seen his closest neighbor's house from the inside, but that might also be due to Singleton's character. While Joey is described as a "lanky white man," and the Leiberts are identified as "the last white family to move off the block," Singleton is never given a racial label.[20] There are specific references to African American naming practices from the generation of Eunettas and Anna Maes to that of Singleton's grandson, whose Arabic name means prince or ruler, as Carole tells her father on the phone. Yet the themes of intergenerational and neighborly alienation, of an aging man's grief and loneliness, belong to Wright's "common themes and burdens of literary expression which are the heritage of all men." Narrative subtlety and the full development of Leslie Singleton's character carry the story, but there is little external action, no dramatic turning point or conflict, no epiphany.

The same is true of Gautier's "Pan Is Dead" (2006), a short story about Blue, a runaway dad who comes back to his wife, son, and stepdaughter (who narrates the story) after a long absence. Blue is still charismatic, but he is *also* still a junkie, and before long he leaves the family once again. Although the story was published two years before Obama's election, one moment in it looks different now from how it might have looked in 2006: the narrator's brother says to her, "I don't want to be a doctor. . . . But I could be a lawyer. Most presidents are lawyers first." She responds, "'Boy, you can't be president.' This much I knew. Everyone knew that the president was always white and never from Brooklyn."[21] Four years later, Gautier's Facebook profile lists her as a member of the "We Love Michelle Obama!!!!" group.[22]

A TRAGIC MOMENT of high tension is the background to Heidi W. Durrow's first novel, *The Girl Who Fell from the Sky* (2010).[23] Durrow, born in 1969, was inspired by Nella Larsen, whose words serve as an epigraph for the novel. Like Larsen, both Durrow and her protagonist, Rachel, are biracial Danish–African American figures.[24] Rachel's mother, Nella, whom she calls "Mor," is Danish; Rachel's grandmother is black; her father, Roger, is a black GI (her parents met at an army base in Germany); and Rachel is biracial. At one point in the novel, Rachel, who now lives with her paternal grandmother, receives a package with two books that symbolize her situation: Frantz Fanon's *Black Skin, White Masks* and Hans Christian Andersen's fairy tales. As the form of the novel indicates, William Faulkner's experiments with point of view in *The Sound and the Fury* (1929) and *As I Lay Dying* (1930), as well as Toni Morrison's reconstruction of a traumatic moment of flying in *Song of Solomon* (1977), undoubtedly also influenced Durrow. The two–part novel is divided into forty-four sections, nineteen of which are told in the first-person present tense by Rachel; seven are told in a more staccato first-person present by her mother, Nella; two are told in the third-person past tense from her father, Roger's, point of view; and the others are told by friends and neighbors, also in the third-person past tense. This chorus of voices surrounding the central presence of Rachel and her mother slowly reveals and offers various attempts to understand, from different points of view, the terrible moment that is the core of the novel: when the deeply depressed Nella takes her three children, Robbie, Ariel, and

Rachel, and jumps off the rooftop with them in an act of utter despair. Only Rachel survives. A first glimpse of the story comes through the eyes of a little boy, Jamie, who loves bird watching and thinks at first that he sees birds when he witnesses the event:

> When he finally reached the courtyard, he saw that his bird was not a bird at all. His bird was a boy and a girl and a mother and a child.
>
> The mother, the girl, the child. They looked like they were sleeping, eyes closed, listless. The baby was still in her mother's arms, a gray sticky porridge pouring from the underside of her head. The girl was heaped on top of the boy's body, a bloody helpless pillow. And yet there was an old mattress, doughy from rain, just ten feet from the bird-boy's right arm, which was folded like a wing beneath him.[25]

The novel moves on to other external perspectives and glimpses of the more distant past (there was an earlier child, Charles, who died; Rachel knew nothing of him) and the later present (Rachel is becoming a woman). Finally, Durrow confronts the event through Nella's and Rachel's voices. Nella claims the children as her own against other people's (and especially her white boyfriend, Doug's) racist perceptions: "They're mine. If people can't see it—how can I keep them safe? . . . They will go where I go." Rachel recounts the jump from the rooftop more fully: "*I saw above me and around, beyond the day's fog. I felt my cells expanding into space and felt larger than ever before. And then I met the ground.*"[26]

In a "Readers' Guide" on her website, Durrow raises the question, "Do you think that in the age of Obama, biracial/bicultural people will continue to experience the same kinds of stereotypes and stigma that Rachel did?"[27] *The Girl Who Fell from the Sky* thematizes not only the still common misperception that a white mother of mixed-race children must be an adoptive parent but also Rachel's sense of biracial and semi-Danish estrangement in her grandmother's black world. Although the novel may ultimately find its source of horror in a good mother's growing mental disturbance more than in social conditions or race relations, there is little hope here that Hughes's American problem of those "who would be kin if they were not Negro" has reached a happy resolution in 2010. Yet the horrifying maternal act that has defined Rachel's life has also given her—she who was not meant to have a future—a new life in which she finally is able to express understanding and love of her mother.

AMONG YOUNG PLAYWRIGHTS who emerged in the first decade of the twenty-first century, Thomas Bradshaw stands out for his satirical edge and his broad, poster-like employment of the repertoire of American racial histories and sexual fantasies in an aggressive black-humor mode that makes audiences initially think that they are watching a comedy.[28] Born in 1980 in New Jersey, Bradshaw wanted to go beyond the mid-century protest tradition:

> There's the black literature of the '40s, '50s and '60s—white oppression is bad, reparations, apologizing. It was awareness building, really. That work was really necessary and important. . . . But there hasn't been much work done since then. What is a modern presentation of race? What kind of issues do upper middle class blacks have to deal with? After you assimilate into the mainstream, what are the issues?[29]

His ironically titled play *Strom Thurmond Is Not a Racist* (2007) addresses the paradox that, at the core of racial segregation, there was also miscegenation.[30] The thinly veiled hypocrisy in the case of South Carolina Senator Strom Thurmond's lifelong but secretive support for his and Carrie Butler's illegitimate biracial daughter, Essie Mae Washington-Williams, provides the source material for the play. Bradshaw follows the story chronologically, from Thurmond's seduction of the sixteen-year-old Carrie to the spiriting away of their child through various encounters he has with his daughter later on, all while his political career as a segregationist and opponent of civil rights unfolds. This path gives Bradshaw the opportunity to contrast Thurmond's infatuation—he recites Wordsworth's "Daffodils" to Carrie—with his prayers for purity and his wish to please his excessively racist father, who says such things as, "We had to lynch a thousand Niggers before they learned their place in the South again!" Later, the play juxtaposes Thurmond's own segregationist statements—"We have segregation because God doesn't want blacks and whites to mix"—with his daughter's sad and critical observation:

You become a different person when you stand in front of cheer-
ing crowds giving campaign speeches. You're unrecognizable to
me. You act and speak completely different from the man I know.
The man I know is loving and wonderful to me, the man on stage
speaks venomously of my kind. It makes me wonder which is the
real you or [if] there's a real you.[31]

In a conversation between Strom and his father, Bradshaw reveals how
the public rhetoric against "nigger-loving" (a phrase employed by both
men) is only the flip side of what Strom's father calls "a right of passage
for most southern gentlemen." His father says, "We learn about women
from the promiscuous nigress. They tantalize us. There's something irresistible about them. We demonize them by day and crawl into their beds
at night." Strom responds, "But we never let the truth be known. It's
our open secret." The play ends with Essie Mae's funeral eulogy for her
father, which she concludes with, "I'm going to miss you daddy."[32] In
explicitly naming the open secret and ending with the word "daddy,"
Strom Thurmond Is Not a Racist crisply illuminates Everett Hughes's notion
of unmet white American "obligations to Negroes who would be kin if
they were not Negro."

Racist obstacles to public recognition and acceptance of interracial
kinship also take center stage in Bradshaw's lurid play *Cleansed*. While
wearing a Klan mask her white grandmother gave her, Lauraul, a mixed-
race daughter who wishes to be white, kills her black father, a heart sur-
geon, for having contaminated her white blood. This play is a ritual-like
revision of black political drama in the wake of the 1960s, in which a
daughter might kill her father for being a sell-out Negro according to
her newly acquired revolutionary black nationalist views (as was the case
with M'Balia in Richard Wesley's *Black Terror* of 1971). But in the twenty-first century of *Cleansed*, the confused biracial daughter is accepted
into a white supremacist group because she hates Negroes even more
than the whites do.

In Bradshaw's theatrical world, an extended interracial family sitting down to a happy Thanksgiving dinner in a postracial setting seems
unthinkable. In a review in the *New Yorker*, Hilton Als confirms the sense
that Bradshaw's plays "take a sharp turn toward strictly racial themes" (in
Wright's formula). "It's fairly easy to get beyond Bradshaw's purposefully
thin surfaces," Als writes, "unless, of course, you're unwilling to look at

what contorts all America: racism, and the bullshit notion that it doesn't affect our view of sex and love in a so-called post-racial country."[33]

BORN IN SOUTH CAROLINA in 1971, the poet Terrance Hayes engages obliquely and self-reflexively with the past as shaped by the Civil Rights Movement, and he does so while experimenting with new poetic forms and with an impressive cultural openness. In his collection of poems *Lighthead* (2010), he finds inspiration in a mélange of greats: from David Bowie, Fela Kuti, and Etta James to Gwendolyn Brooks, Wallace Stevens, and Elizabeth Alexander (who received broader international attention for her inauguration poem for Barack Obama) and *The Hitchhiker's Guide to the Galaxy*.[34] Hayes likes to compose *pecha kucha* poems, a word he explains as "a Japanese adaptation/loanword of the word *picture*, pronounced in three syllables, like 'pe-chack-cha.'"[35] This format, Hayes writes, is derived from Japanese business presentations of twenty connected images of twenty seconds each. Perfect for polished cycles or sequences of poems, the PowerPoint model has inspired a highly contemporary, nontraditional poetic genre that is based in technology and removed from any claims of American or African American authenticity. In one twenty-slide poetic sequence, titled "For Brothers of the Dragon," Hayes imagines Malcolm X's brothers on the day Malcolm was buried, including such self-reflexive slides as

[HOW FICTION FUNCTIONS]

However else fiction functions, it fills you with the sound
of crows chirping, alive alive alive. But that's temporary too.
Tell my story, begs the past, as if it was a prayer
for an imagined life or a life that's better than the life you live.[36]

"What if blackness is a fad?" Hayes asks in "[MALEDICTION]," a slide of another *pecha kucha* with the general title, "Arbor for Butch." It is inspired by the African American artist Martin Puryear, the titles of whose works serve as headings for each of the *pecha kucha*. Hayes suggests that readers search online for these headings and look at the related images. A photograph of Puryear's sculpture *Malediction* is thus to be imagined as the inter-artistic background of Hayes's quatrain that continues, after his opening question, with, "Dear Negritude, I live as you live, / waiting to be better than I am."[37]

Self-reflexive and ironic uneasiness also characterizes his poem "The Avocado," a sustained conceit on the legacy of civil rights and black nationalist actions. The poem casts the avocado as the ideal emblem for a hypothetical abolitionist flag:

> "In 1971, drunk on the sweet, sweet juice of revolution,
> a crew of us marched into the president's office with a list
> of demands," the black man tells us at the February luncheon,
> and I'm pretending I haven't heard this one before as I eye
> black tortillas on a red plate beside a big green bowl
> of guacamole made from the whipped, battered remains
> of several harmless former avocados.[38]

Hayes articulates the distance between the red, black, and green of the black nationalist flag and the commodification of that historical moment, with its sense of political advocacy (a word related to "avocado") for such goals as reparations, into the "money-colored flesh of the avocado." The transformation of the avocado into guacamole provides a visual analogy to a recounting of the past that is so palatable and trite that the listener has to pretend not to have heard the story before.

"AT THE PRESENT MOMENT there is no one dominant note in Negro literary expression": Richard Wright's comment from 1957 echoes still today. Reading Amina Gautier, Heidi Durrow, Thomas Bradshaw, and Terrance Hayes, one encounters rather heterogeneous suggestions about possible story lines for African American literature, as well as diverse approaches to the question whether the country is moving toward a postracial world in the age of Obama. Yet perhaps there never was only one, dominant African American narrative, for writers from Phillis Wheatley and Frank Webb to Albert Murray and Andrea Lee have written about many themes besides race—although racial themes may have been what their readers were looking for most often.

Ironically, no writer makes that more apparent than Richard Wright. Although his most frequently read and taught works emphasize the prototypical African American narrative of victimization, from the legacy of slavery to the ethics of living Jim Crow, he turned away from writing such black proletarian protest poems as "I Have Seen Black Hands" and instead experimented with free-floating and untitled haikus that might be of interest to Hayes—for example, "Crying and crying, / Melodious strings of geese / Passing a graveyard" and "Holding too much rain, / The tulip stoops and spills it, / Then straightens again." Wright also shifted from imagining socially determined and constrained black characters, as in *Uncle Tom's Children* and *Native Son*, to focusing on a much broader range of human motivation and psychology in *The Outsider* and *Savage Holiday*. He expanded from the legacy of American history in *12 Million Black Voices* to take on truly global concerns with tradition and modernity, decolonization, and the emergence of a Third World voice in *Pagan Spain, Black Power*, and *The Color Curtain*.[39] Wright's own willingness to address "strictly racial themes" while also searching for "the common themes and burdens of literary expression which are the heritage of all" is worth remembering, for writers and readers alike, in a world that seems to be postracial and racial at the same time.

Acknowledgments

I AM GRATEFUL to Micah Kleit for suggesting that I put together this book and to Alide Cagidemetrio for her encouragement and help throughout the process of imagining it. Jeffrey Ferguson read the manuscript and suggested the title of this book; Glenda R. Carpio and Rafia Zafar aided me at various stages. David Neustadt helped with image research and permissions. Jamie Wacks proofread, corrected, edited, and formatted the text. Susan Deeks copyedited the manuscript. Kate Nichols designed the layout, and Joan Vidal managed the book's production at Temple University Press.

The essays collected in this volume originally appeared in the sources listed on the copyright page extension and included on the chapter openers, and in the original publications I expressed my gratitude to research assistants, students, writers, and colleagues who helped me find sources and who commented on drafts. In turning each essay into a chapter for this book, I added a descriptive headnote with a date, and where needed I adjusted the chapter title. The texts are reprinted here without significant alteration—with only occasional adjustments, corrections, updates, and deletions as needed for accuracy and consistency and to reduce repetition among the essays.

Notes

INTRODUCTION

1. Richard Wright, *White Man, Listen!* (1957), repr. ed. (Garden City, NY: Double-day Anchor, 1964), 71–72, 102. In the second excerpt, Wright quotes from his own *12 Million Black Voices: A Folk History of the Negro in the United States* (1941), repr. ed. (New York: Thunders Mouth Press, 1988).

2. See Richard Wright's selection in Eugene Woods, ed., *I Wish I'd Written That: Selections Chosen by Favorite American Authors* (New York: McGraw-Hill, 1946).

3. Brian Hochman, "Ellison's Hemingway," *African American Review* 42, nos. 3–4 (Fall–Winter 2008): 513–532.

4. For a reprint of "I Saw Negro Votes Peddled" and "Why the Negro Won't Buy Communism," Hurston's little-known *American Legion Magazine* essays, critically introduced by Ernest Julius Mitchell II, see *Journal of Transnational American Studies* 5, no. 1 (2013), available at https://escholarship.org/uc/acgcc_jtas?volume=5;issue=1.

5. William J. Maxwell published the study *F. B. Eyes: How Hoover's Ghostreaders Framed African American Literature* (Princeton, NJ: Princeton University Press, 2015) and created a publicly accessible website with Freedom of Information Act surveillance documents of African American writers, including Baraka and Wright, The Du Bois files are available at http://omeka.wustl.edu/omeka/exhibits/show/fbeyes/duboisweb (accessed May 14, 2015).

6. I am drawing on Martha Jane Nadell, *Enter the New Negroes: Images of Race in American Culture* (Cambridge, MA: Harvard University Press, 2004), 47–48. See also Jeffrey C. Stewart, *To Color America: Portraits by Winold Reiss* (Washington, DC: Smithsonian Institution Press for the National Portrait Gallery, 1989), as well as the chapter on Reiss in Frank Mehring, *The Democratic Gap: Transcultural Transformations of German Immigrants and the Promise of American Democracy* (Heidelberg, Germany: Universitätsverlag Winter, 2013). Toomer also had a series of photographic portraits taken by Alfred Stieglitz, and a watercolor by Georgia O'Keeffe, *Birch and Pine Trees—Pink*

(1925), has been considered a "surrogate portrait" of Toomer. Van Vechten took several photographs of Hurston that are frequently reproduced.

7. See Emily Bernard, *Carl Van Vechten and the Harlem Renaissance: A Portrait in Black and White* (New Haven, CT: Yale University Press, 2012); Edward White, *The Tastemaker: Carl Van Vechten and the Birth of Modern America* (New York: Farrar, Straus and Giroux, 2014).

CHAPTER 1

1. According to the database of Stephen Behrendt, David Richardson, and David Eltis at the W. E. B. Du Bois Institute, Harvard University, the total number of Africans transported to the Americas was 11,569,000; the figure is based on records for 27,233 voyages by slavers.

2. Nathan Huggins, *Black Odyssey: The Afro-American Ordeal in Slavery* (New York: Pantheon, 1977), 25–56.

3. Paul Edwards, *The Interesting Narrative of the Life of Olaudah Equiano, or Gustavus Vassa, the African. Written by Himself* (1789), Colonial History Series, 2 vols. (London: Dawsons of Pall Mall, 1969). Hereafter, all references are to this edition; page numbers are cited in parentheses in the text.

4. My essay uses the two names interchangeably.

5. Charles Nichols, *Many Thousand Gone: The Ex-Slaves' Account of Their Bondage and Freedom* (Bloomington: Indiana University Press, 1963), xi.

6. Paul Edwards, "Introduction," in Edwards, *The Life of Olaudah Equiano*, 1:xlv–xlvii. As Ernst Robert Curtius's work on "The Book as Symbol" suggests, this topos is also derived from the long legacy of book metaphors going back at least to Isidore of Sevilla (560–636), who had observed in his *Etymologiae* that letters are "signs" that have the "power [to] bring the speech of one absent to our ears": Ernst Robert Curtius, *European Literature and the Latin Middle Ages* (1949), trans. Willard Trask, Bollingen Series 36 (New York: Pantheon, 1953), 302–347, esp. 313.

7. Gates adds the reference to the memoir by John Marrant (1785): Henry Louis Gates Jr., *The Signifying Monkey: A Theory of Afro-American Literary Criticism* (London: Oxford University Press, 1988). For Garcilaso, see *Royal Commentaries of the Incas and General History of Peru, Part One, 1609*, trans. Harold V. Livermore (Austin: University of Texas Press, 1966), 604–605. Invoking a biography of Columbus, Equiano himself later points to the Bible, as if it were magic, to intimidate the Miskito Indians (2:187).

8. Abbé Henri Grégoire was the first to note this in *De la littérature des Nègres; ou, Recherches sur leurs facultés intellectuelles, leurs qualités morales et leur littérature* (Paris: Maradan, 1808).

9. On the "bourgeois subject," see Geraldine Murphy, "Olaudah Equiano: Accidental Tourist," *Eighteenth-Century Studies* 27, no. 4 (July 1994): 551–568. One need only remember David Hume's racist footnote on Negro inferiority in his essay "Of National Characters" (1753–1754) to understand what notions Equiano and other early African writers in England were up against. The passage is reprinted in Wylie Sypher, *Guinea's Captive Kings: British Anti-slavery Literature of the XVIIIth Century* (Chapel Hill: University of North Carolina Press, 1942), 52–53. Sypher points out, however, that Hume also argued against domestic slavery. Many Enlightenment thinkers were contradictory on the subject of African slavery.

10. Eva Beatrice Dykes, *The Negro in English Romantic Thought; or, A Study of Sympathy for the Oppressed* (Washington, DC: Associated Publishers, 1942), and Sypher were the first to stress this aspect. Paul Edwards was skeptical and viewed Equiano as distinct from the "noble savage" tradition.

11. Jean-Jacques Rousseau, *A Discourse upon the Origin and Foundation of the Inequality among Mankind* (London: Dodsley, 1761), 30.

12. Charles-Louis de Secondat, Baron de Montesquieu, *De l'esprit des lois*, ed. Victor Goldschmidt (Paris: Garnier-Flammarion, 1979), book 15, vol. 1, 393. A slightly different English translation can be found in *The Spirit of the Laws*, ed. Franz Neumann (New York: Hafner, 1949), 1:238–240. Whereas Urs Bitterli sees Montesquieu as ironist, Neumann reads him as making a straight comment: Urs Bitterli, *Die "Wilden" und die "Zivilisierten": Die europäisch-überseeische Begegnung* (Munich: C. H. Beck, 1976); Neumann, *The Spirit of the Laws*, 239.

13. Francis Daniel Pastorius, the German American founder of Germantown, articulated the first protest against slavery in British North America as early as 1688. As Alfred Brophy has shown, Pastorius addressed the Quaker Monthly Meeting, calling attention to the inappropriateness of holding humans in bondage, exhorting Quakers to follow the golden rule, and reminding them that they, too, might have been enslaved by Turkish pirates. See Brophy's introduction to Francis Daniel Pastorius, *Bee-Hive* in *The Multilingual Anthology of American Literature*, ed. Marc Shell and Werner Sollors (New York: New York University Press, 2000), 14.

14. John Woolman, *Some Considerations*, 2, 5, 8, available at http://archive.org/stream/considerationson00wool/considerationson00wool_djvu.txt. He also wrote, "When self-love presides in our minds our opinions are biassed in our own favour; and in this condition, being concerned with a people so situated that they have no voice to plead their own cause, there is danger of using ourselves to an undisturbed partiality until, by long custom, the mind becomes reconciled with it and the judgment itself infected": ibid., 6. He worried about the effect of slavery on Quaker children who were educated in "being masters of men in their childhood" and asked, "How can we expect otherwise than that their tender minds will be possessed with thoughts too high for them": ibid., 9. See also the discussion in Winthrop Jordan, *White over Black: American Attitudes toward the Negro, 1550–1812* (1968), repr. ed. (Baltimore: Penguin, 1969), 271–276.

15. Thomas Clarkson, *An Essay on the Slavery and Commerce of the Human Species, Particularly the African*, 3rd ed. (London [printed in Philadelphia], 1787), 52, 155.

16. Ibid., v–vi; Sypher, *Guinea's Captive Kings*, 17. Clarkson's printer, who was a Quaker, advertised, on a page facing the essay's preface, Benezet's works and James Ramsay's *Essay on the Treatment and Conversion of African Slaves* (1784), an essay that Clarkson (and Vassa) defended on rationalist principles against James Tobin's pro-slavery attacks.

17. In his descriptive details concerning his place of birth, Equiano follows closely the idyllic accounts collected in Benezet, even to the extent of incorporating whole sentences. Through Benezet's writings, Equiano drew on eighteenth-century works such as the French traveler Michel Adanson's *Voyage to Senegal* (translated in 1759); Benezet, in turn, in his *Account of Guinea*, drew on Adanson. Adanson's *Voyage* was also cited in authenticating footnotes to Thomas Day and John Bicknell's immensely popular poem *The Dying Negro* (1773), which Equiano quotes in *Narrative*, apparently from memory.

18. As Stefania Piccinato observed, Equiano embodied biculturalism: see Stefania Piccinato, "Olaudah Equiano Gustavus Vassa: Un uomo del '700 fra due culture," in *Il senso del nonsenso*, ed. Lynn Salkin Sbiroli (Rome: Edizioni Scientifiche Italiane, 1994), 237–245.

19. See Murphy, "Olaudah Equiano."

20. See Adam Potkay, "Olaudah Equiano and the Art of Spiritual Autobiography," *Eighteenth-Century Studies* 27, no. 4 (July 1994): 601–614.

21. Even the unfulfilled plans Equiano made to return to West Africa defined his role as commissary of a British resettlement scheme.

22. Houston A. Baker Jr., *Blues, Ideology, and Afro-American Literature: A Vernacular Theory* (Chicago: University of Chicago Press, 1984), 35.

23. In this respect, Equiano was close to Benezet's position.

24. Thomas Browne, "Of the Blackness of Negroes," *Pseudodoxia* (1646), in *The Works of Sir Thomas Browne*, ed. Charles Sayle (London: Grant Richards, 1904), 2:385.

25. John Mitchell, "Essay on the Causes of the Different Colours of People in Different Climates," in Royal Society, *Philosophical Transactions 1744*, vol. 9 (London: C. R. Baldwin, 1809), 65.

26. In the manner of many of his contemporaries who were interested in African color variation, Equiano mentions the red-skinned Oye-Eboe, whose existence complicates notions of color, and he describes an interracial family scene that would seem to appeal to his sense of wonder and express his belief that complexion is merely an accidental human quality: "Soon after my arrival in London, I saw a remarkable circumstance relative to African complexion, which I thought so extraordinary, that I beg leave just to mention it: A white negro woman, that I had formerly seen in London and other parts, had married a white man, by whom she had three boys, and they were every one mulattoes, and yet they had fine light hair" (2:216).

27. "Letter to J. T. [James Tobin]," *Public Advertiser*, January 28, 1788.

28. Charles T. Davis, *Black Is the Color of the Cosmos: Essays on Afro-American Literature and Culture, 1942–1981* (New York: Garland, 1982), 86.

29. For interesting comparisons between Franklin and Equiano, see Rafia Zafar, *We Wear the Mask: African Americans Write American Literature, 1760–1870* (New York: Columbia University Press, 1997); Martin Christadler, "Selbstkonstitution und Lebensgeschichte in der Autobiographie der Aufklärung: Benjamin Franklin und Olaudah Equiano," in *Skepsis, oder das Spiel mit dem Zweifel. Festschrift für Ralph-Rainer Wuthenow zum 65. Geburtstag*, ed. Carola Hilmes, Dietrich Mathy, and Hans-Joachim Piechotta (Würzburg, Germany: Königshausen and Neumann, 1994).

30. Vincent Carretta, "Three West Indian Writers of the 1780s Revisited and Revised," *Research in African Literatures* 29, no. 4 (Winter 1998): 73–86. The corresponding information in Carretta's edition appears in footnote 485, in which the editor argues, "Gustavus Weston was almost certainly Gustavus Vassa," but without drawing any conclusions concerning Equiano's African identity, even though he mentions in footnote 197 that the baptismal record of St. Margaret's Church in Westminster reads, "Gustavus Vassa a Black born in Carolina 12 years old" (February 9, 1759).

31. Vincent Carretta, "Olaudah Equiano or Gustavus Vassa? New Light on an Eighteenth-Century Question of Identity," *Slavery and Abolition* 20, no. 3 (December 1999): 100–102. Carretta suggests as possible carriers the snow *Ogden* for the Middle Passage from the Bight of Biafra to Barbados and the sloop *Nancy* for the voyage from Barbados to the York River, on June 13, 1754. Interestingly, another ship named *Nancy* appears

as the frontispiece to the second volume of the first edition. Robert Allison examined the arrival of slave ships in Virginia in 1756 and found only two that arrived there, one of which, the *Kingston*, did sell two or three slaves; up the York River there also was a plantation owned by a man named Campbell or Kammel: see Olaudah Equiano, *The Interesting Narrative of the Life of Olaudah Equiano, Written by Himself*, ed. Robert J. Allison, repr. ed. (Boston: Bedford Books, 1995), 25n24. See also Vincent Carretta, *Equiano, the African: Biography of a Self-Made Man* (Athens: University of Georgia Press, 2005), and his essay "Methodology in the Making and Reception of *Equiano*," in *Biography and the Black Atlantic*, ed. Lisa A. Lindsay and John Wood Sweet (Philadelphia: University of Pennsylvania Press, 2013), 171–191.

CHAPTER 2

1. Rosemary F. Crockett, "Frank J. Webb: The Shift to Color Discrimination," in *The Black Columbiad: Defining Moments in African American Literature and Culture*, ed. Maria Diedrich and Werner Sollors (Cambridge, MA: Harvard University Press, 1994), 112–122; Allan D. Austin, "Frank Webb," in *Encyclopedia of African-American Culture and History*, ed. Jack Salzman, David Lionel Smith, and Cornel West, vol. 5 (New York: Simon and Schuster Macmillan, 1996), 2796; Rosemary F. Crockett, "'The Garies and Their Friends': A Study of Frank J. Webb and His Novel," Ph.D. diss., Harvard University, Cambridge, MA, June 1998; Eric Gardner, "'A Gentleman of Superior Cultivation and Refinement': Recovering the Biography of Frank J. Webb," *African American Review* 35, no. 2 (Summer 2001): 297–308; Eric Gardner, "Webb, Frank J.," in *American National Biography Online*, July 2002 update, available at http://www.anb.org/arti cles/16/16-03466.html?a=1&n=webb&d=10&ss=9&q=19 (accessed March 9, 2015). See also the chapter on Webb in M. Giulia Fabi, *Passing and the Rise of the African American Novel* (Urbana: University of Illinois Press, 2001).

2. Amber D. Moulton, "'Times Change': Frank J. Webb Addresses Robert Morris on the Promise of Reconstruction," *New England Quarterly* 85, no. 1 (March 2012): 137–144, reproducing a previously unknown letter by Webb dated November 29, 1869, that she found in the Morris Papers.

3. Robert Reid-Pharr, "Introduction," in Frank J. Webb, *The Garies and Their Friends* (Baltimore: Johns Hopkins University Press, 1997).

4. Carla L. Peterson, "Capitalism, Black (Under)development, and the Production of the African-American Novel in the 1850s." *American Literary History* 4 (1992): 559–583.

5. Blyden Jackson, *A History of Afro-American Literature, Volume 1: The Long Beginning, 1746–1895* (Baton Rouge: Louisiana State University Press, 1989). Hugh Gloster read the roles of Walters and the Ellises differently. "In contradistinction to the Garies," he writes, "a humble dark-skinned family struggles to a degree of mediocre security and contentment": Hugh M. Gloster, *Negro Voices in American Fiction* (Chapel Hill: University of North Carolina Press, 1948), 27.

6. Robert S. Levine, "Disturbing Boundaries: Temperance, Black Elevation, and Violence in Frank J. Webb's *The Garies and Their Friends*," *Prospects* 19 (1994): 349–373.

7. Theodore Hershberg, "Free Blacks in Antebellum Philadelphia: A Study of Ex-Slaves, Freeborn, and Socioeconomic Decline," in *African Americans in Pennsylvania: Shifting Historical Perspectives*, ed. Joe William Trotter Jr. and Eric Ledell Smith (University Park: Pennsylvania State University Press, 1997), 123–147. See also Sam Bass War-

ner, *The Private City: Philadelphia in Three Periods of Its Growth* (Philadelphia: University of Pennsylvania Press, 1968); Noel Ignatiev, *How the Irish Became White* (New York: Routledge, 1995).

8. Philip Lapsansky, "Afro-Americana: Frank J. Webb and His Friends," in *Annual Report of the Library Company of Philadelphia for the Year 1990* (Philadelphia: Library Company of Philadelphia, 1991), 27–43.

9. See Mary Maillard, "'Faithfully Drawn from Real Life': Autobiographical Elements in Frank J. Webb's *The Garies and Their Friends*," *Pennsylvania Magazine of History and Biography* 137, no. 3 (July 2013): 261–300.

10. In 1856, Webb also wrote a biographical sketch of his first wife. In 1870, he wrote a letter he sent to the journalist Mary Wager Fisher about his second novel, "Paul Sumner," which was lost in manuscript. The political piece "The Benefits of Co-operation," from the *New Era* of February 3, 1870, was published anonymously and consists of a conversation about the advantages of joining a cooperative. Since a "Mary" and her husband "Frank" are the protagonists in the piece, it may be related to the Webbs.

11. Arthur P. Davis, "Introduction," in Frank J. Webb, *The Garies and Their Friends* (New York: Arno Press, 1969). Earlier on, Gloster devoted a paragraph-length discussion to Frank Webb, finding his novel "unlike most other early fiction by Negroes in that it analyzes the effect of race prejudice above the Mason-Dixon line": Gloster, *Negro Voices in American Fiction*, 27.

12. See, e.g., James H. DeVries, "The Tradition of the Sentimental Novel in *The Garies and Their Friends*," *College Language Association Journal* 17, no. 2 (1973): 241–249; Anna Engle, "Depictions of the Irish in Frank Webb's *The Garies and Their Friends* and Frances E. W. Harper's *Trial and Triumph*," *MELUS* 26, no. 1 (Spring 2001): 151–171; Anna Mae Duane, "Remaking Black Motherhood in Frank J. Webb's *The Garies and Their Friends*," *African American Review* 38, no. 2 (Summer 2004): 201–212; Gene Andrew Jarrett, *African American Literature beyond Race: An Alternative Reader* (New York: New York University Press, 2006); Samuel Otter, "Frank Webb's Still Life: Rethinking Literature and Politics through *The Garies and Their Friends*," *American Literary History* 20, no. 4 (Winter 2008): 29–58; Tess Chakkalakal, "Free, Black, and Married: Frank J. Webb's *The Garies and Their Friends*," in *Novel Bondage* (Champaign: University of Illinois Press, 2011), 47–63.

CHAPTER 3

1. Charles W. Chesnutt, *The Conjure Woman*, repr. ed. with an introduction by Robert M. Farnsworth (Ann Arbor: University of Michigan Press, 1969). Hereafter, all references are to this edition (abbreviated *TCW*); page numbers are cited in parentheses in the text.

2. *Webster's Third New International Dictionary* (1961); Alan Dundes, ed., *Mother Wit from the Laughing Barrel* (Englewood Cliffs, NJ: Prentice-Hall, 1973), 371n.

3. The best biographical account is in Frances Richardson Keller, *An American Crusade: The Life of Charles Waddell Chesnutt* (Provo, UT: Brigham Young University Press, 1978), 25–85.

4. Sylvia Lyons Render, *The Short Fiction of Charles W. Chesnutt* (Washington, DC: Howard University Press, 1974). Hereafter, all references are to this edition (abbreviated *TSF*); page numbers are cited in parentheses in the text.

5. Robert A. Smith, "A Note on the Folktales of Charles W. Chesnutt," *College Language Association Journal* 5 (March 1962): 232.

6. William Dean Howells, "Mr. Charles W. Chesnutt's Stories," *Atlantic Monthly*, May 1900, 699–701, cited in Robert A. Bone, *Down Home: A History of Afro-American Short Fiction from Its Beginning to the End of the Harlem Renaissance* (New York: G. P. Putnam's Sons, 1975), 105.

7. Richard E. Baldwin, "The Art of *The Conjure Woman*," *American Literature* 43 (1971): 385–398; Bone, *Down Home*, 86–88; Robert Hemenway, "Gothic Sociology: Charles Chesnutt and the Gothic Mode," *Studies in the Literary Imagination* 7 (Spring 1974): 101–119. A useful survey of Chesnutt criticism is in William L. Andrews, "Charles Waddell Chesnutt: An Essay in Bibliography," *Resources for American Literary Study* 6, no. 1 (Spring 1976): 3–22.

8. Newbell Niles Puckett, *The Magic and Folk Beliefs of the Southern Negro* (1926), repr. ed. (New York: Dover, 1969), 474–475.

9. Wayland D. Hanel, Anna Cassetta, and Sondra Thiederman, eds., *Popular Beliefs and Superstitions: A Compendium of American Folklore*, 3 vols. (Boston: G. K. Hall, 1981). Hereafter, all references to this edition, citing number and year, are in parentheses in the text.

10. See Gustav Jahoda, *The Psychology of Superstition* (Harmondsworth, UK: Penguin, 1969), 4–8.

11. Bone, *Down Home*, 86.

12. See Jahoda, *The Psychology of Superstition*, 4–8.

13. Robert Bone, lecture given at Columbia University, New York, September 24, 1975.

14. James R. Giles, "Chesnutt's Primus and Annie: A Contemporary View of *The Conjure Woman*," *Markham Review* 3 (October 1971): 46–49.

15. Theodore Hovet, "Chesnutt's 'The Goophered Grapevine' as Social Criticism," *Negro American Literature Forum* 7 (Fall 1973): 86–88.

16. Reprinted in Dundes, *Mother Wit*, 369–376, esp. 372, 375.

17. Robert B. Stepto, "'The Simple but Intensely Human Inner Life of Slavery': Storytelling, Fiction, and the Revision of History in Charles W. Chesnutt's 'Uncle Julius Stories,'" in *History and Tradition in Afro-American Culture*, ed. Günter Lenz (Frankfurt, Germany: Campus-Verlag, 1984), 54n27. See also Robert B. Stepto and Jennifer Lee Greeson, eds., *Charles W. Chesnutt, The Conjure Stories: A Norton Critical Edition* (New York: W. W. Norton, 2012). Perhaps it deserves mention that Chesnutt explained in an interview he gave in 1899 that one model for John (at least, the John of "The Goophered Grapevine") was his father-in-law:

> My father-in-law had made enough to buy one of the old Southern houses—a town house it was—but there was a great garden around it. One day an old colored man came to work in this garden, and as he leaned on his how he told me of an old man who had anointed his bald head with scuppernong grape-juice which had the remarkable effect of producing a luxuriant crop of hair. This hair grew with the rising sap of the scuppernong vines and fell away periodically with the shrivelling of the grapes, occasioning a yearly repetition of the anointing process. That was the foundation of "The Goophered Grapevine."

Quoted in Pauline Carrington Bouvé, "An Aboriginal Author: The Work and Personality of Charles W. Chesnutt," *Boston Transcript*, August 22, 1899. Perhaps the figure of the father-in-law accounts for some of the obvious ambivalence with which Chesnutt approaches the narrator of *The Conjure Woman*.

18. Smith, "A Note on the Folktales of Charles W. Chesnutt," 232.

19. William Andrews, "The Significance of Charles W. Chesnutt's 'Conjure Stories,'" *Southern Literary Journal* 7 (Fall 1974): 85n19.

20. Jules Chametzky, *Our Decentralized Literature: Cultural Mediation in Selected Jewish and Southern Writers* (Amherst: University of Massachusetts Press, 1986), 39.

21. Melvin Dixon, "The Teller as Folk Trickster in Chesnutt's *The Conjure Woman*," *College Language Association Journal* 18 (December 1974): 186–197.

22. Claudia de Lys, *A Treasury of American Superstitions* (New York: Philosophical Library, 1948), 117–118.

23. David Britt, "Chesnutt's Conjure Tales: What You See Is What You Get," *College Language Association Journal* 15 (March 1972): 274.

24. Bone, *Down Home*, 86, 88.

25. Hemenway, "Gothic Sociology," 112.

26. The German translator of *The Conjure Woman*, Monika Plessner, chose the title *Der verwunschene Weinberg* (The Goophered Grapevine) because conjure women or witches of European fairy tales usually represent evil powers.

27. Josef F. Thiel and Jürgen Frembgen call attention to the origins of the word "fetish." (Derived from the Portuguese "feitiço," akin to "factitious," it was used as early as 1600 in West African travel accounts.) They stress the negative uses of (commodity and sexual) "fetishism" in Marxist and Freudian thought and suggestively describe the Western equivalents of fetishes (among them, according to Marcel Mauss, money) in *Was sind Fetische?* (Frankfurt, Germany: Museum für Völkerkunde, 1986), 9–47.

28. Hemenway, "Gothic Sociology," 116.

29. Ibid., 117. Now (in 2015), thanks to Google Books, we know that the excerpt comes from Herbert Spencer, "The Instability of the Homogeneous Exemplifying Instability at Large," in *First Principles of a New System of Philosophy* (New York: D. Appleton, 1883).

30. See Karen Magee Myers, "Mythic Patterns in Charles Waddell Chesnutt's *The Conjure Woman* and Ovid's *Metamorphoses*," *Black American Literature Forum* 13, no. 1 (Spring 1979): 13–17; Christopher E. Koy, "African American Vernacular Latin and Ovidian Figures in Charles Chesnutt's Conjure Stories," *Litteraria Pragensia: Studies in Literature and Culture* 21, no. 41 (July 2011): 50–70.

31. For a Virgilian reading of Chesnutt, see Sarah Wagner-McCoy, "Virgilian Chesnutt: Eclogues of Slavery and Georgics of Reconstruction in the Conjure Tales," *ELH* 80, no. 1 (Spring 2013): 199–220.

32. Monika Plessner, "Nachwort," in Charles W. Chesnutt, *Der verwunschene Weinberg und andere Sklavenmärchen aus Nordamerika* (Frankfurt, Germany: Insel, 1979), 132–133.

33. Jahoda, *The Psychology of Superstition*, 138–147. Compare the NCTE language ruling for college teachers which suggests that to avoid offensiveness, writers should say "superstition" instead of "old wives' tale."

34. In this context, one could profitably interpret Chesnutt's statement in a letter of 1889 to Tourgée that he tried to make "the transition from the 'realm of superstition' to that of 'feeling and passion'" in "Dave's Neckliss": quoted in William L. Andrews, *The*

Literary Career of Charles W. Chesnutt (Baton Rouge: Louisiana State University Press, 1980), 21.

35. One need only remember the meaning of "goofer dust," the "graveyard" rabbit, and the resurrection motif in some of the metamorphoses. This aspect makes the rabbit's foot part of the rituals that "socially dead" people could invoke in order to undergo symbolic rebirths: see Orlando Patterson, *Slavery and Social Death: A Comparative Study* (Cambridge, MA: Harvard University Press, 1982), 214–239; Klaus Heinrich, *Vernunft und Mythos* (Frankfurt, Germany: Fischer, 1983), 7–9.

CHAPTER 4

1. Jean Toomer, *Cane* (1923), repr. ed. with an introduction by Arna Bontemps (New York: Harper and Row, 1969), title page. This is a facsimile of the text of the first edition of 1923. Hereafter, all references are to this edition; page numbers are cited in parentheses in the text. Toomer's important epigraph to *Cane* has been carelessly omitted in some modern reprints.

2. Henry F. May, *The End of American Innocence: A Study of the First Years of Our Own Time 1912–1917* (London: Jonathan Cape, 1960).

3. See Michael Soto, *The Modernist Nation: Generation, Renaissance, and Twentieth-Century American Literature* (Tuscaloosa: University of Alabama Press, 2004).

4. Waldo Frank, *Our America* (New York: Boni and Liveright, 1919), cited in the context of the correspondence between Frank and Toomer in Daniel Terris, "Waldo Frank and the Rediscovery of America, 1889–1929," Ph.D. diss., Harvard University, Cambridge, MA, 1992, 306.

5. On Frank and Toomer, see Terris, "Waldo Frank and the Rediscovery of America." At least one reviewer believed *Holiday* and *Cane* were written by the same author.

6. From an autobiographical sketch cited in Darwin T. Turner, ed., *Cane*, Norton Critical Edition (New York: W. W. Norton, 1988), 141–142. A larger excerpt appears in Darwin T. Turner, ed., *The Wayward and the Seeking: A Collection of Writings by Jean Toomer* (Washington DC: Howard University Press, 1980), 121.

7. Jean Toomer, *Essentials* (1931), repr. ed. with introduction by Rudolph P. Byrd (Athens: University of Georgia Press, 1991), xxxii.

8. Turner, *The Wayward and the Seeking*, 129. Cynthia Kerman and Richard Eldridge also call attention to this passage: Cynthia Kerman and Richard Eldridge, *The Lives of Jean Toomer: A Hunger for Wholeness* (Baton Rouge: Louisiana State University Press, 1987), 116.

9. Excerpted in Turner, *Cane*, 152.

10. The play was published in Turner, *The Wayward and the Seeking*, 243–325. See also the discussions in Nellie Y. McKay, *Jean Toomer, Artist: A Study of His Literary Life and Work, 1894–1936* (Chapel Hill: University of North Carolina Press, 1984); Rudolph P. Byrd, *Jean Toomer's Years with Gurdjieff* (Athens: University of Georgia Press, 1990); Terris, "Waldo Frank and the Rediscovery of America."

11. Turner, *The Wayward and the Seeking*, 290.

12. Undated letter to Waldo Frank, in Frederik L. Rusch, ed., *A Jean Toomer Reader: Selected Unpublished Writings* (New York: Oxford University Press, 1993), 25.

13. Robert Jones suggests that "Avey" is reminiscent of Joyce's "Araby." He also links the story's theme of the modern woman's indifference to men's sexual advances

to Eliot's *Waste Land*: Robert B. Jones, *Jean Toomer and the Prison-House of Thought: A Phenomenology of the Spirit* (Amherst: University of Massachusetts Press, 1993), 42,

14. Toomer sometimes employs two-point (rather than three-point) ellipses. I have retained his usage.

15. The tale may go back to an incident reported in Walter White, *Rope and Faggot* (1929), repr. ed. (New York: Arno Press, 1969), 20–21: "In the ten years from January 1, 1918, through 1927, American mobs lynched 454 persons. Of these, 38 were white, and 416 were coloured. Eleven of the Negro victims were women, three of them at the time of lynching with child." White gives a detailed account of the lynching of Mary Turner (the pregnant wife of Hayes Turner, who had been killed by a mob), writing, "Securely they bound her ankles together and, by them, hanged her to a tree. Gasoline and motor oil were thrown upon her dangling clothes; a match wrapped her in sudden flames. . . . The clothes burned from her crisply toasted body, in which, unfortunately, life still lingered, a man stepped towards the woman and, with his knife, ripped open the abdomen in a crude Caesarean operation. Out tumbled the prematurely born child. Two feeble cries it gave—and received for answer the heel of a stalwart man, as life was ground out of the tiny form": ibid., 28–29.

16. Excerpted in Turner, *Cane*, 152. The letter is also cited and perceptively discussed in, among others, McKay, *Jean Toomer*, and Byrd, *Jean Toomer's Years with Gurdjieff.*

17. Robert A. Bone, *The Negro Novel in America* (New Haven, CT: Yale University Press, 1958); McKay, *Jean Toomer.* John Reilly and Patricia Watkins are among the critics who have developed aspects of the unity of *Cane.* As Turner suggests, names also recur from one section to another: John Stone in "Becky" is the father of Bob Stone in "Blood-Burning Moon," and David Georgia also appears in both of these tales; "Barlo" appears in "Becky" and "Esther"; the "Dixie Pike" in "Carma" and "Fern." For a concise statement of elements that complicate a unifying reading of *Cane*, see Byrd, *Jean Toomer's Years with Gurdjieff*, 15–18.

18. John Reilly, "The Search for Black Redemption: Jean Toomer's *Cane*," reprinted in Turner, *Cane*, 198.

19. See Jones, *Jean Toomer and the Prison-House of Thought*, 47. The question is repeated three more times and served as inspiration for Farah Jasmine Griffin, *"Who Set You Flowin'?" The African-American Migration Narrative* (New York: Oxford University Press, 1994).

20. Turner and Byrd, among others, have briefly discussed imagist aspects of Toomer's work. Flint's and Pound's maxims are cited in William Pratt, ed., *The Imagist Poem: Modern Poetry in Miniature* (New York: Dutton, 1963), 18.

21. T. E. Hulme, cited in ibid., 28. Du Bois's review of *Cane* is reprinted in Frank Durham, ed., *Merrill Studies in Cane* (Columbus, OH: Merrill, 1971), 40–42, and excerpted in Turner, *Cane*, 170–171.

22. Cited in Kerman and Eldridge, *The Lives of Jean Toomer*, 95.

23. Charles C. Eldredge, *Georgia O'Keeffe* (New York: Harry N. Abrams, 1987), 44. For a full analysis of Toomer's literary work in relationship to O'Keeffe's and Stieglitz's visual arts, see Martha J. Nadell, *Enter the New Negroes: Images of Race in American Culture* (Cambridge, MA: Harvard University Press, 2004).

24. Rusch, *A Jean Toomer Reader*, 280–281.

25. Jean Toomer, "Race Problems and Modern Society," in *Man and His World: Northwestern University Essays in Contemporary Thought*, ed. Baker Brownell (New York: Van Nostrand, 1929), 98–99. This essay, reprinted in Werner Sollors, ed., *Theories of*

Ethnicity: Classic Essays (Basingstoke, UK: Macmillan, 1996), 168–190, has not received much attention by Toomer scholars. See, however, Diana Irene Williams, "Jean Toomer's Art and Ideology: Echoes of Eugenics," *Harvard College Forum* 9 (Spring 1995): 1–12; Kathryne Lindberg, "Raising *Cane* on the Theoretical Plane: Jean Toomer's Racial Personae," in *Cultural Difference and the Literary Text: Pluralism and the Limits of Authenticity in North American Literatures*, ed. Winfried Siemerling and Katrin Schwenk (Iowa City: University of Iowa Press, 1996).

26. Rusch, *A Jean Toomer Reader*, 107–108.

27. Undated letter to Waldo Frank in Rusch, *A Jean Toomer Reader*, 25; also excerpted in Turner, *Cane*, 151. Toomer's view of black culture as prototypically American culture prefigures the thinking of Ralph Ellison, *Shadow and Act* (New York: Random House, 1964) and Albert Murray, *The Omni-Americans: New Perspectives on Black Experience and American Culture* (New York: Outerbridge and Dienstfrey, 1970).

28. For an excellent discussion of Toomer in this context, see George Hutchinson, "Jean Toomer and American Racial Discourse," *Texas Studies in Literature and Language* 35, no. 2 (Summer 1993): 226–250.

29. Rusch, *A Jean Toomer Reader*, 109.

30. Toomer, *Essentials*, xxiv.

31. One thinks, for example, of Man Ray's portrait of Marcel Duchamp as Rrose (1921) or of Anton Räderscheidt's doubling self-portrait of 1928.

32. Turner, *The Wayward and the Seeking*, 121.

33. Toomer to Samuel Pessin, cited in Kerman and Eldridge, *The Lives of Jean Toomer*, 99.

34. The biographical information is derived from Turner, *Cane*, 121–145; Robert Bone, *Down Home: A History of Afro-American Short Fiction from Its Beginning to the End of the Harlem Renaissance* (New York: G. P. Putnam's Sons, 1975); Onita Estes-Hicks, "Jean Toomer: A Biographical and Critical Study ('Cane')," Ph.D. diss., Columbia University, New York, 1982; conversations with the late Marjorie Content Toomer; and Kerman and Eldridge, *The Lives of Jean Toomer*. See also Onita Estes-Hicks, "Jean Toomer and the Politics and Poetics of National Identity," *Contributions to Black Studies* 7 (1985–1986): 22–44.

35. Certificate and Record of Marriage, Mount Vernon, New York State Department of Health, no. 17277, dated August 21, 1905.

36. Certificate and Record of Death, New Rochelle Hospital, Ward 4, State of New York, Bureau of Vital Statistics, no. 25735, June 9, 2009.

37. W. Edward Farrison argues, however, that "thy son" need not be identified as Toomer: W. Edward Farrison, "Jean Toomer's *Cane* Again," reprinted in Turner, *Cane*, 179.

38. Bontemps, "Introduction," viii–ix. The latter part of this important letter is included in Turner, *Cane*, 128–129, and cited in Kerman and Eldridge, *The Lives of Jean Toomer*, 96.

39. Toomer's granddaughter Sharon D. Toomer rightly stressed that "Toomer said he wanted to be identified as an American. That is different from deciding to pass for white": *New York Times*, January 8, 2011.

40. Rusch, *A Jean Toomer Reader*, 105.

41. As Lindberg comments on this passage, "Toomer is not even a writer, but simply a Negro looking for a new race through (dread) miscegenation": Lindberg, "Raising *Cane* on the Theoretical Plane," 73n17. Michael North describes the "almost hysterical"

reaction to Toomer's marriage to Latimer in *Time* magazine, which "quoted his idea about the new American race with scorn and affected alarm under the ironic title of 'Just Americans.' The article suggested that some states, like Wisconsin, where Toomer and Latimer were married, were insufficiently vigilant against marriages between the races": Michael North, *Dialect of Modernism: Race, Language, and Twentieth-Century Literature* (New York: Oxford University Press, 1994), 163. For other responses, see Kerman and Eldridge, *The Lives of Jean Toomer*, 202.

42. Other important black American writers such as Countée Cullen, James Weldon Johnson, William Stanley Braithwaite, Jessie Fauset, and Claude McKay also responded enthusiastically to Toomer's *Cane*, as McKay has shown: McKay, *Jean Toomer*, 238. In addition, Byrd cites a letter by Sterling Brown describing *Cane* as "one of the most beautiful and moving books of contemporary American literature" and discusses Toomer's influence on Langston Hughes, on Michael Harper's "Cryptograms," on Alice Walker's *Meridian*, on Ernest J. Gaines's *The Autobiography of Miss Jane Pittman*, and on Gloria Naylor's *The Women of Brewster Place*: Byrd, *Jean Toomer's Years with Gurdjieff*, 183–189.

43. See McKay, *Jean Toomer*, 46–50. Byrd quotes Toomer's letter to Cunard dated February 8, 1930 as saying, "Though I am interested in and deeply value the Negro, I am not a Negro. And though I have written about the Negro, and value the material and the art that is Negro, all my writings during the past seven years have been on other subjects. In America I am working for a vision of this country as composed of people who are Americans first, and only of certain descents as secondary matters": Byrd, *Jean Toomer's Years with Gurdjieff*, 97.

44. "Blood-Burning Moon" and "Avey" are reprinted in the section on short stories, and "Song of the Son" and "Georgia Dusk" are reprinted in the part on poetry, in *The Negro Caravan: Writings by American Negroes*, ed. Sterling A. Brown, Arthur P. Davis, and Ulysses Lee (New York: Citadel, 1941). The first headnote states that Toomer had "startled literary America with its unusual subject matter and its unique approach": ibid., 41–42.

45. Cited in Kerman and Eldridge, *The Lives of Jean Toomer*, 97.

46. Toomer to Frank, April 26, 1922, cited in ibid., 87.

47. Cited in ibid., 96; Bontemps, "Introduction," viii; Turner, *Cane*, 128.

48. Toomer to McClure, July 22, 1922, cited in Kerman and Eldridge, *The Lives of Jean Toomer*, 96.

CHAPTER 5

1. See Michel Fabre, *From Harlem to Paris: Black American Writers in Paris, 1840–1980* (Urbana: University of Illinois Press, 1991); Maria Diedrich, *Love across Color Lines: Ottilie Assing and Frederick Douglass.* (New York: Hill and Wang, 1999); Christoph Lohmann, *Radical Passion: Ottilie Assing's Reports from America and Letters to Frederick Douglass* (New York: Peter Lang, 1999). In 2015, Kerstin Rudolph presented a paper at the University of Mississippi on Mary Church Terrell's German diaries from the 1890s, which include the account of a relationship with Otto von Dewitz.

2. Jessie Fauset, *Plum Bun: A Novel without a Moral* (1929), repr. ed. (Boston: Beacon, 1990), 340.

3. Benito Mussolini [Richard Washburn Child], *My Autobiography* (New York: Scribner's Sons, 1928).

4. Gerald Early, ed., *My Soul's High Song: The Collected Writings of Countee Cullen* (New York: Anchor, 1990), 24.

5. For "bookoo," see Zora Neale Hurston, *Mules and Men* (1935), repr. ed. with an introduction by Robert Hemenway (Bloomington: Indiana University Press, 1978), 16. "Toot sweet" appears in Rudolph Fisher's short story "City of Refuge." For the returning veteran theme, see Richard Wright, "Long Black Song," in *Uncle Tom's Children: Four Novellas* (New York: Harper and Brothers, 1938), 192–193; Frantz Fanon, *The Wretched of the Earth*, trans. Constance Farrington (New York: Grove, 1968), 231–232.

6. David Levering Lewis, *When Harlem Was in Vogue* (New York: Vintage, 1982), 15. Lewis also calls attention to the U.S. "War Department's insistence that Afro-American soldiers not be depicted in the heroic frieze displayed in France's Panthéon de la Guerre."

7. *The Crisis*, vol. 26, 1929, 119; reprinted in Early, *My Soul's High Song*. Cullen continues, "Then off to Algiers by way of Marseilles to rest there for a day or two in the hope of meeting and exchanging a word with Claude McKay, but he was too deep in the beauties of Seville to get to Marseilles before we sailed for Algiers." Actually, we learn from the biography by Wayne Cooper that McKay was in Barcelona at the time, accompanying a West Indian boxer who had a bout there, and finishing the novel *Banjo*: Wayne Cooper, *Claude McKay: Rebel Sojourner in the Harlem Renaissance* (Baton Rouge: Louisiana State University Press, 1987), 238.

8. Early, *My Soul's High Song*, 553. See also Blanche E. Ferguson, *Countee Cullen and the Negro Renaissance* (New York: Dodd, Mead, 1966), 108.

9. Early, *My Soul's High Song*, 205, 554.

10. Ferguson, *Countee Cullen and the Negro Renaissance*, 109.

11. Early, *My Soul's High Song*, 565.

12. Nancy Sloan Goldberg, "From Whitman to Mussolini: Modernism in the Life and Works of a French Intellectual," *Journal of European Studies* 26 (June 1996): 153–173. Claire Goll made headlines when she accused Paul Celan of having plagiarized her husband, Yvan Goll's, poetry, including even the famous phrase "schwarze Milch."

13. According to J. A. Rogers, the title character of the novel *Der Neger Jupiter raubt Europa* was based on Prince Benhanzin of Dahomey: J. A. Rogers, *Sex and Race: Negro-Caucasian Mixing in All Ages and All Lands*, vol. 1 (1941), 9th. ed. (St. Petersburg, FL: J. A. Rogers, 1967), 261. The novel appeared in French as Claire Goll, trans., *Le Nègre Jupiter enlève Europe* (Paris: Crès et Cie, 1928). A Spanish translation was published in Chile in 1935.

14. Claire Goll, *Die neue Welt* (Berlin: S. Fischer, 1921), 9. Goll praised Vachel Lindsay for his opposition to war, and she included Fenton Johnson's "Tired," four anonymous African American songs, and eleven Indian poems.

15. Claire Goll, "Nachwort," in *Der gläserne Garten: Prosa von 1917–1939* (Berlin: Argon, 1989), 335.

16. Early, *My Soul's High Song*, 568.

17. Ibid.

18. Claude McKay, *A Long Way from Home* (1937), repr. ed. (New York: Harcourt Brace Jovanovich, 1970), 312. McKay also thought that Cullen was the "most outstanding" of the black writers in Paris.

19. Ibid., 240. The letters in the Grosz Papers at the Akademie der Künste, Berlin, suggest that their friendship continued when Grosz planned a visit to the United States: see, e.g., Grosz to "Mr. Claude McKay, Grand Paris Hotel, Moskau," letter no. 133,

December 8, 1922, and letter no. 136, January 21, 1923, in which Grosz also mentions the inflation.

20. McKay, *A Long Way from Home*, 312–313. McKay had sent his poem "Mulatto" to Alain Locke for inclusion in the special issue of the *Survey Graphic*, which became the *New Negro*, but Locke declined it "for its bitterly radical tone" (as Cooper reported). McKay wrote an angry letter to Locke dated October 7, 1924 (quoted in Cooper, *Claude McKay*, 225), in which he said:

> You know of course that I am suicidally frank. Your letter has angered me. Your attitude is that of Booker T. Washington in social reform. . . . It's a playing safe attitude—the ultimate reward of which are dry husks and ashes! . . . There are many white people who are longing and hoping for Negroes to show they have guts. I will show you by getting a white journal to take Mulatto. . . . No wonder the Negro movement is in such a bad way. When Negro intellectuals like you take such a weak line. . . . Send me back all the things— and I do not care to be mentioned at all—don't want to—in the special Negro number of the Survey. I am not seeking mere notoriety and publicity. Principles mean something to my life.

If Locke published only the other poems and not "Mulatto," McKay warned him, "You may count upon me as an intellectual enemy for life!" He ended by saying that he was not too surprised by Locke's action, since Locke was "a dyed-in-the-wool pussy-footing professor." Locke ignored McKay's request and further angered him by printing the sonnet "The White House" under the title "White Houses."

21. Alain Locke, "Spiritual Truancy," in *Voices from the Harlem Renaissance*, ed. Nathan Irvin Huggins (New York: Oxford University Press, 1976), 404–406.

22. McKay, *A Long Way from Home*, 139–140.

23. Ibid., 186–187.

24. Ibid., 208.

25. Claude McKay, *Negroes in America*, ed. Alain L. McLeod, trans. Robert J. Winter (Port Washington, NY: Kennikat, 1979), 7.

26. McKay, *A Long Way from Home*, 208.

27. McKay, *Negroes in America*, 10.

28. Horace R. Cayton, *Long Old Road* (1964), repr. ed. (Seattle: University of Washington Press, 1970), 208. Hereafter, page numbers are cited in parentheses in the text.

29. This encounter, or non-encounter, was not mentioned in Anne Chisholm, *Nancy Cunard: A Biography* (New York: Knopf, 1979), in which chapters 18–21 cover the period around the publication of *Negro*.

30. On the sterilization campaign, see Reiner Pommerin, *Sterilisierung der Rheinlandbastarde: Das Schicksal einer farbigen deutschen Minderheit 1918–1937* (Düsseldorf, Germany: Droste, 1979).

31. Alain Locke, "The Black Watch on the Rhine," *Opportunity* 2: no. 13 (January 1924): 6. Hereafter, page numbers are cited in parentheses in the text. See also Sally Marks, "Black Watch on the Rhine: A Study in Propaganda, Prejudice and Prurience," *European Studies Review* 13 (1983): 297–334; Jonathan Wipplinger, "Germany, 1923: Alain Locke, Claude McKay and the New Negro in Germany," *Callaloo* 36, no. 1 (Winter 2013): 106–124.

32. René Maran, letter, *Opportunity* 2, no. 21, (September 1924): 261–262. See also Locke's response: ibid., 262–263. Maran was the author of the Goncourt Prize–winning novel *Batouala* (1921) that Jessie Fauset was offered but refused to translate into English. Michel Fabre writes that Maran "exposed forced participation of African 'volunteers' as well as the sellout of African deputies condoning colonial exploitation": Fabre, *From Harlem to Paris*, 148–149.

33. Reproduced in Katharina Oguntoye, May Opitz, and Dagmar Schultz, *Farbe bekennen: Afro-deutsche Frauen auf den Spuren ihrer Geschichte* (1986), repr. ed. (Frankfurt, Germany: Fischer Taschenbuch, 1992), 50.

34. S. Frederick Starr, *Red and Hot: The Fate of Jazz in the Soviet Union, 1917–1980* (New York: Oxford University Press, 1983), 89–90.

35. Martin Bauml Duberman, *Paul Robeson* (New York: Knopf, 1988), 133.

36. Ibid., 184–185.

37. Mike Zwerin, *La Tristesse de Saint Louis: Swing under the Nazis* (London: Quartet, 1985). The original—"Was ist Niggerjazz?" taken from the *Preußische Zeitung*—reads, "[Es ist eine] Musik, die entweder einer krankhaften Seelenverfassung entspringt, oder aber . . . nur mit dem Verstande ergrübelt ist. . . . [Sie] kann . . . günstigstenfalls von volksfremden Snobs als 'interessant' empfunden werden. . . . Kennzeichnend für den Jazz ist weiter das starke Hervortreten des Saxophons, das . . . aufdringlich allein die Melodie führt, während alle anderen Instrumente lediglich den Rhythmus betonen und hetzen. Eine solche Orchestrierung gibt der Tanzweise ein fratzenhaftes Gesicht. Sie sucht sich durch den Rhythmus einzuhämmern und systematisch jedes Gefühl für Wohllaut abzustumpfen."

38. George Hutchinson, *In Search of Nella Larsen: A Biography of the Color Line* (Cambridge, MA: Harvard University Press, 2006), 71–72.

39. Nella Larsen, *Quicksand* (1928), repr. ed. (New York: Dover, 2006), 83.

40. Hutchinson refers to Martin Urban, *Emil Nolde: A Catalogue Raisonné of the Oil Paintings*, 2 vols. (London: Sotheby's, 1987); Peter Selz, *Emil Nolde* (New York: Museum of Modern Art and Doubleday, 1963); Werner Haftmann, *Emil Nolde*, trans. Norbert Guterman (New York: Abrams, 1959). Hutchinson points out, however, that the Danish section of Larsen's novel *Quicksand* is not a consistently autobiographical fictionalization and is inspired by later events, including Josephine Baker's popularity in the second half of the 1920s.

41. Langston Hughes, *I Wonder as I Wander: An Autobiographical Journey* (1956), repr. ed. (New York: Hill and Wang, 1964), 81–82.

42. Langston Hughes, "Going South in Russia" (1934), in *Good Morning, Revolution: Uncollected Writings of Social Protest*, ed. Faith Berry (New York: Lawrence Hill, 1973), 255.

43. Maxim Gorky, "The Music of the Degenerate," trans. Marie Budberg, *Dial* 85 (1928): 480–484.

44. Hughes, "Going South in Russia," 103. See also Arnold Rampersad, *The Life of Langston Hughes, Volume 1, 1902–1941: I, Too, Sing America* (New York: Oxford University Press, 1986), 349.

45. Hughes, "Going South in Russia," 104.

46. James Yates, *From Mississippi to Madrid: Memoir of a Black American in the Abraham Lincoln Brigade* (Seattle: Open Hand, 1989), 176–177.

47. Ibid., 112.

48. Ibid., 137; also cited in Kathryne V. Lindberg, "W. E. B. Du Bois's 'Dusk of Dawn' and James Yates's 'Mississippi to Madrid,' or 'What Goes Around Comes Around and Around' in Autobiography," *Massachusetts Review* 35, no. 2 (Summer 1994): 283–308.

49. Wayne F. Cooper, ed., *The Passion of Claude McKay: Selected Poetry and Prose, 1912–1948* (New York: Schocken, 1973), 231.

50. In *My Life: An Attempt at an Autobiography* (New York: C. Scribner's Sons, 1930), the exiled Trotsky reports the Americans' annoying habit of asking him casually at cocktail parties how he lost power. Mike Gold, who had hailed Trotsky when he was still in power, commented on the assassination, "I . . . can shed no tears for him; I care for something greater that Trotsky's fate; the proletarian revolution": Mike Folsom, ed., *Mike Gold: A Literary Anthology* (New York: International Publishers, 1972), 194.

51. The publication of two books based on fresh archival researches suggests that the internationalization of African American studies is well under way. Kate Baldwin examines the Soviet travels of Hughes, Du Bois, McKay, and Robeson, and Brent Hayes Edwards analyzes René Maran, Alain Locke, Jessie Fauset, the Nardal sisters, Claude McKay, W. E. B. Du Bois, and Nancy Cunard's *Negro* through a meticulous focus on interactions in and outside the francophone world: see Kate A. Baldwin, *Beyond the Color Line and the Iron Curtain: Reading Encounters between Black and Red, 1922–1963* (Durham, NC: Duke University Press, 2002); Brent Hayes Edwards, *The Practice of Diaspora: Literature, Translation, and the Rise of Black Internationalism* (Cambridge, MA: Harvard University Press, 2003). See also Jonathan Wipplinger, *The Jazz Republic: Music, Race, and American Culture in Weimar Germany* (Ann Arbor: University of Michigan Press, forthcoming).

CHAPTER 6

1. W. E. B. Du Bois, *The Autobiography of W. E. B. Du Bois: A Soliloquy on Viewing My Life from the Last Decade of Its First Century* (New York: International Publishers, 1986), 431–437, 439. The text about the period moves on quickly: see, e.g., ibid., 302–303. None of the index references to Germany is about 1936.

2. W. E. B. Du Bois, *Dusk of Dawn: An Essay toward an Autobiography of a Race Concept* (1940), reprinted in *Writings*, ed. Nathan Huggins (New York: Library of America, 1986), 790–791.

3. Kathryne V. Lindberg, "W. E. B. Du Bois's 'Dusk of Dawn' and James Yates's 'Mississippi to Madrid' or 'What Goes Around Comes Around and Around and Around' in Autobiography," *Massachusetts Review* 35, no. 2 (Summer 1994): 283–308; Russell Berman, "Marian Anderson and Paul Robeson," lecture given at the Conference on African-American Artists and Writers in Europe (1919–1939), Washington University, St. Louis, March 27, 1999. The Library of America edition of *Writings* mentions Du Bois's trip in the Chronology for 1936–1937: "Leaves United States in June; visits England, France, Belgium, and Austria, spends five months in Germany in autumn and winter of 1936. Reports on Germany for the *Pittsburgh Courier*, attributing Hitler's success to his use of socialist methods in reducing unemployment and his skill at propaganda; denounces anti-Semitic persecutions as cruel and barbaric. . . . Begins never-finished novel 'A Search for Democracy,' about black American professor exploring fascism, communism, and democracy" (Du Bois, *Writings*, 1298–1299).

4. W. E. B. Du Bois, *The Correspondence of W. E. B. Du Bois, Volume II: Selections 1934–1944*, ed. Herbert Aptheker (Amherst: University of Massachusetts Press, 1976),

135–136. Letters are dated April 22, May 5, and May 11 (two), 1936. On March 31, 1936, Du Bois also responded to Victor Lindeman, a Jewish businessman from New Jersey, writing, "My investigations in Germany do not commit me to any set conclusions or any attitude. Sixty-six million people are always worth studying": W. E. B. Du Bois, *The Papers of W. E. B. Du Bois, 1877–1963* (Sanford, NC: Microfilming Corporation of America, 1980–1981), 46/52. He also indicated his Berlin address as care of Dr. Georg Kartzke at the Oberlaender Trust.

5. Memorandum to the Board of Directors of the Oberlaender Trust, February 8, 1935, in Du Bois, *The Papers of W. E. B. Du Bois*, 46/260.

6. The annual report of the Carl Schurz Foundation for May 1, 1935–April 30, 1936, lists Du Bois as the recipient of a special grant for the topic "The Relation of Education and Industry." The minutes of the Oberlaender Trust for April 10, 1935, state, "Dr. Frank Tannenbaum, Dr. Anson Phelps Stokes, Dr. Will Alexander, Dr. James E. Drake, and President A. A. Moton were consulted about DuBois's application. Some questioned the value of the particular project which Dr. DuBois has in mind, but all were agreed that Dr. DuBois would make good use of an opportunity to revisit Germany. VOTED to make a grant to Dr. DuBois, provided the sum involved is not too large. Referred to Mr. Thomas with power to act": Carl Schurz Memorial Foundation Papers, Balch Institute, Philadelphia. The grant was set at $1,600. On Oberlaender's politics and encounters with Hitler and Goebbels, see scrapbook 1 of the Oberlaender Trust (e.g., "Hitler empfängt Oberländer," *Staatszeitung*, August 15, 1933, and U.S. Department of Interior report on the foundation, signed by [Saul K.?] Padover, June 24, 1940: Carl Schurz Memorial Foundation Papers, Balch Institute. See also Philip Jenkins, *Hoods and Shirts: The Extreme Right in Pennsylvania, 1925–1950* (Chapel Hill: University of North Carolina Press, 1997), 56. I am extremely grateful to Karl Krueger, director of Library and Archives at the Balch Institute, for his help in researching this matter.

7. The very same *S.S. St. Louis* became infamous three years later when, under Captain Gustav Schroeder, it carried German Jewish refugees leaving Germany on May 13, 1939, who were then refused entry into Cuba and were returned on the *St. Louis* to Europe.

8. In solidarity with Jewish athletes who had been excluded from the Olympics, liberal and leftist sports clubs around the world staged boycotts, even planning a counter-Olympics in Barcelona that fell victim to the Spanish Civil War, and the African American athletes who did participate hoped that their achievements would put Nazi race theories to rest. For background on the Berlin Olympics with a focus on a black American athlete, see William J. Baker, *Jesse Owens: An American Life* (New York: Free Press, 1986), 73–128.

9. "Farbiger bereist Nazi-Deutschland," *New York Staats-Zeitung und Herold*, January 29, 1937, clipping in Du Bois, *The Papers of W. E. B. Du Bois*.

10. W. E. B. Du Bois to Leo Stein, AJC, letter, March 10, 1937, in Du Bois, *The Papers of W. E. B. Du Bois*. In a letter to Stein dated February 25, 1937, Du Bois mentioned that his views had been reported in a "somewhat garbled" way in a *New York Post* interview. The article in question, "Hitler Far ahead of Simon Legree: Negro Educator Finds Persecution of Jews Worse than South's Abuses," *New York Post*, January 27, 1937, however, is in its key statements similar to that in the *Staats-Zeitung*. According to its archivist, the AJC does not have any files on Du Bois. His interlocutor Leo Stein "was born in Stettin, Germany on December 13, 1884. He was a lawyer in Germany from 1912–1929. He began his employment at AJC on November 25, 1930, in the capacity

of archivist for the library where he worked until his retirement August 1948": Miriam Tierney, e-mail to the author, May 14, 1999. It is not clear how the interview was conducted. Du Bois refers to a telephone call he received from the *Staats-Zeitung* after an inaccurate and misleading interview had appeared elsewhere, but the *Staats-Zeitung* describes Du Bois stroking his graying "Van Dyke beard" as he was contemplating the question of whether the German population was happy; this creates the impression that the journalist interviewed Du Bois in person.

11. The second volume of David Levering Lewis's biography, *W. E. B. Du Bois: The Fight for Equality and the American Century* (New York: Henry Holt, 2000), treats this period more fully.

12. A recent study of George Schuyler is Jeffrey B. Ferguson, *The Sage of Sugar Hill: George S. Schuyler and the Harlem Renaissance* (New Haven, CT: Yale University Press, 2004). I focus here on only selected *Pittsburgh Courier* pieces directly related to Germany. Du Bois also wrote on such topics as the color line in England (incomparably less harshly drawn than in the United States), and offered travel impressions from Austria, Poland, Russia, Manchuria, China, Japan, and Hawaii. In his massive collection of Du Bois's writings, David Levering Lewis reprinted a couple of these pieces without editorial comment or introductory contextualization. These essays have, to my knowledge, never been examined fully. They are quoted from the microfilm edition of the *Pittsburgh Courier*; the dates are in parentheses in the text.

13. According to the archivist of Siemens, no records of Du Bois's visit have survived (Alexandra Kinter, e-mail to the author, May 12, 1999). The detailed history by Wolfgang Robe and Wolfgang Schächte, *Die Siemensstadt: Geschichte und Architektur eines Industriestandortes* (Berlin: Ernst und Sohn, 1985), gives an excellent sense of the industrial city Du Bois visited and contains numerous photographs from the 1930s.

14. Huggins gives the translation, "Faithfully led, be drawn to that place / Where the blessings of love watch over you!" and comments that "Du Bois changes Treulich (faithfully) to Freudig (joyfully)": Huggins, *Writings*, 1323.

15. Erik Levi shows that Wagner and Verdi were the two most popular operatic composers in the 1930s and that by 1940 Verdi had taken over Wagner's "pre-eminent position as the most performed composer in the Reich," while "Wagner actually suffered a steady decline in popularity, in spite of the exceptionally high profile he enjoyed in Nazi propaganda": Erik Levi, *Music in the Third Reich* (Basingstoke, UK: Macmillan, 1994), 192. Whereas in 1932–1933 there were still 1837 Wagner productions as opposed to 1265 Verdi operas, by 1939–1940 the figures had changed to 1440 for Verdi and only 1154 for Wagner.

16. Kenneth O'Reilly and David Gallen's *Black Americans: The FBI Files* (New York: Carroll and Graf, 1994) contains a chapter on Du Bois in which a statement he made in Japan appears, although the trip to Germany does not. The FBI provided me with a copy of the Du Bois dossier that starts only after his 1936 trip to Germany. Inquiries at the Bundesarchiv, the Geheimes Staatsarchiv, the Landesarchiv Berlin, and the Archiv des Auswärtigen Amts yielded no documents.

CHAPTER 7

1. Richard Wright, *Native Son* (1940), repr. ed. (New York: Harper and Row, 1966), 7. Hereafter, all references are to this edition; page numbers are cited in parentheses in the text. Robert Redfield, *Tepoztlán: A Mexican Village* (Chicago: University of Chicago

Press, 1930), 1–6. Herbert Gutman has also traced the importance of clocked time for the consciousness of laborers, minorities, and immigrants in the modern United States: see Herbert G. Gutman, *Work, Culture, and Society in Industrializing America* (New York: Random House, 1977). Robert Stepto lists the symbolism of "various timepieces" as one of the predictable staples in interpretations of *Native Son*: Robert Stepto "I Thought I Knew These People: Richard Wright and the Afro-American Literary Tradition," *Massachusetts Review* 18, no. 3 (Autumn 1977): 537.

2. Keneth Kinnamon, *The Emergence of Richard Wright: A Study in Literature and Society* (Urbana: University of Illinois Press, 1972), 127.

3. See also the parallels between such famous autobiographical statements as, "This was the culture from which I sprang. This was the terror from which I fled" (Richard Wright, *Black Boy* [1945], repr. ed. [New York: Harper and Row, 1966], 281) and the statement's racial generalization, "But the American Negro, child of the culture that crushes him, wants to be free in a way that white men are free" (Richard Wright, "Introduction," in St. Clair Drake and Horace R. Cayton, *Black Metropolis: A Study of Negro Life in a Northern City* (1945), repr. ed. (New York: Harper Torchbooks, 1962), xxv). As Carla Cappetti has argued, Richard Wright was his own participant observer and case study: Carla Cappetti, "Sociology of an Existence: Richard Wright and the Chicago School," *MELUS* 12, no. 2 (Summer 1985): 25–43; Carla Cappetti, *Writing Chicago: Modernism, Ethnography, and the Novel* (New York: Columbia University Press, 1993), 198–210.

4. Zora Neale Hurston, *Dust Tracks on a Road* (1942), 2d ed., ed. Robert Hemenway (Urbana: University of Illinois Press, 1984), 324–325.

5. Zora Neale Hurston, *Mules and Men* (1935), repr. ed. with an introduction by Robert Hemenway (Bloomington: Indiana University Press, 1978), 40.

6. Ibid., 33.

7. Wright shared the outline of Boris Max's interpretation in "How Bigger Was Born"—his favorite piece of his own writing. It was his contribution to Whit Burnett's *This Is My Best: Over 150 Self-Chosen and Complete Masterpieces, together with Their Reasons for Their Selections* (New York: Dial, 1942), 448–458.

8. Richard Wright, "Long Black Song," in *Uncle Tom's Children: Four Novellas* (New York: Harper and Brothers, 1938), 169–217.

9. Richard Wright, "How 'Uncle Tom's Children' Grew," *Writers' Club Bulletin* 2 (1938): 17.

10. For a typological reading of the religious significance of Sarah and Silas, see John Lowe, "Wright Writing Reading: Narrative Strategies in *Uncle Tom's Children*," *Journal of the Short Story in English/Les Cahiers de la Nouvelle*, no. 11 (Autumn 1988): 62.

11. Wright, "Long Black Song," 192.

12. See the manuscripts in the James Weldon Johnson Collection, Beinecke Rare Book and Manuscript Library, Yale University, New Haven, CT, JWJ Wright 962, 964.

13. "It is the story of a rape or seduction of a black peasant woman by a white traveling salesman": Margaret Walker, *Richard Wright, Daemonic Genius: A Portrait of the Man, a Critical Look at His Work* (New York: Warner Communications, 1988), 117. See also Sherley Anne Williams, "Papa Dick and Sister-Woman: Reflections on Woman in the Fiction of Richard Wright," in *American Novelists Revisited: Essays in Feminist Criticism*, ed. Fritz Fleischmann (Boston: G. K. Hall, 1982), 394–415. Williams argues that the "threat of physical force" has "conditioned" black woman "to an almost un-

conscious submissiveness in the presence of white men, and it is this threat that helps to make 'seduction,' rather than rape, possible between Sarah and the white man": Williams, "Papa Dick and Sister-Woman," 409. For a different view, see Joyce Ann Joyce, "Richard Wright's 'Long Black Song': A Moral Dilemma," *Mississippi Quarterly* 42, no. 4 (Fall 1989): 379–385.

14. Max Weber ascribed the maxim to Benjamin Franklin, although he actually took it from Ferdinand Kürnberger's novel *Der Amerikamüde* (1836)": see Max Weber, *The Protestant Ethic and the Spirit of Capitalism* (1904–1905), trans. Talcott Parsons (New York: Scribner's, 1958), 48–65.

15. Quoted in Peter Wollen and Joe Kerr, eds., *Autopia: Cars and Culture* (London: Reaktion Books, 2002), 66–67. See also http://xroads.virginia.edu/~MUSIC/blues/pb.html for an alternative version, with such lines as. "Now, we played it on the sofa, now / we played it 'side the wall / My needles have got rusty, baby / they will not play at all." For a broader discussion of the blues, see Jeffrey B. Ferguson, "A Blue Note on Black American Literary Criticism and the Blues," *Amerikastudien/American Studies* 55, no. 4 (2010): 699–714.

16. Some plot summaries make the salesman's death a certainty: see, e.g., Edwin Berry Burgum, "The Art of Richard Wright's Short Stories" (1963), reprinted in *Five Black Writers: Wright, Ellison, Baldwin, Hughes, and LeRoi Jones*, ed. Donald Gibson (New York: New York University Press, 1970), 44.

17. Wright, *Uncle Tom's Children*, 178–180.

18. Wright, "How 'Uncle Tom's Children' Grew," 17. This is analogous to Wright's comment about his own autobiography, "I wrote the book to tell a series of incidents strung through my childhood, but the main desire was to render a judgment on my environment. . . . That judgment was this: the environment the South creates is too small to nourish human beings, especially Negro human beings": *P.M. Magazine*, April 4, 1945, 3, cited in Michel Fabre, *The Unfinished Quest of Richard Wright*, trans. Isabel Barzun (New York: William Morrow, 1973), 252. Wright uses the figure of a *salesman* as the modernizer and that of a peasant as the premodern one. In a related fashion, Wright also mocks the roles Negro writers had to play, writing, "But even if Negro writers found themselves through some 'ism,' how would that influence their writing? Are they being called on to preach? To be "salesmen"? To "prostitute" their art? Richard Wright, "Blueprint for Negro Literature" (1937), in *Amistad*, vol. 2, ed. John A. Williams and Charles F. Harris (New York: Vintage, 1971), 13.

19. James Giles refers to Jean Toomer and William Faulkner: James Giles, "Richard Wright's Successful Failure: A New Look at *Uncle Tom's Children*," *Phylon* 4, no. 3 (1973): 256–266. Edward Margolies, *The Art of Richard Wright* (Carbondale: Southern Illinois University Press, 1969), 66–67. The creation of a black Mother Earth figure may also reflect the literal meaning of the name "Melanctha." Wright singles out Stein's "Melanctha" for praise in Wright, "Introduction," xxxi. And in *American Hunger* (New York: Harper and Row, 1977), 22, Wright describes his own efforts to sound like Gertrude Stein in his early attempts to write prose. Wright defended Stein against Mike Gold's attack of 1936, titled "Gertrude Stein: A Literary Idiot," and claimed not only that Stein was loved by dockworkers but also that her style brought back Wright's grandmother's voice. Michel Fabre calls attention to Wright's identification of Stein's language and his own grandmother's diction, as well as to similarities between "Long Black Song" and Toomer's *Cane*, in *The World of Richard Wright* (Jackson: University of Mississippi Press, 1985), 18–19. See also Wright's reviews "Gertrude Stein's Story Is Drenched in Hitler's

Horrors, *P.M. Magazine*, March 11, 1945, 15, and "American G.I.s' Fears Worry Gertrude Stein," *P.M. Magazine*, July 26, 1946, 15–16; Eugene E. Miller, "Richard Wright and Gertrude Stein," *Black American Literature Forum* 16, no. 3 (Fall 1982): 107–112; M. Lynn Weiss, *Gertrude Stein and Richard Wright: The Poetics and Politics of Modernism* (Jackson: University Press of Mississippi, 1998).

20. See, e.g., "CRASH!" and "Bloom!" in Wright's early story "Superstition," *Abbot's Monthly Magazine*, vol. 2, April 1931, 45–47, 64–66, 72–73, and "CRACK!" in "Big Boy Leaves Home," the first story in *Uncle Tom's Children*.

21. Kinnamon has paid special attention to this image of the clock: "Wright makes his white salesman a college student studying science in Chicago, certainly antithetical to Sarah as he intrudes his profit-motivated, clock-regulated values on her natural order. But even before his appearance, the conflict is suggested by the symbol of the clock. Sarah's baby finds pleasure in striking an old broken clock: 'Bang! Bang! Bang!' The refrain is repeated no fewer than eleven times in the first section of the story"— that is, one time less than the number of hours on the face of a clock. Kinnamon gives a detailed account of the symbol of the clock and the "Bang! Bang! Bang!" but generalizes it into a racial contrast when he writes, "Blacks need no clock, for their lives are close to the pulse of the earth itself, unlike whites, whose mechanical, rational civilization is sterile and artificial. The clock symbol suggests this": Kinnamon, *The Emergence of Richard Wright*, 96–97. Kinnamon thus writes that one "of the difficulties between the races is the cultural difference between black rural folk and 'modern,' urban whites," yet he has to add, correcting himself, that "in point of fact, most whites in Mississippi in 1919 were also rural folk." In fact, Wright is probably thinking of the opposition mostly in terms of modern versus premodern (although it is not uninteresting that he also casts it in terms of white versus black and male versus female). Kinnamon continues (ibid., 98):

> The symbol of the clock is a complex one. "Bang! Bang! Bang!" suggests also the passing of time, important to the plot because of Silas's impending arrival. The refrain is clearly related, too, to Sarah's libido. When it sounds the second through the sixth times, she thinks longingly of Tom or Silas, and when it sounds the seventh time, she hears the approaching noise of the salesman's automobile. On the penultimate repetition, the sound is quite specifically associated with sex. . . . The last time is even more overtly sexual. . . . When one observes, finally, that the sound may also prefigure the gunshots of the fight between Silas and the white men, the fact that the resources of Wright's prose go beyond a simple, prosaic naturalism becomes apparent.

From this observation, Kinnamon generalizes that Wright "shared the common misgivings of so many American writers about the intrusion of the machine into the American garden." According to Kinnamon, Wright "shared to some degree, at least in 'Long Black Song,' [the southern agrarians'] emotional nostalgia for the pastoral tranquillities of rural life": ibid., 99–100.

22. Both wrote compelling tales. Thus, Edward Margolies views "Long Black Song" as perhaps Wright's best story, and Robert E. Hemenway in his influential *Zora Neale Hurston: A Literary Biography* (Urbana: University of Illinois Press, 1977), 188, considers "The Gilded Six-Bits" among the best and Robert Bone, *Down Home: A History of Afro-American Short Fiction from Its Beginnings to the End of the Harlem Renaissance* (New

York: G. P. Putnam's Sons, 1975), 149, considers it *the* best of Hurston's stories. According to Hurston's account, the publication of "The Gilded Six-Bits" (combined with the "missionary work" done by Martha Foley and Whit Burnett) was an important step toward the writing of her first novel: Hurston, *Dust Tracks on a Road*, 209. "The Gilded Six-Bits" is included in Bob Callahan, ed., *Spunk: The Selected Stories of Zora Neale Hurston* (Berkeley, CA: Turtle Island Foundation, 1985), 54–68. Hereafter, all references are to this edition, and page numbers are cited parenthetically in the text.

23. In the story, Slemmons kept the other two bits of the title on his stickpin. See, however, Robert E. Hemenway, *Zora Neale Hurston: A Literary Biography* (Urbana: University of Illinois Press, 1977), 188. The difference between Joe's take-home pay in the first scene ($9) and the last scene ($15) is the same number in dollars that Slemmons had only in bits.

24. It is telling that Robert Bone's interpretation of Hurston closely parallels Kinnamon's reading of Wright. Bone (*Down Home*, 150) writes:

> The shallowness of urban culture is conveyed through Slemmons' attitude toward time. In the modern world of progress and improvement, of which the ice cream parlor is an emblem, time is a commodity. The capitalist ethos, with its obligation to convert time into money, is symbolized by Slemmons' golden watch charm. But the peasant world of Joe and Missie May responds to natural rather than artificial rhythms: "Finally the sun's tide crept upon the shore of night and drowned its hours." In this world, time has a moral and theological rather than economic significance. It is primarily a healing force, repairing the breach that guilt has opened in the human soul. "The Gilded Six-Bits" thus reveals the central core of Hurston's values. In this story, written in the depths of the Depression, she attacks the acquisitive society from a standpoint not unlike that of the Southern Agrarians. For the first time her social conservatism . . . finds in pastoral an appropriate dramatic form. A mature style emerges whose metaphors, drawn from folk speech, function as a celebration of agrarian ideals."

25. Richard Wright's worst nightmare recorded in *Black Boy*, which occurs after he has been beaten to unconsciousness, seems to describe the horrible transformation of a nourishing breast into a terrifying vehicle of torture and destruction. He writes, "Whenever I tried to sleep I would see huge wobbly white bags, like the full udders of cows, suspended from the ceiling above me. Later, as I grew worse, I could see the bags in the daytime with my eyes open and I was gripped by the fear that they were going to fall and drench me with some horrible liquid. Day and night I begged my mother and father to take the bags away, pointing to them, shaking with terror because no one saw them but me": Wright, *Black Boy*, 13.

26. Hurston invites a reading of the birth of the child as an event possibly caused by Slemmons rather than the faithful employee of the G and G fertilizer works, although Hemenway kindly rescues Missie May's honor by stating that she and Joe "work during the next year to recapture their love": Hemenway, *Zora Neale Hurston*, 188. In Hurston's text, however, the time that has passed between the woman's act of infidelity and the birth of the baby is given less precisely. We are told only that Joe and Missie May live estranged from each other for three months; that weeks and days later, Joe notices that she is pregnant; and that six months after that she delivers a baby.

27. See Zora Neale Hurston, "Characteristics of Negro Expression," in *Negro: An Anthology*, ed. Nancy Cunard (London: Wishart, 1934), 229.

28. Wright was equally aware of the mixed blessings of modernity and wrote in the introduction to *Black Metropolis* about the city in which the salesman intended to study: "There is an open and raw beauty about that city that seems either to kill or endow one with the spirit of life": Wright, "Introduction," xvii.

29. Compare such readings as Darwin Turner's, on the one hand, with Alice Walker's and Mary Helen Washington's, on the other: Darwin T. Turner, "Zora Neale Hurston: The Wandering Minstrel," in *In a Minor Chord: Three Afro-American Writers and Their Search for Identity* (Carbondale: Southern Illinois University Press, 1971), 89–120; Alice Walker, ed., *I Love Myself When I Am Laughing . . . and Then Again When I Am Looking Mean and Impressive: A Zora Neale Hurston Reader*, introduction by Mary Helen Washington (Old Westbury, NY: Feminist Press, 1979).

30. Walker, *I Love Myself*, 171.

31. JWJ Wright Misc. 281. Unpublished ms., James Weldon Johnson Collection, Beinecke Rare Book and Manuscript Library, Yale University, New Haven, CT. This blurb parallels Boris Max's effort to interpret his client in *Native Son*. "Let me, Your Honor, explain further the meaning of Bigger Thomas' life. In him and men like him is what was in our forefathers when they first came to these strange shores hundreds of years ago. We were lucky. They are not" (362–363).

32. The thematic (though not the formal) alternative of representing black life in the period is also captured in William Siegel, "The White Bourgeois Version of the Negro" and "—As the White Worker Knows Him," two-part illustration for *New Masses*, the May 1930, 7. The first image represents singing, comedy, jazz, gambling, and so forth, while the second shows somber scenes of labor and oppression and a lynching.

33. Wright, "Long Black Song," 192–193. and the much longer passages in the manuscript version of the story: JWJ Wright 962, 20. See also Wright's general comments about war in Wright, "Introduction," xxi. See Hurston, *Mules and Men*, 16, with a footnote explaining "bookooing." The word also appears later, in LeRoi Jones/Amiri Baraka, *Tales* (New York: Grove, 1967), which is dedicated to "Lanie whose heard boo coos."

34. "But at my back in a cold blast I hear / The rattle of the bones, and chuckle spread from ear to ear"; "some old white woman over in Paris said a rose is a rose is a rose is a rose": Richard Wright, *Lawd Today* (New York: Walker, 1963), 150, 162.

35. Wright, *American Hunger*, 1.

36. Wright, "Blueprint for Negro Writing," 10. For a thourough analysis of Wright's reading, see Fabre,*Unfinished Quest*, 111–112; Michel Fabre, "Wright's First Hundred Books," in *The World of Richard Wright* (Jackson: University Press of Mississippi, 1985), 12–26.

37. Kinnamon, *The Emergence of Richard Wright*, 116.

38. Wright, *American Hunger*, 22.

39. Wright, "Introduction," xxxi. In *Native Son*, Wright also employed such Toomer-like phrasings as "the room was black-dark and silent; the city did not exist" (221) and a Faulknerian paragraph-length single sentence that takes off from the sound of a distant church bell while Bigger is asleep (155–156):

It sounded suddenly directly above his head and when he looked it was not there but went on tolling and with each passing moment he felt an urgent need to run and hide as though the bell were sounding a warning and he stood on a street corner in a red glare of light like that which came from the furnace and he had a big package in his arms so wet and slippery and heavy that he could scarcely hold onto it and he wanted to know what was in the package and he stopped near an alley corner and unwrapped it and the paper fell away and he saw—it was his *own* head—his own head lying with black face and half-closed eyes and lips parted with white teeth showing and hair wet with blood and the red glare grew brighter like light shining down from a red moon and red stars on a hot summer night and he was sweating and breathless from running and the bell clanged so loud that he could hear the iron tongue clapping against the metal sides each time it swung to and fro and he was running over a street paved with black coal and his shoes kicked tiny lumps rattling against tin cans and he knew that very soon he had to find some place to hide but there was no place and in front of him white people were coming to ask about the head from which the newspapers had fallen and which was now slippery with blood in his naked hands and he gave up and stood in the middle of the street in the red darkness and cursed the booming bell and the white people and felt that he did not give a damn what happened to him and when the people closed in he hurled the bloody head squarely into their faces *dongdongdong.*

40. Hurston, *Dust Tracks on a Road*, 54–56, 238–243. However, see also references to the Bible, to Milton, and to Lorenzo Dow Turner's course on English poetry: ibid., 54, 127, 166. In her "Story in Harlem Slang" (1942), Hurston uses the sentence, "Dat broad I seen you with wasn't no pe-ola." In the glossary, she explains "pe-ola" as "a very white Negro girl," probably alluding to the character of the same name in Fannie Hurst's once popular novel *Imitation of Life* (1933): Callahan, *Spunk*, 85, 945.

41. Wright, "Blueprint for Negro Writing," 14, with slight variations from the *New Challenge* version that is reprinted in Michel Fabre, ed., *The Richard Wright Reader*, ed. Ellen Wright and Michel Fabre (New York: Harper and Row, 1978), 36–49.

42. Hurston, *Dust Tracks on a Road*, 345.

43. Richard Wright, "Between Laughter and Tears," *New Masses*, October 5, 1937, 22.

44. Zora Neale Hurston, "Stories of Conflict," *Saturday Review of Literature*, April 2, 1938, 32.

45. Zora Neale Hurston, "What White Publishers Won't Print," in Walker, *I Love Myself When I Am Laughing*, 171. Wright also criticized Hurston in *New Masses* somewhat puzzlingly for having "no theme." This charge becomes clearer in the context of his "Blueprint for Negro Writing," in which he explicates, "Theme for Negro writers will emerge when they have begun to feel the meaning of the history of their race as though they in one lifetime had lived it themselves throughout all the long centuries": Wright, "Blueprint for Negro Writing," 16.

46. This context rarely was mentioned in such widely circulating media as the *New York Times Book Review*, Sandra Gilbert and Susan Gubar's *The Norton Anthology of Literature by Women: The Tradition in English* (New York: W. W. Norton, 1985), and Emory Elliott's *Columbia Literary History of the United States* (New York: Columbia University Press, 1988), all of which stressed Wright's antagonism to Hurston's novel without mentioning Hurston's attitude toward Wright.

47. See Bone, *Down Home*; Robert Bone, "Richard Wright and the Chicago Renaissance," *Callaloo* (1987): 446–468; Günter Lenz, "Southern Exposures: The Urban

Experience and the Reconstruction of Black Folk Culture and Community in the Works of Richard Wright and Zora Neale Hurston," *New York Folklore* 7 (Summer 1981): 3–39; Cappetti, "Sociology of an Existence." The extent of Wright's and Hurston's exposure to the social sciences is made clear in Fabre, *The Unfinished Quest*, 127, 201, 232–234, and Hemenway, *Zora Neale Hurston*, 21, 62–63, 81, 88–91.

48. Wright, *American Hunger*, 7. As is well known, *American Hunger* was originally written as the last third of Wright's autobiography but was cut from the book that became *Black Boy* in the galley stage.

49. Wright, "Introduction," xvii–xviii. *American Hunger* also contains specific references to Wright's interest in the social sciences: see, e.g., Wright, *American Hunger*, 19–20. Compare also Cayton's recollection (see Herbert Hill, ed., "Reflections on Richard Wright: A Symposium on an Exiled Native Son," in *Anger, and Beyond: The Negro Writer in the United States* [New York: Harper and Row, 1966], 198, reprinted in Gibson, *Five Black Writers*, 58–60):

> I think that [Wright] had more influence on me than anyone else except Dr. Robert Park. . . . I was research assistant to the brilliant sociologist, Louis Wirth, at the University of Chicago, and one day there came a tapping on the door of his office. I opened the door and there was a brown-skinned Negro, and I said, "Hello. What do you want?" He looked like an undergraduate, so I was perhaps condescending in a polite fashion, and, of course, he *was* also colored. He said, "My name is Richard Wright. Mrs. Wirth made an appointment for me to see Dr. Wirth." That made me a little more respectful. I told him to come in. "Mrs. Wirth said that her husband might help me. I want to be a writer."
>
> Well, I thought that was a little pretentious, a brown-skinned boy coming in to the University and saying he wanted to be a writer. Who didn't want to be a writer? But who could write? I began showing him the files in the office—I would not say that we were totally statistically oriented at the University at the time, but we were very empirical. We were going out studying every facet of the city. We were discovering the Italian district, the Polish district, the Irish district, the Negro community. We were studying the vast complex of human beings who make up that monster of Chicago, and Dick said, "you've got all of your facts pointed, pinned to the wall like a collector would pin butterflies." I looked at him. He was a poetic little Negro. . . . Some years later Dick came to me and said, "I've come to write a picture book [which was later *12 Million Black Voices*]. I want to get into your files. I want your sociological concepts." I explained to him the idea of urban versus rural, of culture versus civilization, or a sacred versus a secular society. I talked about the differences between societies in which folkways determine the way of life and those which are governed by contracts rather than promises, and from those two concepts Dick came up with this lovely, poetic formulation: "The Lords of the Land," who characterized the rural, sacred society in the South, and "The Bosses of the Buildings," describing the forces of the cold, impersonal cities of the North.

50. She adds, "But I found that it did not do to be too detached as I stepped aside to study them. I had to go back, dress as they did, talk as they did, live their life, so that I could get into my stories the world I knew as a child": Sally McDougall, "author Plans to Upbraid Own Race," *New York World Telegram*, February 6, 1935, quoted in

Hemenway, *Zora Neale Hurston*, 215. While she is trying to bridge the gulf, the very distinction between "their life" and "my story" points to a separation, just as she is no longer a child when she is writing this.

51. Hurston, *Mules and Men*, 3. In "Folklore," a Florida WPA typescript from 1938, Hurston writes that folklore comes out of a people's "first wandering contact with natural law": quoted in Hemenway, *Zora Neale Hurston*, 159. While Wright expressed his indebtedness to both anthropology and sociology, Hurston seemed to assume that anthropology was compatible with her writing, while sociology was explicitly perceived to be antithetical to it. She thus polemicized against publishers who shied away from printing black love stories unless they involved racial tension and "could then be offered as a study in Sociology": Hurston, "What White Publishers Won't Print," 170. In a letter from 1943 to the journalist Douglas Gilbert, she explained, "I hate talking about the race problem. I am a writer, and leave sociological problems to sociologists, who know more about it than I do": quoted in Hurston, *Dust Tracks on a Road*, xxix. Yet at the same time, it was a sociologist, Charles S. Johnson, who printed Hurston's first story in *Opportunity* (1924) and helped her launch her literary career: Hurston, *Dust Tracks on a Road*, 167–168, 312. In 1934, Robert Park wrote the introduction to Johnson's *Shadow of the Plantation* (Chicago: University of Chicago Press, 1934).

52. Wright, "Introduction," xxii.

53. Hurston, *Dust Tracks on a Road*, 206.

54. Horace R. Cayton, "Robert Park: A Great Man Died, but Leaves Keen Observation on Our Democracy," *Pittsburgh Courier*, February 26, 1944, 7.

55. Cayton in Hill, *Anger, and Beyond*, 198, cited in Gibson, *Five Black Writers*, 60.

56. John M. Reilly, ed., *Richard Wright: The Critical Reception* (New York: Burt Franklin, 1978), 104–105, 184–188. See also the following introduction from one of the volumes on race that appeared during World War II: "Richard Wright's *Native Son* showed by the techniques of fiction how Bigger Thomas reacted to his lot as a Negro youth in Chicago's South Side "Black Belt." . . . As the author of a novel must often do, Wright was obliged to simplify facts and generalize freely in his interpretation. The present volume, *Color and Human Nature*, which is not limited to the story of one Negro youth in Chicago, includes facts about hundreds of lives on which generalizations may be established." Robert L. Sutherland, "Preface," in W. Lloyd Warner, *Color and Human Nature* (Washington, DC: American Council on Education, 1941).

57. Hurston, *Dust Tracks on a Road*, 170.

58. Zora Neale Hurston to Franz Boas, letter, August 20, 1934, cited in Hemenway, *Zora Neale Hurston*, 163. See also Carla Kaplan's comprehensive edition, *Zora Neale Hurston: A Life in Letters* (New York: Anchor Books, 2002), 308–309.

59. Franz Boas, "Preface," in Hurston, *Mules and Men*, 5.

60. *Opportunity*, April 16, 1938, 120–121, quoted in Kinnamon, *The Emergence of Richard Wright*, 109. Sterling Brown, *The Negro in American Fiction* (1937), repr. ed. (New York: Atheneum, 1969), 160–161.

61. Philip Gleason, "Americans All: World War II and the Shaping of American Identity," *Review of Politics* 43, no. 4 (1981): 483–518. See also the chapters on W. I. Thomas and Robert Redfield in Cappetti, *Writing Chicago*, 59–108.

62. Redfield, *Tepoztlán*, 193.

63. Robert Redfield, "The Folk Society and Culture," *American Journal of Sociology* 45, no. 5 (March 1940): 732.

64. Louis Wirth, "Urban Society and Civilization," *American Journal of Sociology* 45,

no. 5 (March 1940): 744. Incidentally, several of the social scientists were themselves newcomers to the cities of New York and Chicago, whether from immigrant (Wirth and Boas) or small-town (Thomas and Park) backgrounds. And like some American authors, social scientists also took an existentialist turn in the 1940s. Thus, E. B. Reuter wrote in 1945 in an essay on racial theory, "Apparently, the development of intelligence and personality has always come in the collective struggle for ends manifestly absurd, useless, undesirable, and impossible of achievement": E. B. Reuter, "Racial Theory," *American Journal of Sociology* 50 (1945): 461.

65. Burgum, "The Art of Richard Wright's Short Stories," 44.

66. This makes an interesting contrast with the Shorty scenes in Wright, *Black Boy*, 248–250, and Wright, *American Hunger*, 6, but parallels the use of money in an erotically charged scene in Hurston, *Dust Tracks on a Road*, 253. Other parts of *Dust Tracks on a Road*, too, throw some light on "The Gilded Six-Bits"—for example, the porch discussion about city ways (*Dust Tracks on a Road*, 23–25), the use of meal sacks as towels (*Dust Tracks on a Road*, 26, and *Spunk*, 55), the presence of gardenias under the name "cape jasmine" (*Dust Tracks on a Road*, 18, and *Spunk*, 55), or the imitation millionaire ethos (*Dust Tracks on a Road*, 303–304).

67. In *Jonah's Gourd Vine*, written in the wake of "The Gilded Six-Bits," Hurston puts the phrase "'bout in spots and places" into John Pearson's mouth to make the character (often thought to resemble John Hurston, the author's father) appear as an experienced traveler before his first train trip.

68. Wright, *American Hunger* 31–35; Hurston, *Mules and Men*, 3–9. The contrast between Hurston's and Wright's work was probably symptomatic of the directions black and ethnic writing took in the 1930s and 1940s. Many figures—Langston Hughes, Sterling Brown, Michael Gold, Henry Roth, and William Saroyan come to mind—combined elements of both visions or hovered between images of home as arcadia or as a place from which one had to escape. Each perspective seems to rest on an assertion, as well as a denial and occasionally the other side comes through. For example, Hurston's beloved Eatonville is once described as a "dull village": Hurston, *Dust Tracks on a Road*, 46.

69. Hurston, *Mules and Men*, 91–92.

70. Wright, *12 Million Black Voices*, 41.

71. Hurston, *Mules and Men*, 20.

72. Wright, *Lawd Today* (New York: Walker, 1963), 154; Wright, *12 Million Black Voices*, 88. The following version, reported in 1915–1916 from Auburn, Alabama, is reprinted in Newman I. White, *American Negro Folk-Songs* (Cambridge, MA: Harvard University Press, 1928), 289:

> I'd rather be in the cottonfield
> Working hard,
> Than be a buck-private in the
> National Guard.

This is a text that rhymes like Hurston's yet has a social perspective similar to Wright's.

73. Hurston, *Mules and Men*, 19.

74. Lawrence W. Levine, *Black Culture and Black Consciousness: Afro-American Folk Thought from Slavery to Freedom* (New York: Oxford University Press, 1977), 266, from Timely Records TI-112, collection of Lawrence Gellert.

75. It is noticeable that she varied dialect transcriptions and expanded the story considerably; moved the scene from a clear paradise setting with a tree of life to a more

idiosyncratic one with a sea of life; and changed the punchline with which the story concludes. Hemenway's interpretation of the story pays some attention to the variants and resembles Kinnamon's reading of the meaning of time in "Long Black Song": see Hemenway in Hurston, *Dust Tracks on a Road*, xxii–xxiii.

76. Hurston, *Mules and Men*, 32–33. In 1937, God called everybody up and said, "Now, I want everybody around the throne at seven o'clock sharp tomorrow morning and I want everybody here on time. I got a lot more creating to do and I want to give out this color and be through with that": Earlier version of "My People, My People!" in Hurston, *Dust Tracks on a Road*, 305.

77. Hurston, *Dust Tracks on a Road*, 67.

78. Wright, *Black Boy*, 33.

79. Like Hurston, Wright changed the punchlines when he retold stories, a strategy that is noticeable in his use of autobiographical materials, first in "The Ethics of Living Jim Crow," and then in *Black Boy*. Most striking is the transformation of the guilt-ridden memoir of a friend's drowning that appears in early manuscript versions of Wright's autobiography and is turned into the story "Big Boy Leaves Home": see Fabre, *The Unfinished Quest*, 43–44.

80. Corrected manuscript of *Native Son*, New York Public Library Archives and Manuscripts ScMicro R-1234, 1.

81. Wright, "Blueprint for Negro Writing," 14.

CHAPTER 8

1. Leo Marx, "Pastoralism in America," and Henry Nash Smith, "Symbol and Idea in *Virgin Land*," in *Ideology and Classic American Literature*, ed. Sacvan Bercovitch and Myra Jehlen (New York: Cambridge University Press, 1986), 21–69; David M. Schneider, *American Kinship: A Cultural Account*, 2d ed. (Chicago: University of Chicago Press, 1980).

2. Werner Sollors, "A Critique of Pure Pluralism," in *Reconstructing American Literary History*, ed. Sacvan Bercovitch, Harvard English Studies 13 (Cambridge, MA: Harvard University Press, 1986), 250–279. Gunnar Myrdal, "A Parallel to the Negro Problem," app. 5 in *An American Dilemma: The Negro Problem and Modern Democracy* (New York: Harper and Brothers, 1944), 1073–1078.

3. Zora Neale Hurston, "Court Order Can't Make Races Mix," *Orlando Sentinel* August 11, 1955. Darwin T. Turner, "Zora Neale Hurston: The Wandering Minstrel," in *In a Minor Chord: Three Afro-American Writers and Their Search for Identity* (Carbondale: Southern Illinois University Press, 1971), 97. In this pre–Hurston revival essay, Turner is quite critical of Hurston, and although he advances several hypotheses that might justify or, at least, explain her stance, he concludes that "no single explanation eases the disappointment": Turner, "Zora Neale Hurston," 98. Robert Hemenway, *Zora Neale Hurston: A Literary Biography* (Urbana: University of Illinois Press, 1977), 336.

4. Mary Helen Washington, "Introduction," in *I Love Myself When I Am Laughing . . . and Then Again When I Am Looking Mean and Impressive*, ed. Alice Walker (Old Westbury, NY: Feminist Press, 1979), 19.

5. Sandra M. Gilbert and Susan Gubar, eds., *The Norton Anthology of Literature by Women: The Tradition in English* (New York: W. W. Norton, 1985), 1639.

6. Elaine Showalter, "Women Writers between the Wars," in *Columbia Literary*

History of the United States, ed. Emory Elliott (New York: Columbia University Press, 1988), 838.

7. Quoted from a microfilm copy in the Orange County (Florida) Library System, provided by R. B. Murray.

8. Hurston, "Court Order Can't Make Races Mix." She had used the parable similarly in "Why the Negro Won't Buy Communism," a startling contribution to the *American Legion Magazine,* June 1951, 14–15, 55–60, which features photographs of communists such as Paul Robeson, W. E. B. Du Bois, Langston Hughes, and Howard Fast. Hurston argues that, to "mount their world rule on Black American backs," communists took for a blueprint "an ancient and long-discarded folk piece. The analogy of the 'white mare.' It got to be said during the Reconstruction that the highest ambition of every Negro man was to have a white woman": Hurston, "Why the Negro Won't Buy Communism," 56. Here she concludes the parable with the interpretation that analogies are dangerous, because it is "possible, and even probable that we might not be mules," although "the reds evidently thought so." Hurston finds in what she terms the party's "'pig-meat' crusade"—when Harlem "swarmed with party-sent white women"—an explanation for the frequency of mixed couples in party councils and suspects that it was by "such whoopdedoo" that the Lincoln Brigade was "recruited to go to Spain in a vain attempt to place the Russian Bear at Gibraltar": Hurston, "Why the Negro Won't Buy Communism," 57.

9. Hurston, "Court Order Can't Make Races Mix"; Mario Materassi, "Gli avvenimenti storici e le icone letterarie: Alcune osservazioni sulla 'roba' della letteratura near" (Historic events and literary icons: Some observations on the "stuff" of black literature), *Rivista di Studi Anglo-Americani* 4, no. 6 (1986): 161–168.

10. Hurston, "Court Order Can't Make Races Mix." Having received her first training from a student of Booker T. Washington, and having defended Washington against Du Bois as late as 1940, Hurston here may be recapitulating Washington's adaptation of the court's earlier "separate but equal" doctrine in *Plessy v. Ferguson* (1896). Worried that she might be denounced "in certain quarters" as a "handkerchief head" for seeking "to deny Negro children their rights," she emphatically denies that she is selling out her own people.

11. Ibid. In a contribution to the April 21, 1958, issue of *New Leader,* Sidney Hook—who once was a strenuous and principled supporter of enforcing school desegregation but now appears in the *Congressional Record* as an opponent of affirmative action (as Philip Gleason notes in *Speaking of Diversity: Language and Ethnicity in Twentieth-Century America* [Baltimore: Johns Hopkins University Press, 1992], 190–221)— summarized conservative white southerners' critique of integration. Hurston's views were compatible with the three major thrusts of that critique: (1) that integration meant a change in the established way of life; (2) that integration constituted a usurpation of congressional functions by the court, interfering also with states' rights; and (3) that integration was a violation of the "separate but equal" ruling in *Plessy v. Ferguson.*

12. Hurston associated efforts at racial integration with the political left long before McCarthy and *Brown v. Board of Education.* Thus, in a letter dated February 21, 1944, to her friend, the writer Bob Wunsch (to whom she had dedicated her first novel), she supported the position of the more cautious part of the experimental Black Mountain College faculty *not* to admit black students, writing, "Even at this distance I can see the dynamite in the proposal to take Negro students *now.* Confidentially, some of these Left-

wing people get me down. They always want to spring some sensation that gives *them* great publicity, but which does *us* no good. Sometimes *positive* harm": see Martin Duberman, *Black Mountain: An Exploration in Community* (New York: E. P. Dutton, 1972), 180.

13. Cornel West argues that "Hurston's reactionary essays . . . and Republican Party allegiance . . . are often overlooked by her contemporary feminist and womanist followers": Cornel West, "Demystifying the New Black Conservatism," *Praxis International* 7, no. 2 (July 1987): 143. In the absence of a manuscript, the possibility exists that the essay was tampered with by the newspaper editors, although the similarities with Hurston's article for *American Legion Magazine* piece speak against it.

14. Hannah Arendt, "Reflections on Little Rock," *Dissent* 6, no. 1 (Winter 1959): 45–55. Rebuttals by David Spitz and Melvin Tumin appeared in same issue: see David Spitz, "Politics and the Realms of Being," *Dissent* 6, no. 1 (Winter 1959): 56–64; Melvin Tumin, "Pie in the Sky . . . ," *Dissent* 6, no. 1 (Winter 1959): 65–71. A response by Sidney Hook, letters by readers, and Arendt's follow-up piece ("A Reply to the Critics") were published in the journal's next issue. For Arendt's quote, see "A Reply to the Critics," *Dissent* 6, no. 2 (Spring 1959): 179. Hereafter, references to these articles are in parentheses in the text. Background information, especially her correspondence with *Commentary* and *Dissent*, is from the Arendt papers at the Library of Congress (thanks to Charles J. Kelly) and from Elisabeth Young-Bruehl, *Hannah Arendt: For Love of the World* (New Haven, CT: Yale University Press, 1982).

15. The Supreme Court's decision in *Loving v. Virginia* (388 US 1, 1967) would echo Arendt's point: "Marriage is one of the basic civil rights of man, fundamental to our very existence and survival. . . . Under our Constitution, the freedom to marry or not to marry, a person of another race resides with the individual and cannot be infringed upon by the State."

16. See *New Leader*, April 21, 1958.

17. Wilhelm Reich observed that Hitler made no semantic distinction between incest and miscegenation: both were "Blutschande": Wilhelm Reich, *The Mass Psychology of Fascism* (1933), trans. Vincent R. Carfagno (New York: Farrar, Straus and Giroux, 1970), 78–79. Simone Vauthier explores the connection between incest and miscegenation in literature: Simone Vauthier, "Textualité et stéréotypes: Of African Queens and Afro-American Princes and Princesses in *Old Hepsy*," in *Regards sur la littérature noire américaine*, ed. Michel Fabre (Paris: Publications du Conseil Scientifique de la Sorbonne Nouvelle—Paris III, 1980), 65–107. Eva Saks reports the vicinity of prohibitions of incest and of miscegenation in law books: Eva Saks, "Representing Miscegenation Law," *Raritan* 8, no. 2 (Fall 1988): 39–69.

18. Ralph Ellison, *Shadow and Act* (New York: Signet Books, 1966), 116. In the context of his debate with Howe, Ellison noted that Arendt's essay was a "dark foreshadowing" of the blowup caused by her Eichmann book. As Young-Bruehl notes, in his interview in Robert Penn Warren, *Who Speaks for the Negro?* (New York: Random House, 1965), Ellison also disputed Arendt's misunderstanding of the ideal of sacrifice and parental responsibility of those who sent their children through lines of hostile people, and Arendt agreed with him in a letter dated July 29, 1965.

Myrdal included the finding that intermarriage was lowest on the black man's (but highest on the white man's) rank order of discrimination: Myrdal, *An American Dilemma*, 60–67, as readers of *Dissent* also noted (205). Yet throughout history, Afro-American intellectuals have fairly consistently opposed legal restrictions on intermarriages (without therefore necessarily *advocating* such unions). Thus, David Walker compared biblical slavery as embodied in Joseph's marriage story (Genesis 41:45) favorably to American slavery, because in America marriages between black and white were outlawed. Yet Walker goes on to say that he "would not give a *pinch of snuff* to be married to any white person": David Walker, *Appeal* (Boston, 1829), art. 1. Charles W. Chesnutt described the proscription of intermarriage as a forcible expression of southern race prejudice, and he discussed it *first*, before segregation in transportation, education, and politics, in his article "The Future American," *Boston Evening Transcript*, September 1, 1900. W. E. B. Du Bois gave readers of *The Crisis* moral and social reasons for opposing the motions in state legislatures for anti-intermarriage bills but, most important, cited the *"physical reason that to prohibit such intermarriage would be publicly to acknowledge that black blood is a physical taint*—a thing that no decent, self-respecting black man can be asked to admit": W. E. B. Du Bois, editorial, *The Crisis*, February 1913, 180. He concluded the editorial with the strong admonition that non-intermarriage laws must be killed "not because we are anxious to marry white men's sisters, but because we are determined that white men shall let our sisters alone": Du Bois, editorial, 181. In his autobiography, James Weldon Johnson cited with admiration Frederick Douglass's statement, "In my first marriage I paid my compliments to my mother's race; in my second marriage I paid my compliments to the race of my father": James Weldon, *Along This Way: The Autobiography of James Weldon Johnson* (New York: Viking, 1933), 61. And J.A. Rogers made the criticism of American attitudes toward, and legal restrictions of, racial mixing his lifelong concern, culminating in such works as the three-volume *Sex and Race: Negro-Caucasian Mixes in All Ages and All Lands*, 9th. ed. (St. Petersburg, FL: J. A. Rogers, 1967). See also Calvin Hernton, *Sex and Racism in America* (New York: Grove, 1966).

19. A further investigation of the reverberations of the discussion in *Dissent* in other journals and correspondence, as well as of reactions in the black press and Orlando press to Hurston's piece might add new dimensions to this debate.

20. Elliott, *Columbia Literary History of the United States*, xxi.

21. Gilbert and Gubar, *The Norton Anthology of Literature by Women*, xxvii.

22. Ibid., 21.

23. Ibid., 1637.

24. Thomas J. Ferraro, *Ethnic Passages: Literary Immigrants in Twentieth-Century America* (Chicago: University of Chicago Press, 1993).

25. Otelia Cromwell, Eva B. Dykes, and Lorenzo Dow Turner, eds., *Readings from Negro Authors for Schools and Colleges* (New York: Harcourt, Brace, 1931), iii.

26. Sterling A. Brown, Arthur P. Davis, and Ulysses Lee, eds., *The Negro Caravan: Writings by American Negroes* (New York: Citadel, 1941), 5. Hereafter, page numbers for this volume are cited in parentheses in the text. Interestingly, when Alain Locke reviewed *The Negro Caravan* in *Opportunity* in 1942, he praised the editors' wisdom in giving "some notion of the important correlation of Negro creative effort with that of white authors treating Negro themes; which somewhat offsets the inconsistency of the anthology's non-racialist critical platform and its actual restriction to Negro authorship": Leonard Harris, ed., *The Philosophy of Alain Locke* (Philadelphia: Temple University Press, 1989), 215.

27. It was as palpable in Hurston's voice as in that of her political opponent Richard Wright, whose publicity statement for *Black Boy* is cited above.

28. "Anthropological Instruction in Columbia University," in *A Franz Boas Reader: The Shaping of American Anthropology, 1883–1911*, ed. George W. Stocking Jr. (Chicago: University of Chicago Press, 1974), 291.

29. Andrew Delbanco, *New Republic*, January 16, 1989.

30. Julius Lester, "Introduction to This Edition," in *The Negro Caravan*, repr. ed., ed. Sterling A. Brown, Arthur P. Davis, and Ulysses Lee (New York: Arno Press [paperback reprint], 1970), unpaginated. Lester's introduction was adapted from his review of *The Negro Caravan* for the *New York Times*, November 30, 1969, BR 71.

31. See the careful annotations in Nathan Huggins's edition of Du Bois's *Writings* (New York: Library of America, 1986), and his suggestive essay "W. E. B. Du Bois and Heroes," *Amerikastudien* 34, no. 2 (1989): 167–174. See also Shamoon Zamir, *Dark Voices: W. E. B. Du Bois and American Thought* (Chicago: University of Chicago Press, 1995); Gerald L. Early, ed., *Lure and Loathing: Essays on Race, Identity, and the Ambivalence of Assimilation* (New York: A. Lane, 1993).

32. Albert Murray, *The Omni-Americans: New Perspectives on Black Experience and American Culture* (New York: Discus/Avon, 1971), 112.

33. Fredrik Barth, "Introduction," in *Ethnic Groups and Boundaries: The Social Organization of Culture Difference* (Boston: Little, Brown, 1969), 9–38; Abner Cohen, "Introduction: The Lesson of Ethnicity," *Urban Ethnicity* (London: Tavistock, 1974), ix–xxiv; George Devereux, "Ethnic Identity: Its Logical Foundations and Its Dysfunctions," in *Ethnic Identity: Cultural Continuities and Change*, ed. George de Vos and Lola Romanucci-Ross (Palo Alto, CA: Mayfield, 1975), 42–70; Herbert J. Gans, "Symbolic Ethnicity: The Future of Ethnic Groups and Cultures in America," in *On the Making of Americans: Essays in Honor of David Riesman* (Philadelphia: University of Pennsylvania Press, 1979), 193–220.

34. LeRoi Jones, letter to the editor, *Evergreen Review* 8 (1959), 255. The discussion that follows draws on Werner Sollors, *Amiri Baraka/LeRoi Jones: The Quest for a "Populist Modernism"* (New York: Columbia University Press, 1978).

35. "Jazz and Revolutionary Nationalism," *Jazz* 5, no. 1 (November 1966): 38.

36. Richard Gilman, "White Standards and Negro Writing," *New Republic*, vol. 158, March 9, 1968, 25. Hereafter, page numbers for this article are cited in parentheses in the text.

37. See Mark Silk, "Notes on the Judeo-Christian Tradition in America," *American Quarterly* 36, no. 1 (Spring 1984): 65–85.

38. Richard Handler, "Boasian Anthropology and the Critique of American Culture," *American Quarterly* 42 (June 1990): 266–280.

39. Richard Gilman, "More on Negro Writing," *New Republic*, vol. 158, April 13, 1968, 26. Hereafter, page numbers for this article are cited in parentheses in the text.

40. Randall Kennedy, "Racial Critiques of Legal Academia," *Harvard Law Review* 102 (1989): 1798–1799. For another critique of Gilman's argument, see Theodore L. Gross, "Our Mutual Estate: The Literature of the American Negro," in *The Black American Writer*, ed. C. W. E. Bigsby, vol. 1: Fiction (Baltimore: Penguin, 1969), 51–61. See also James W. Tuttleton, "The Negro Writer as Spokesman," in Bigsby, *The Black American Writer* 245–259.

41. H. C. Porter, "Reflections on the Ethnohistory of Early Colonial America," *Journal of American Studies* 16 (August 1982): 245–246.

CHAPTER 9

1. W. E. B. Du Bois, *The Autobiography of W. E. B. Du Bois: A Soliloquy on Viewing My Life from the Last Decade of Its First Century* (New York: International Publishers, 1968), 413. Hereafter, references are to this edition; page numbers are cited in parentheses in the text.

2. On the contexts of "double consciousness," see Shamoon Zamir, *Dark Voices: W. E. B. Du Bois and American Thought, 1888–1903* (Chicago: University of Chicago Press, 1995), 113–119.

3. David Levering Lewis, "The Autobiographical Legacy of W. E. B. Du Bois," in *Living Our Stories, Telling Our Truths: Autobiography and the Making of the African-American Intellectual Tradition*, ed. V. P. Franklin (New York: Scribner, 1995), 223–274. See also David Levering Lewis, *W. E. B. Du Bois: Biography of a Race, 1868–1919* (New York: Holt, 1993); David Levering Lewis, *W. E. B. Du Bois: The Fight for Equality and the American Century, 1919–1963* (New York: Holt, 2000).

4. Irving Howe, "Remarkable Man, Ambiguous Legacy," *Harper's Magazine*, March 1968, 143–148.

5. Howe, "Remarkable Man, Ambiguous Legacy."

6. Richard Kostelanetz, "W. E. B. Du Bois: Perhaps the Most Important Black in American Intellectual History," *Commonweal*, November 1968, 161–162.

7. Hugh Davis Graham, *Journal of Southern History* 34, no. 4 (November 1968): 640–641.

8. Truman Nelson, "A Life Style of Conscience," *Nation*, April 29, 1968, 574–575.

9. William E. Cain, "W. E. B. Du Bois's Autobiography and the Politics of Literature," *Black American Literature Forum* 24, no. 2 (Summer 1990): 299–313.

10. Gilbert Osofsky, "The Master of the Grand Vision," *Saturday Review*, February 29, 1968, 42.

11. Keith Eldon Byerman, *Seizing the Word: History, Art, and Self in the Work of W. E. B. Du Bois* (Athens: University of Georgia Press, 1994), 205.

12. For additional reviews of Du Bois's *Autobiography*, see Martin Duberman, "Du Bois as Prophet," *New Republic*, March 23, 1968, 36–39; Louis Filler's review in *American Historical Review* 74, no. 1 (October 1968): 315–316.

13. For a recent assessment of the bildungsroman, see Jesse Raber, "Progressivism's Aesthetic Education: The *Bildungsroman* and the Struggle for the American School, 1890–1920," Ph.D. diss., Harvard University, Cambridge, MA, 2014.

CHAPTER 10

KEY TO ABBREVIATIONS

Original Plays

B   *A Beast Story* (1966), in *Kuntu Drama*, ed. Paul Carter Harrison (New York: Grove, 1974), 191–201.

F   *Funnyhouse of a Negro* (1964), in *Black Drama: An Anthology*, ed. William Brasmer and Dominick Consolo (Columbus, OH: Charles E. Merrill, 1970), 251–272.

I   *In One Act* (Minneapolis: University of Minnesota Press, 1988); contains all of these plays (except *B*) and the Euripides adaptions.

L   *A Lesson in Dead Language* (1966), in *Collision Course*, ed. Edward Parone (New York: Vintage, 1968), 33–40.

M   *A Movie Star Has to Star in Black and White* (1976), in *Performing Arts Journal: Wordplay* 3 (1984): 51–68.

O   *The Owl Answers* (1965), in *Kuntu Drama*, ed. Paul Carter Harrison (New York: Grove, 1974), 169–190.

Adaptations

E   Electra and Orestes (1980), typescript.

W   *In His Own Write* (1968), in *The Lennon Play: In His Own Write*, ed. Adrienne Kennedy, John Lennon, Victor Spinetti (London: Jonathan Cape, 1968).

Autobiographical Sources

G   "A Growth of Images" (interview), ed. Lisa Lehman, *Drama Review* 21, no. 4 (1977): 41–48.

K   "A *MELUS* Interview: Adrienne Kennedy" (with an analytical preface by the interviewer Wolfgang Binder), *MELUS* 12, no. 3 (1985): 99–108.

P   *People Who Led to My Plays* (New York: Knopf, 1987).

S   "Sketches: People I Have Met in the Theatre," *Quilt* 5 (1986): 1–34.

1. I thank Adrienne Kennedy for correspondence and conversations. Page references to primary works are cited in the text and endnotes in parentheses, preceded by the one-letter abbreviations of titles listed in the key. In two cases, passages are cited from galley proofs (e.g., *P* galleys) because they do not seem to appear in the first printed edition. The plays reprinted (with variants) in *In One Act* are identified both by original publication and by page number in the anthology. For Kennedy's view of the theater scene of 1964, see *S*, 5–11.

2. This is common in the lyrical drama tradition of Stéphane Mallarmé, Hugo von Hoffmannsthal, Villiers de l'Isle-Adam, and Maurice Maeterlinck, on whose play *L'oiseau bleu* (1908) the film *The Blue Bird* (*P*, 3) was based. See Peter Szondi, *Das lyrische Drama des Fin de Siècle* (Frankfurt, Germany: Suhrkamp, 1977); Edmund Wilson, *Axel's Castle: A Study in the Imaginative Literature of 1870–1930* (New York: Scribner, 1931).

3. Rosemary K. Curb, "Fragmented Selves in Adrienne Kennedy's *Funnyhouse of a Negro* and *The Owl Answers*," *Theatre Journal* 32 (1980): 182; Lorraine A. Brown, "'For the Characters Are Myself': Adrienne Kennedy's *Funnyhouse of a Negro*," *Negro American Literature Forum* 9 (1975): 86–88; Ruby Cohn, *New American Dramatists, 1960–1980* (London: Macmillan, 1982), 109–111.

4. See Kennedy's earlier statement about how amazed she was "that one person could have a whole era named after" her (*G*, 46).

5. Geneviève Fabre has emphasized that *Funnyhouse of a Negro* does not permit a single summary because Sarah, for example, "imagines various fates for her father: either she herself kills him for having given her a taste of the jungle, or he commits suicide upon hearing of the death of Lumumba, or again he lives with a white prostitute." Even when an action is presented on stage, its "reality" is dubious. Thus, Sarah "hangs herself as the curtain falls, and her death becomes as real or imaginary as the games she has just played": Geneviève Fabre, *Drumbeats, Masks, and Metaphor: Contemporary Afro-American Theatre* (Cambridge, MA: Harvard University Press, 1983), 119–120.

6. Ibid., 119; see also Yemi Ogunbiyi, "New Black Playwrights in America (1960–1975): Essays in Theatrical Criticism," Ph.D. diss., New York University, 1976, 133–134; Samuel Larry Grossman, "Trends in the Avant-Garde Theatre of the United States during the 1960s," Ph.D. diss., University of Minnesota, Minneapolis, 1974, 154; Brown, "For the Characters Are Myself," 88n.

7. The play could be divided into the following clusters: "Returning father" dialogue (Duchess and Victoria, Mother); Poetic voice and "Roman ruins" monologue (Sarah); "Returning father" description (the Funnylady); "Returning father" dialogue (the Funnyman and Duchess); "Returning father" monologue (Man turning into Lumumba); "Roman ruins" monologue (Lumumba); "African savior-white dove" monologue (Sarah); "Returning father" dialogue (Duchess and Jesus); "African savior" monologue (the Funnylady); perverted "African savior" monologue (Jesus); "Returning father" chorus (all selves); "Roman ruins" variation (the Funnyman and the Funnylady).

8. See Curb, "Fragmented Selves in Adrienne Kennedy's *Funnyhouse of a Negro* and *The Owl Answers*," 191; Robert L. Tener, "Theatre of Identity: Adrienne Kennedy's Portrait of the Black Woman," *Studies in Black Literature* 6, no. 2 (Summer 1975): 2; Kimberly W. Benston, "*Cities in Bezique*: Adrienne Kennedy's Expressionistic Vision," *College Language Association Journal* 20 (1976): 240.

9. Cited in Grossman, "Trends in the Avant-Garde Theatre of the United States during the 1960s," 159. See also Paul K. Bryant-Jackson, "Interview with Gerald Freedman," in *Intersecting Boundaries: The Theatre of Adrienne Kennedy*, ed. Paul K. Bryant-Jackson and Lois More Overbeck (Minneapolis: University of Minnesota Press, 1992), 215n2.

10. Kennedy uses Ingram Bywater, trans., *Poetics* (New York: Modern Library, 1954), 255, with slight variants.

11. Hence Curb's and Tener's disagreement about whether "Bastard's Black Mother" and "Reverend's Wife" count as two different characters: see Tener, "Theatre of Identity," 1; Curb, "Fragmented Selves in Adrienne Kennedy's *Funnyhouse of a Negro* and *The Owl Answers*," 184. See also James V. Hatch and Ted Shine, eds., *Black Theater, U.S.A.: Forty-Five Plays by Black Americans* (New York: Macmillan, 1974), 756.

12. Tener ("Theatre of Identity," 1–3), referred to by Curb and Benston, stresses the owl's opposition to the white bird of Christianity; its connection to fig trees (see also Matthew 21:19); its association with death, sterility, and barrenness; and its sacred aspect. Ogunbiyi ("New Playwrights in America [1960–1975]," 142–143) reports the earlier interpretation of the "owl" as the bird who asks "who" and thus questions identity; he adds his own view that the owl's changing color is what makes it meaningful and notes Kennedy's association of owls with "West African night noises": "If you be awake all night, the owls are answering your thoughts, are talking to you, your psychic state." Curb ("Fragmented Selves in Adrienne Kennedy's *Funnyhouse of a Negro* and *The Owl Answers*," 193) sees owls as symbols of women, "dark as night, warm, round, maternal, and possessors of intuitive female wisdom which men fear because they cannot fathom it." Herbert Blau ("The American Dream in American Gothic: The Plays of Sam Shepard and Adrienne Kennedy," *Modern Drama* 27 [1984]: 532–533) invokes the Gothic tradition of Poe's "Raven": cf. *P*, 117–118. As Athena's bird, the owl also constitutes a connection to Aeschylus's *Oresteia*, in which Athena has to cast her vote and settle the dispute on the fate of Orestes who is tragically caught in conflicting family claims: Curb, "Fragmented Selves in Adrienne Kennedy's *Funnyhouse of a Negro* and *The Owl Answers*," 192.

13. *The Owl Answers* and *A Beast Story* were performed together under the title *Cities in Bezique* at the New York Public Theater in January 1969. "Bezique" may refer to the card game in which the combination of the queen of spades and the jack of diamonds counts for forty points and is called bezique: see Cohn, *New American Dramatists*, 112. Yet neither play makes any further mention of bezique. Clearing up part of the mystery, Kennedy wrote that in 1967 Joseph Papp commissioned her to write a drama

for the New York Public Theater. She sent him the (unpublished) play *Cities in Bezique*, but he asked to use only the title, as he preferred to produce the two earlier plays *The Owl Answers* and *A Beast Story* (*S*, 28). Kennedy did not include *A Beast Story* in her collection *In One Act* but said that *The Owl Answers* was her favorite play and "much better that the other play that goes with it" (*K*, 104–105). It may thus be closest to the author's original intentions to regard *The Owl Answers* and *A Beast Story* as separate plays. A detailed reading of *A Rat's Mass* was presented by Paul Carter Harrison, *The Drama of Nommo* (New York: Grove, 1972), 116–120; see also Blau, "The American Dream in American Gothic," 536–538.

14. Curb sees in the play "horrors attendant on female adolescent rites of passage under patriarchy": Rosemary K. Curb, "'Lesson I Bleed': Female Adolescent Rites of Passage in Adrienne Kennedy's Plays," in *Women in American Theatre*, ed. Helen Krich Chonoy and Linda Walsh Jenkins (New York: Crown, 1980), 56.

15. Jeanne Thomas Allen, "Introduction: *Now, Voyager* as Woman's Film: Coming of Age Hollywood Style," in *Script of Now, Voyager*, ed. Jeanne Thomas Allen (Madison: University of Wisconsin Press, 1984), 33.

16. The drowning of Alice Tripp as George Eastman stares at her (*M*, 68) is also an inversion of a scene in *Leave Her to Heaven* (1945), a film Kennedy mentions (*P*, 48).

17. Cohn, *New American Dramatists*, 114–115; Ruby Cohn, "Twentieth-Century Drama," *Columbia Literary History of the United States*, ed. Emory Elliott (New York: Columbia University Press, 1988), 1124. Kennedy's plays *The Ohio State Murders* and *She Talks to Beethoven* show the more overtly political side of her work while presenting her familiar division of a lyrical persona into antithetical selves, a Nkrumah and a Beethoven, a Thomas Hardy and a Frantz Fanon, whereas the lyrical monologue *The Film Club* specifically continues her exploration of the power of popular culture—the movies in particular, and Bette Davis most especially. In all three plays, the central character is Suzanne Alexander, and it is fitting that the plays were published, together with *The Dramatic Circle*, a dramatization of the monologue *The Film Club*, as *The Alexander Plays* (Minneapolis: University of Minnesota Press, 1992).

CHAPTER 11

1. "LeRoi Jones—A Fierce and Blazing Talent," *New York Herald Tribune*, April 12, 1964, 26; Howard Taubman, "The Theatre: 'Dutchman,'" *New York Times*, March 25, 1964, 46. The play was directed by Edward Parone and produced by Theater 1964, an enterprise dedicated to the promotion of American plays in the European absurdist tradition. Started by Richard Barr, Clinton Wilder, and Edward Albee, Theater 1964 was originally called Theater 1960 and changed its name every year. For the first month of the Cherry Lane production, *Dutchman* was performed in conjunction with Arrabal's *The Two Executioners* and Beckett's *Play*; these two plays were subsequently replaced by Albee's *The American Dream*. *Dutchman* was successful, received the *Village Voice* Obie Award as Best New American Play, ran well into 1965, and toured several cities in the United States and in Europe. Except for the difficulties the show had when performed on a double bill with *The Toilet* in Los Angeles at the time of the Watts riots (a production I saw), there are few reported interferences by authorities with *Dutchman*. In 1965, one of the American backers of the Italian theater festival at Spoleto "emerged from the first performance of *Dutchman* outraged by the violence of the language and indignant

at what he described as the irresponsibility of the dramatist's point of view": "Poets Applauded at Spoleto Fete," *New York Times*, June 28, 1965, 34. A French production of *Dutchman* at the Dramatic Center in Montpellier in 1968 was banned by the city's mayor as "audacious, erotic, politically violent": "Drama Is Banned; Theater Head Quits," *Minneapolis Star*, January 8, 1968, 11B. In New York, attempts to film *Dutchman* were boycotted by subway authorities, and it became easier to shoot the film in England: Gene Persson, "Arguing 'Dutchman,'" *New York Times*, March 3, 1967, sec. 2, 14. In 1969, *Dutchman* was barred from a reading list of a high school course on black authors in San Francisco by Max Rafferty, superintendent of public instruction in California: Wallace Turner, "Books by Two Negroes Barred from San Francisco Schools," *New York Times*, August 26, 1969, 24. In 1970, a Washington theater filed a complaint with the Federal Communications Commission against a television station that had stopped videotaping a performance of *Dutchman* because "the language was bad" and "there is too much kissing and we have young children watching this show": *Studies in Black Literature* 1, no. 2 (Summer 1970): 87–88.

2. For descriptions of the formal characteristics of the theater of the absurd and the one-act play, cf. Martin Esslin, *The Theatre of the Absurd*, rev. ed. (Garden City, NY: Doubleday and Anchor, 1969); Diemut Schnetz, *Der moderne Einakter: Eine poetologische Untersuchung* (Bern, Switzerland: Francke, 1967).

3. LeRoi Jones, *Dutchman and The Slave* (New York: William Morrow, 1964), 3–4. Hereafter, references are to this edition; page numbers are cited in parentheses in the text.

4. This resembles the structure of Jones's earlier male-on-male plays. In *The Eighth Ditch*, the hostile closeness of Otis-62 and the group of Boy Scouts transforms the relationship of 64 and 46, and in *The Toilet*, Ora's gang code inverts Ray Foots's love for James Karolis into violence.

5. Philip Roth criticized *Dutchman*, charging that the silent acquiescence of the other passengers to the murder was "not a truth anyway; it is a fact we already know from the newspapers": Philip Roth, "Channel X: Two Plays on the Race Conflict," *New York Review of Books* 2, no. 8 (May 28, 1964): 12. What *Dutchman* might have revealed was not simply that such atrocities are practiced in this country—as, of course, they are—but what it is to be a Negro man and a white woman meeting in a country where these possibilities constantly impinge on the consciousness and so cannot but distort every encounter between the two angry races." Baraka responded to Roth's interpretation: see Amiri Baraka, letter to the editor, *New York Review of Books* 2, no. 11 (July 9, 1964): 23.

6. Willene P. Taylor, "The Fall of Man Theme in Imamu Amiri Baraka's (LeRoi Jones') *Dutchman*," *Negro American Literature Forum* 7 (1973): 127–130. The absurdist situation of *Dutchman* is a two-fold inversion of *The Toilet*. On the one hand, the physical victims have changed: instead of the white Karolis, who could be comforted by Ray Foots in the end, the Negro Clay has irrevocably become the victim of Lula's (and America's) violent racism. On the other hand, the sequence of action elements has been inverted, and thereby the statement of Dutchman has become much less ambiguous: the conciliatory ending of *The Toilet* corresponds to the ostensibly harmless idyll at the end of scene 1 in *Dutchman*, and the violence in the course of *The Toilet* is paralleled by the murder at the end of *Dutchman*. These changes allow no hope for a solution to the race problem through "love," as at least one reading of *The Toilet* suggested.

7. Edward Parone, who directed the Cherry Lane Production, included *Dutchman* in his anthology *New Theatre in America* (New York: Dell-Delta, 1965), 191–214. In "Le-

Roi Jones' *Dutchman*: A Brief Ride on a Doomed Ship," *Educational Theatre Journal* 20, no. 1 (February 1968): 53, Hugh Nelson argued that there are "a few significant differences between the two texts." He therefore based his discussion on the "later version" of the Parone text. However, all of his quotations are identical in both versions, and instead of Nelson's reference to "beauties dashing along through the city's entrails" at the bottom of page 56, both versions read "beauties smashing." Here are some representative variants between the first edition, published by Morrow (Jones, *Dutchman and The Slave*, 31; below left), and Parone's edition (Parone, *New Theatre in America*, 208; below right):

Lula: "like your ol' rag-head   Lula: "like our ol' rag-head
  mammy   mammy"

There is a typographical error in the Morrow text (27) that can be emendated with the help of Parone (206):

Clay: "Morbid. Morbid. You sure   Clay: "I will. And is this all of our
  you're not an actress? All scribed?   life together you've described?"

The most significant departure of the Parone text from the Morrow version of *Dutchman* is the absence of the conductor from the last scene, though not from the list of characters (37–38; Parone, *New Theatre in America*, 213–214).

8. Cf. Gerald Weales, *The Jumping-Off Place: American Drama in the 1960s* (New York: Macmillan, 1969), 139.

9. Earlier attempts to interpret *Dutchman* as drama of self include that of Diane Weisgram, who sees Baraka as "both Clay and Lula" (Diane H. Weisgram, "LeRoi Jones' *Dutchman*: Interracial Ritual of Sexual Violence," *American Imago* 29, no. 3 [Fall 1972]: 231), and that of Albert Bermel ("The Poet as Solipsist: *Dutchman* by LeRoi Jones [1964]," in *Contradictory Characters: An Interpretation of the Modern Theatre* [New York: Dutton, 1973], 284), who interprets Clay's death as a poetic suicide and Lula as "the fears and doubts that torment Clay."

10. See, e.g., the poems "Consider This," in Daisy Allen, ed., *A New Folder* (New York: Folder Editions, 1959), 31–32, and "The Disguise," *Penny Poems* 155 (1961).

11. "Lula would make a better 'critic,' and is already, if you dig it, for say East Village Other and SDS (viz Grokville Estab.), she at least, is, at the time of. Crowther never knew what hit him": "Movie Mailbag: Fur Still Flies on 'Dutchman.' From LeRoi Jones," *New York Times*, March 12, 1967, sec. 2, 17.

12. Parone, *New Theatre in America*, 209; cf. Jones, *Dutchman and The Slave*, 31.

13. In his letter to the editor of the *New York Times*, Baraka defended Clay's speech and identified with it to such an extent as to make it appear even more black nationalist than it is: "The 17 minutes of the play he [i.e., Crowther] missed are the 17 minutes it takes for the black man to say his long speech. (We are a different species, with different 'zones' of response, &c.)."

14. André Breton, *Manifestoes of Surrealism*, trans. Richard Seaver and Helen R. Lane (Ann Arbor: University of Michigan Press, 1969), 125.

15. Cf. Pierre Billard, ed., *Masculine Feminine: A Film by Jean-Luc Godard* (New York: Grove, 1969), 52–57.

16. Cf. this section of Baraka's earlier poem "The A, B, C's (for Charles)", *Yugen* no. 6 (1960): 38: "Safe now, within the poem, I make my / Indiscreet avowals, my

indelicate assumptions / As if this gentle fire that bathed my flesh / was rancor, or fear, or any other of life's idiot progeny."

17. George Knox, "The 'Mythology' of LeRoi Jones's *Dutchman*," in *Interculture: A Collection of Essays and Creative Writing Commemorating the 20th Anniversary of the Fulbright Program at the Institute of Translation and Interpretation, University of Vienna*, ed. Sy M. Kahn and Martha Raetz (Vienna: n.p., n.d.), 246–250.

18. Cf. Knox, "The 'Mythology' of LeRoi Jones's *Dutchman*"; Tom S. Reck, "Archetypes in LeRoi Jones' *Dutchman*," *Studies in Black Literature* 1, no. 1 (1970): 66–68; John Gassner and Bernard F. Dukore, eds., *A Treasury of the Theatre*, 4th ed., vol. 2 (New York: Simon and Schuster, 1970), 1274. George Adams, who published a psychoanalytic interpretation of *Dutchman* as "a literary expression of id-activity," also attempted a typological interpretation: see George R. Adams, "Black Militant Drama," *American Imago* 28, no. 2 (Summer 1971): 116–121; George R. Adams, "'My Christ' in *Dutchman*," *College Language Association Journal* 15, no. 1 (September 1971): 54–58; cf. Nelson, "LeRoi Jones' *Dutchman*." The archetypes in *Dutchman* are also indebted to popular culture.

19. Cf. Julian C. Rice, "LeRoi Jones' *Dutchman*: A Reading," *Contemporary Literature* 12, no. 1 (Winter 1971): 43; Herbert Grabes, "LeRoi Jones (Imamu Amiri Baraka): *Dutchman*," in *Das amerikanische Drama der Gegenwart* (Kronberg, Germany: Atheneum, 1976), 193.

20. Cf. Janheinz Jahn, *Muntu: The New African Culture*, trans. Marjorie Grene (New York: Grove, 1961), 45.

21. James Weldon Johnson, ed., *The Book of American Negro Poetry* (1922), repr. ed. (New York: Harcourt, 1931, 120–122. I am indebted to Robert Bone for suggesting this parallel. The *White Witch* is also the name of a ghost ship.

22. Nelson's approach is criticized in Robert L. Tener, "Role Playing as a Dutchman," *Studies in Black Literature* 3, no. 3 (Autumn 1972): 17–21.

23. Sherley Anne Williams, *Give Birth to Brightness: A Thematic Study in Neo-Black Literature* (New York: Dial, 1972), 106–107. Cf. Theodore Hudson, *From LeRoi Jones to Amiri Baraka: The Literary Works* (Durham, NC: Duke University Press, 1973), 152.

24. Further interpretations of the title are of minor relevance. Since the days of Dutch-English rivalries, the word "Dutch" has retained a derogatory connotation in the English language. If Clay has "Dutch courage," Lula gives him "Dutch consolation." With the geographic ambiance of Harlem and Amsterdam Avenue, *Dutchman* may also obliquely refer to a Harlemite. Knox called attention to the use of a poster for Dutch Master cigars in the movie version and to Larry Rivers's painting *Dutchmaster and Cigars* (1964): see Knox, "The 'Mythology' of LeRoi Jones's *Dutchman*," 250–251. Rivers designed the set of *The Toilet*.

25. John Leyden, *Scenes of Infancy: Descriptive of Teviotdale*, 2d ed. (Edinburgh: Ballantyne, 1811), "Flying Dutchman" in the notes, 176. The poem is quoted in J. Logie Robertson, ed., *The Poetical Works of Sir Walter Scott: With the Author's Introductions and Notes* (London: Henry Frowde, 1906), 389. Another connection between the Flying Dutchman and the slave trade is made in Celia Thaxter's "The Mystery," quoted in Fletcher S. Bassett, *Legends and Superstitions of the Sea and of Sailors in All Lands and at All Times* (London: Sampson Low, 1885), 360 (a reference to the *White Witch* as a spectral ship is on 354). Cf. John Livingston Lowes, *The Road to Xanadu: A Study in the Ways of the Imagination* (1927), repr. ed. (Boston: Houghton Mifflin, 1964), 512–516.

26. Baraka explained how he related the myth of the Flying Dutchman to his play in an interview with me on September 1, 1974: "The title is from the Flying Dutchman

. . . not from Wagner, but from the myth, wherever I picked up the myth from, that myth of a ship that sailed around forever." He also said that the *situation* really was the Dutchman, not Lula or Clay.

CHAPTER 12

1. Wright's spirit surely was present in the *Daedalus* issues—in comments on Negroes and communism in the 1930s; in discussions of the importance of decolonization in the Third World for African American civil rights in the 1950s; and in an essay by St. Clair Drake and references to Horace Cayton, for whose joint study, *Black Metropolis*, Wright had written an introduction in 1945. Furthermore, the African American writers who were cited in the issues, Ralph Ellison and James Baldwin, started their careers under the wings of the older Wright.

2. See Charles Johnson, "The End of the Black American Narrative," *American Scholar* 77, no. 3 (Summer 2008), available at http://www.theamericanscholar.org/the-end-of-the-black-american-narrative (accessed March 24, 2009).

3. The essay was originally published in *Daedalus* 94, no. 4 (Fall 1965): 1133–1147. I quote from the expanded paperback reprint: Everett C. Hughes, "Anomalies and Projections" in *The Negro American*, ed. Talcott Parsons and Kenneth B. Clark (Boston: Beacon, 1967), 694–708. Hughes also reprinted his essay in *The Sociological Eye: Selected Papers* (Chicago: Aldine-Atherton, 1971).

4. Hughes, "Anomalies and Projections," in Parsons and Clark, *The Negro American*, 698, 700.

5. Skeptics may wish to consult the original passage in Hughes, "Anomalies and Projections," *Daedalus*, 1139; the quote here is from Hughes, "Anomalies and Projections," in Parsons and Clark, *The Negro American*, 700. See also Hughes's interventions in the discussions of the papers included in *Daedalus* 95, no. 1 (Winter 1966): 287–441. No one seems to have asked a question about this passage in Hughes's essay from the first *Daedalus* issue, although Hughes reiterated his reflections on American kinship in the second issue: see p. 352.

6. Hughes, "Anomalies and Projections," in Parsons and Clark, *The Negro American*, 700, 705–706.

7. Transcript of Barack Obama's speech on race, available at http://www.npr.org/templates/story/story.php?storyId=88478467 (accessed February 28, 2010).

8. Available at http://www.nytimes.com/interactive/2009/10/08/us/politics/20091008-obama-family-tree.html (accessed February 28, 2010).

9. Available at http://www.nytimes.com/2009/10/08/us/politics/08genealogy.html?_r=1 (accessed February 28, 2010).

10. Available at http://www.nytimes.com/interactive/2009/01/21/us/politics/20090121-michelle-audioss/index.html (accessed February 28, 2010).

11. Available at http://www.huffingtonpost.com/david-wallechinsky/flashback-the-first-black_b_159301.html (accessed May 7, 2010).

12. Irving Wallace, *The Man* (New York: Simon and Schuster, 1964), unpaginated front matter. I do not know of a novel by an African American author that anticipated the emergence of a black president.

13. Ibid., 62–63.

14. Andrew Lam, *East Eats West: Writing in Two Hemispheres* (Berkeley, CA: Heyday Books, 2010), 115. A slightly different version of the essay is available at http://

news.newamericamedia.org/news/view_article.html?article_id=e96674231b31155c9a
e5adeca7c1ec08 (accessed October 24, 2010).

15. Lam, *East Eats West*, 121.

16. Ishmael Reed, *Barack Obama and the Jim Crow Media: The Return of the Nigger Breakers* (Montreal: Baraka Books, 2010), 75, 80; quoted from page proofs.

17. Two first novels from the twenty-first century should also be mentioned. Edward P. Jones's Pulitzer Prize–winning *The Known World* (New York: Amistad, 2003) is a sweeping historical novel set in Virginia during the time of slavery that untypically represents slaveholding blacks. Michael Thomas's *Man Gone Down* (New York: Black Cat, 2007), the winner of the International Dublin/IMPAC Literary Award and one of the *New York Times's* "Top Ten Best Books of 2007," is a breezy first-person singular account narrated by an interracially married black father living in Brooklyn who confronts his crisis-ridden past and present in four intense days.

18. Originally published in the *Southwest Review* (2008): 287–297. "Been Meaning to Say" was included in *Best African American Fiction 2010*, ed. Gerald Early and Nikki Giovanni (New York: One World, 2010), 106–116. The quotes are from this edition.

19. Amina Gautier, "Been Meaning to Say," in Early and Giovanni, *Best African American Fiction 2010*, 109, 115.

20. Ibid., 106, 110.

21. Amina Gautier, "Pan Is Dead," *Chattahoochee Review* (Fall 2006): 6, available at http://www.gpc.edu/~gpccr/gautier.php (accessed February 26, 2010).

22. Available at http://www.facebook.com/people/Amina-Gautier/1339033752 (accessed May 15, 2010).

23. Heidi W. Durrow, *The Girl Who Fell from the Sky* (Chapel Hill, NC: Algonquin Books, 2010).

24. Heidi W. Durrow, "Dear Ms. Larsen, There's a Mirror Looking Back," *PMS—poem—memory—story* 8 (2008): 101–109.

25. Durrow, *The Girl Who Fell from the Sky*, 19–20.

26. Ibid., 238, 247.

27. Available at http://heidiwdurrow.com/readers-guide/ (accessed May 10, 2010).

28. This aspect of Bradshaw's work has affinities with the raucously irreverent tradition delineated and analyzed in Glenda R. Carpio, *Laughing Fit to Kill: Black Humor in the Fictions of Slavery* (New York: Oxford University Press, 2008).

29. Available at http://www.brooklynrail.org/2006/12/theater/pushing-buttons -an (accessed May 14, 2010).

30. Thomas Bradshaw, *Strom Thurmond Is Not a Racist* and *Cleansed* (New York: Samuel French, 2007).

31. Ibid., 20, 26, 29.

32. Ibid., 32, 39.

33. Available at http://www.newyorker.com/arts/critics/notebook/2009/09/28/ 090928gonb_GOAT_notebook_als#ixzz0o1GF6dV6 (accessed May 15, 2010).

34. Terrance Hayes, *Lighthead* (New York: Penguin, 2010). See also http://www pbs.org/newshour/video/module.html?mod=0&pkg=24042008&seg=4 (accessed May 12, 2010).

35. Hayes, *Lighthead*, 94.

36. Ibid., 18.

37. An image of *Malediction* is available at http://updateslive.blogspot.com/2008/06/ martin-puryear-exhibition-at-national.html (accessed May 10, 2010). Hayes, *Lighthead*, 18.

38. Ibid., 27.

39. Because Wright included observations about the Western dress of Eurasian elites in *The Color Curtain*, one is tempted to imagine how he might have reacted to Michelle Obama's dress at the inauguration ball. The fact that her white gown was designed by the Asian American Jason Wu might have added a mediating or "third" dimension to the black-white divide that had dominated the discussion of race at a time that the new Asian immigration wave had not yet started—all the more so since Wu commented on the color choice by saying, "White is the most powerful non-color": see http://www.huffingtonpost.com/2009/01/20/jason-wu-michelle-obamas_n_159519 .html (accessed February 28, 2010).

Index

Werner Sollors is Henry B. and Anne M. Cabot Research Professor of English Literature at Harvard University and Global Professor of Literature at New York University Abu Dhabi. He is the co-editor (with Greil Marcus) of *A New Literary History of America* and the author of *Beyond Ethnicity, Neither Black nor White yet Both,* and *The Temptation of Despair.*

Chapter 1: From Werner Sollors, "Introduction," in *The Interesting Narrative of the Life of Olaudah Equiano, or Gustavus Vassa, the African. Written by Himself: Norton Critical Edition*, ed. Werner Sollors (New York: W. W. Norton, 2001), ix–xxxi. Copyright © 2001 by W. W. Norton and Company, Inc. Used by permission of W. W. Norton and Company, Inc.

Chapter 2: Werner Sollors, "Introduction," in *Frank J. Webb: Fiction, Essays and Poetry* (New Milford, CT: Toby Press, 2005), 1–24. Copyright © 2005 by Werner Sollors.

Chapter 3: Werner Sollors, "The Goopher in Charles Chesnutt's Conjure Tales: Superstition, Ethnicity, and Modern Metamorphoses," *Letterature d'America* 6, no. 27 (Spring 1985): 107–129.

Chapter 4: Werner Sollors, "Jean Toomer's *Cane*: Modernism and Race in Interwar America," in *Dream-Fluted Cane: Essays on Jean Toomer and the Harlem Renaissance*, ed. Geneviève Fabre and Michel Feith (New Brunswick, NJ: Rutgers University Press, 2001), 18–37. Copyright © 2001 by Werner Sollors.

Chapter 5: Werner Sollors, "African American Intellectuals and Europe between the Two World Wars," in *Regards Croisés sur les Afro-Américains: Hommage à Michel Fabre*, ed. Claude Julien (GRAAT No. 27) (Tours, France: Presses Universitaires François Rabelais, 2003), 41–57. Copyright © 2003 by Werner Sollors.

Chapter 6: Werner Sollors, "W. E. B. Du Bois in Nazi Germany, 1936," *Amerikastudien/American Studies* 44, no. 2 (1999): 207–222.

Chapter 7: Werner Sollors, "Modernization as Adultery: Richard Wright, Zora Neale Hurston, and American Culture of the 1930s and 1940s," *Hebrew University Studies in Literature and the Arts* ("Women and American Ideology," special issue, ed. Emily Budick) 18 (1990): 109–155. A similar version was published as Werner Sollors, "Anthropological and Sociological Tendencies in American Literature of the 1930s and 1940s: Richard Wright, Zora Neale Hurston, and American Culture," in *Looking Inward, Looking Outward: From the 1930s through the 1940s*, ed. Steven Ickringill, vol. 18 of *European Contributions to American Studies* (Amsterdam: VU Press, 1990), 22–66.

Chapter 8: Werner Sollors, "Of Mules and Mares in a Land of Difference; or, Quadrupeds All?" *American Quarterly* 42, no. 2 (1990): 167–190. Reprinted with permission by Johns Hopkins University Press. Copyright © 1990 American Studies Association.

Chapter 9: Werner Sollors, "Introduction," in *The Autobiography of W. E. B. Du Bois: A Soliloquy on Viewing My Life from the Last Decade of Its First Century*, by W. E. B. Du Bois (New York: Oxford University Press, 2007), xxiii–xxx. Copyright © 2007 by Werner Sollors.

Chapter 10: Extract from Werner Sollors, "Owls and Rats in the American Funnyhouse: Adrienne Kennedy's Drama," *American Literature* 63, no. 3 (September 1991): 507–532. Copyright © 1991 by Duke University Press. Republished by permission of the publisher.

Chapter 11: Werner Sollors, "Dutchman," in *Amiri Baraka/LeRoi Jones: The Quest for a "Populist Modernism,"* by Werner Sollors (New York: Columbia University Press, 1978), 117–133, 284–288. Copyright © 1981 by Werner Sollors.

Chapter 12: Werner Sollors, "Obligations to Negroes Who Would Be Kin if They Were Not Negro," *Daedalus* (special issue on "Race in the Age of Obama," ed. Gerald Early) 140, no. 1 (Winter 2011): 142–153.